A Bottle of Rain

ALSO BY MICHAEL KAYE

<u>Novels</u>

One Monday
From The Cradle To The Grave
The Choice
Never The Light Of Day
The Feral Girls
The Hands Of Memory
Riddle

<u>Poetry</u>

Covering The Cracks
Lovers And Losers

A Bottle of Rain

a novel by
Michael Kaye

authorHOUSE®

AuthorHouse™
1663 Liberty Drive
Bloomington, IN 47403
www.authorhouse.com
Phone: 833-262-8899

Published by AuthorHouse 02/28/2023

ISBN: 979-8-8230-0200-4 (sc)
ISBN: 979-8-8230-0199-1 (e)

Print information available on the last page.

Interior Graphics/Art Credit: Richard Drake & Kristine Kaye

This book is printed on acid-free paper.

This book is for my other 'sister', Sandra Rist, with love.

ACKNOWLEDGMENTS

My thanks and deep appreciation to Clint Moon for sharing some meaningful, personal thoughts and observations with me.

I'm grateful to Darlene Martino for providing details of some fun, interesting and thought provoking grade school activities, which certainly encompass the general theme of the book.

Richard Drake's pen and ink artistry on the front cover enhances the book beyond measure. He has my profound gratitude.

Editing and technical expertise are essential requirements for the writing process. My wife, Kristine, has my love and eternal thanks for helping with these tasks, as well as for her contributions to the final cover art.

We must believe that we are gifted for something.

Marie Curie

CHAPTER ONE

So, the question is... what do you see yourself doing twenty years from now? Tell me about your hopes and dreams. Where will you be? What will your life be like? What will make you a happy person? How will you help a stranger, brighten a day or even make someone feel better? Try to imagine yourself twenty years from now and then write it all down. Have fun with this assignment but always remember to be honest and thoughtful. Now, go! Go ahead and write.

ANNIE LEE CAVALLARO SMILED AS she recalled the second grade writing project from all those years ago. That was the first time she had admitted to anyone the very real ambition burning brightly inside her head and heart. Being eight years of age mattered not in the slightest to Annie. It was what she wanted to do and somehow in the years to come she would make it happen.

Now, at age twenty-five, she was a doctoral student at the prestigious Fitzgerald University, enrolled in their world renowned biotechnology training program. For Annie, the seventeen years since putting pencil to paper in second grade, with her optimistic hopes and dreams, now seemed to have passed by in a flash of hard work, encouragement and on-going possibilities.

Not one to second guess herself, for Annie was nothing but

self-confident about her work, she caught this quiet moment in the lab genuinely amazed at how far she'd come. And yet, she still felt this joyous journey she was on hadn't really begun; hadn't truly answered her calling whatever that might be.

Her musings were suddenly brought to a halt by the familiar voice of her professor and now friend and mentor, Dr. Virginia West.

"Annie, a word, if I may?"

Annie looked up and smiled. She was always glad when Virginia bothered her. Usually it meant something of note was about to happen.

"Fire away," she replied, giving Virginia her full attention. "What d'you want me to discover now?"

"Ha. Ha. Very funny," Virginia answered, poking out her tongue. "This is going to break up your summer plans somewhat, but I've signed you up for an advanced biotech conference at Harvard in July. Lots of great speakers, including one of my favorites, Dr. Gail Stephens, and it'll also give you a chance to compare notes with some of the other attendees. Good chance to broaden your horizons. Okay?"

"Well, yes, if you think I'm ready?"

"Wouldn't have put your name forward otherwise."

"All right, then." Annie answered, secretly taken aback by Virginia's faith in her, "Harvard, here I come."

"Good. Good. I'll send you all the details in a few days. You won't regret it." As she was about to leave, Virginia turned and asked, "By the way, how's the book coming along?"

"Surprisingly well," Annie responded, nodding her head, "just chapter by chapter, lots of research but fascinating, revealing and so inspiring."

"Good. Good," Virginia offered. "I can understand why you picked her. Can't wait to read it. I know it'll be amazing."

"She's always been my hero – or heroine, I should say, so let's hope I don't mess it up."

"*She's* your heroine!" Virginia replied, in mock horror. "And what about *yours truly* here?"

Annie poked out *her* tongue this time.

"I promise you the first copy," she responded, holding out her hands. "Would that make up for my apparent disloyalty?"

Both women laughed as Virginia went on her way.

Home for the summer meant precious weeks with her beloved family. Annie arrived in mid-May and, apart from the week-long course at Harvard in July, would get to spend the rest of the time catching up with her mother and father, chilling and continuing to write her biography.

Both her parents were professionals; Blythe taught third grade at the local primary school, while Clive, a lawyer, ran his own practice. Each would have plenty of quality time with Annie, something they had missed so much while she was in school.

Blythe, still teaching until late June, planned on taking Annie in with her a few times a week to expose her daughter to her working life, as well as hoping to inspire her students with all sorts of possibilities from someone nearer their own age. Annie loved the idea and was already thinking of a million different ways to fire up the kids' imaginations.

She particularly wanted to focus on math and science and would suggest to her mother some fun and innovative projects to stretch and motivate their young minds.

Just to have Annie around for a few months thrilled Blythe beyond measure. The time would give them a chance to reconnect, not only in a mother/daughter way but also in an adult, almost sisterly manner. Their whole relationship was so important and crucial to Blythe considering her own experience of growing up without the close, personal love and friendship of either of her parents.

The memories still haunted and stung her. She determined, if she ever became a mother, her child or children would never go through a day in their lives not knowing they were loved unconditionally and beyond measure. Now Annie was coming home, if only for a while, and Blythe waited for the moment like one of her excited third graders.

"There's my baby girl!" Blythe exclaimed, hurrying to greet her, as Annie struggled through the door with her bags. "Dad, give the poor thing a hand," she motioned to her husband, who quickly put down his glass of wine and trotted over.

"Leave them right there, Honey," he ordered, "and I'll take them to your room in a second. But first, we need hugs all round."

Annie, while glad to be home, was less enthusiastic about the overwhelming welcome. That she dearly loved her parents could never be questioned, but her emotions were always a notch or two below theirs.

"You're just in time for dinner," Blythe said, taking Annie by the hand and leading her into the kitchen. "But first, let me look at you," she continued, grinning.

"Mother," Annie countered with a frown, "I haven't been gone *that* long! And I really need to change and use the bathroom."

"I know. I know," replied her mother. "But I've missed you so much. All right, run along but hurry back. Dinner's in twenty."

Annie quickly disappeared while Blythe smiled ruefully to herself. *It's really happening*, she thought. *Three whole months with my baby. Wow!*

Dinner and catch-up time lasted well past midnight. It was tiring for Annie since her mom and dad peppered her with almost non-stop questions. But their interest was understandable and always encouraging given their daughter's passion for her chosen field.

She brought them up to date with her graduate work under Virginia West's guidance, which both baffled and amazed them with the seemingly complex array of projects with which she was involved. They didn't profess to comprehend most of Annie's detailed descriptions of her work. They just knew it was important research both to the world and to Annie herself.

"Harvard!" Blythe exclaimed, when Annie told them about the July conference for which Virginia West had signed her up. "Oh, my gosh, Annie, that's just wonderful."

"I know," Annie answered, raising her eyebrows. "Little scary to tell the truth, but Ginny feels I'm ready. She wants me to broaden my horizons, see what's out there and talk to some of the other attendees. Oh, and one of her favorite researchers is due to speak, so I'm doubly looking forward to that."

"It'll be an amazing experience," chimed in her father. "I've been a couple of times myself for law symposiums. It's a great place to see let alone learn some stuff."

"That's what Ginny said. And she also said she'd let some people know I'd be coming so they could look me up and discuss the work I'm currently involved with. And, heaven knows, I need all the help I can get right now!"

Dinner wound down and the dishes were left until morning. When

Annie had settled in bed, her mother went in and sat with her for a while.

Holding her hand, she said, "We're very proud of you, you know. We never imagined in our wildest dreams you'd be where you are today."

"Thanks to you and Dad," Annie answered, nodding.

"No, that's not what I mean," her mother offered. "When you were a baby, when we brought you all the way from China, we just wanted to give you a better life; a good life. As long as you were happy and healthy then, hopefully, all of the other stuff would follow eventually.

"We hoped, of course, you'd blossom and find your own way. We decided early on that whatever road you followed, whatever person you turned out to be, that that would be fine with us.

"What you've done with your life so far, Sweetie, with your hard work and dedication to those things you love, has been such a blessed bonus for your dad and me. I couldn't have wished for a better daughter if I could've had a hundred."

Annie frowned before raising her eyebrows once again.

"Mom, really, you're embarrassing me. I've only been able to do all those things because of you and Dad always supporting me, always ready to buck me up and always willing to go the extra mile to make sure I had what I needed to succeed."

Sitting up, she reached her arms around her mother's neck.

"I think…no, I *know* I got the better part of the deal. All I'm trying to do is to make you proud of me."

The two held each other for the longest time, until Blythe broke away and headed to the door, brushing away a tear as she went.

"And we are, Sweetie, we are. Never, ever forget that. Okay?"

"Okay," Annie nodded.

"Goodnight, Sweetheart," Blythe said, before adding one more piece of advice. "Oh, by the way, just to bring you down to earth a little, just remember on Monday, in my classroom, I'm Mrs. Cavallaro to you!"

Annie, poking out her tongue, replied she'd try very hard to remember.

CHAPTER TWO

OVER THE WEEKEND BLYTHE BROUGHT Annie up to speed with the latest and last curriculum topics of the school year her kiddos were trying to master. Again, the moment sent Annie spinning back to her own time in third grade. As she listened to her mother explaining where they were in the various subjects and their contents, Annie marveled at the improvements and strides that had been taken since she was a third grade student.

All the kiddos now had Chromebooks with which they could not only write their reports but also, within certain defined parameters, research the particular subject matter for facts and guidance. Annie was especially interested, of course, in where they were in math and science, as well as their writing projects in English class. Her mother had gently suggested she might be prepared to share with them some of her insights as she was writing her own biography of a famous, historical person.

In that connection, Blythe told her one of the end of year assignments was for her students to select an historical figure from a small list she had given them, research the person's life and then compile a meaningful biography. From the work the class had previously done in this area, Blythe told Annie, the kids seemed to really enjoy the whole concept.

After listening to her mother describe the positive atmosphere in her classroom, Annie couldn't wait for Monday morning to arrive.

"Boys and girls," Blythe began, standing in front of her kiddos with a broad smile covering her face, "I'd like you all to meet my daughter,

Miss Annie Cavallaro. Miss Annie, as she will be known to you all, will be coming in a few days a week to help us all out. Right now, she is a graduate student at Fitzgerald University studying biotechnology. She loves math, science and writing, so I know she will be able to help us all out with her knowledge. And besides all that, she's a lot of fun, too!"

The kiddos giggled at Blythe's last remark.

"Now, I'm going to ask Miss Annie to introduce herself and tell you a little bit about what she has in mind for all of you. Miss Annie…"

Annie stepped before the class, a lot more nervous than she expected. She looked out at the sea of faces staring expectantly back at her, took a deep breath, smiled and began.

"This is *so* exciting for me! Mom…I mean Mrs. Cavallaro…" the kiddos giggled as Annie corrected herself, "has told me what a great group of students you are. She also told me you all love math, science and writing which are some things I hope I'll be able to help you with.

"Right now, I'm in college studying those subjects, too. They're hard work but also a lot of fun. And, you know what else is cool about them? You get to learn a lot of really neat ways to solve all sorts of problems.

"Now, Mrs. Cavallaro mentioned you were researching and writing reports on some famous historical people, which is exactly what I'm doing! I'm trying to write a biography, which is telling a person's life story, about someone called Marie Curie…"

"Oh, I've heard of her," a young lady in the back said, proudly. "She invented stuff, didn't she?"

"She kinda did," Annie replied, impressed that someone in the class knew who she was. "But she didn't invent them, she actually discovered them. They're elements called radium and polonium and they've made such a difference in people's lives. So, anyway, I can help you all with some of the reports you'll be writing.

"Now, I don't want to take up too much more of our precious time but if anyone has a question then fire away."

Hands shot up like rockets going off. Since the kiddos' names were on the front of their desks, Annie could call on each child by name.

"Amy, in the back. What's your question?"

Annie's mom instructed the kids to stand and speak in a loud, confident voice, so Amy stood and almost shouted her question which made the whole class laugh.

"Miss Annie, why do you like science so much?"

Annie beamed at Amy before answering, "That is a really great question, Amy. I guess I love science so much because learning about it helps you understand neat things about our incredible world.

"I mean, think about it for a second…where would we be today without all those amazing scientific discoveries in medicine, space exploration, plants and animals? We'd probably still be living in caves!"

The whole class laughed at that image.

"And, oh my, learning about all this stuff is just so interesting, right? I know from talking with your teacher that you guys have covered so many great topics this year. Ecology, ecosystems, all sorts of matter such as gasses, water and solids and lots more. I have to tell you, I'm very impressed."

"Does anyone have a math question for Miss Annie?" Mrs. Cavallaro asked, glancing around the room.

From the front row, Noah raised his hand.

"Yes, Noah, go ahead."

"Why is math so hard sometimes?" he asked, frowning.

"Good question again," Annie replied, knowing this class had covered multiplication and division this year. "But let me ask you a question, Noah. If everything was easy would you ever manage to learn anything?"

Noah frowned again as he thought about the question.

"Guess not," he said, shaking his head.

"No, you wouldn't," Annie confirmed. "Math is all about numbers and building step by step until you can solve a problem. For instance, if you all didn't know how to count past ten, and I asked you to count the jelly beans in a full jar and tell me how many were in there, you couldn't because you only knew how to count to ten.

"Math is so interesting because it helps you solve everyday problems like figuring out how much money you can spend at the store, or knowing how to divide a pizza up so everyone gets the same share."

After a few more questions, Annie told the kids that one of their assignments would be to write a report on their favorite science lesson they'd had this school year.

"I will help you, but your report should describe the topic in detail, why you liked it so much and how you think it will help the world."

Mrs. Cavallaro then stepped up, thanked her daughter and asked the kids to get ready for their English lesson.

Over the next days and weeks Annie, true to her word, immersed herself in helping her mother's students with science, math and English. She went in three days a week, spending the other days working on her biography of Marie Curie.

Those days were exhilarating, full of joy and enthusiasm. Annie, when starting the project, was acutely aware of its enormity and scope, and hoped she possessed the necessary drive, time and patience to complete such an ambitious undertaking.

After four months of intermittent writing Annie had managed to cover the first fifteen years of Marie's life. For someone born in 1867, as Marie was, Annie learned that that short time on earth for her must have been full of uncertainty and bewilderment.

As the fifth and youngest child, Marie, before the age of eleven, experienced numbing and depressive situations within her family. When she was not quite eight years of age her oldest sibling, Zofia, died of typhus, an acute infectious disease transmitted by lice, ticks and fleas in whose bodies they live as parasites.

"She is with God," her devout Catholic parents told her, which Marie accepted at face value. And yet, even at her tender age, Marie could only wonder why such a god would take away someone so close to her.

It was also around this time that her family began losing their property and wealth. Their homeland of Poland – in those days called the Kingdom of Poland – was part of the Russian Empire and her parents were involved in the Polish national uprising springing up around the country. They were part of a movement to restore Poland to independence, but their actions left them with a difficult struggle to get ahead.

Marie's father was a man of educational distinction. A teacher of math and physics, he was also the director of two secondary schools for boys. But when the Russian authorities took away laboratory instruction he brought the equipment home and taught his own children.

"We shall investigate today," her father began, with a broad smile, "the properties of water, gas and solids."

The three children watching attentively were transfixed by all the various glass bottles and tubes spread over their father's desk. Marie couldn't wait to see what her father was going to do with them all.

Mrs. Sklodowska, Marie's mother, who before Marie was born

operated a prestigious Warsaw boarding school for girls, helped her husband with the experiments as well as ensuring all the children paid attention.

"It was like home-schooling," Annie remarked to her mother, as she took a break between chapters. "But this was nearly one hundred fifty years ago. Amazing."

"Not really," Blythe countered, dropping a plate of freshly baked cookies in front of Annie. "You have to remember in those days girls were denied a formal education. You, young lady, don't know how lucky you are," she grinned, while raising her eyebrows. "Virginia Woolf had the same problem. She basically taught herself from her father's vast library."

But Annie did know how lucky she was on so many fronts. As her mother left her to the cookies and her biography, she reflected on how she had never felt discriminated against on account of her sex. Nor did she feel her achievements had been attained for the same reason. Indeed, Annie knew how hard she'd worked for everything earned, thanking whatever gods there were for the brain she'd been blessed with.

Soon, her thoughts drifted back to Mr. Sklodowski's makeshift laboratory and the eager children awaiting his magic. Boiling water, she imagined him telling them to watch, observe and note what happened. Next, she saw him take a fresh piece of ice the iceman had delivered earlier that morning and slowly heat it. Again, she could clearly hear him instruct the children to pay attention to the result and note it in their books. Finally, he placed a tube of water in the middle of a tubful of ice.

"This experiment will take a little longer," Annie fancied him saying. During the two hours they waited their father awed them with a demonstration about gravity and the effect it had on an apple.

Of all the children, Marie asked the most questions and by far seemed to be the most interested. She actually helped her father with his experiments, which he noted with surprise and hope. In the coming months Mr. Sklodowski began using Marie more and more to assist with his demonstrations, often discussing them with her beforehand so that his explanations could be more easily understood.

He also was well aware of the limited opportunities for girls to advance in the field of science and mathematics, and was determined to give his daughters the benefit of his vast knowledge.

Marie, under his close tutelage, blossomed despite the lingering sadness she felt over Zofia's death. Both her parents now hoped her depressive moments would ease and eventually disappear as she grew both in mind and body. And for a while that direction seemed to be the smooth road ahead. But sometimes the unthinkable happens again. When Marie was ten, curious and bright-brained, another disaster befell her and the family which sent her spinning towards more than despair.

Annie stopped her writing at this point. She tried hard to put herself in Marie's position, imagining how she would have felt and coped with such a devastating situation. Annie needed time to think and process this next part of Marie's life so that she could do justice to all involved; Marie; herself and her prospective readers. For that she would have to talk to her parents.

CHAPTER THREE

ITIS THE WEEKEND, A Saturday, and Annie walks a little nervously to the patio where her parents are enjoying their coffee on a soft summer morning. The lawn, freshly mowed, provides the air with a strong scent of earthy lushness which Annie always finds intoxicating. She breathes in deeply, filling her lungs and senses with… what?…the mere satisfaction, perhaps, of just being alive.

Her father, looking up from his paper, asks, "Coffee, Sweetheart?" and starts to rise.

Annie pats his arm, sits, smiles and shakes her head. "I'm good, Dad, but thanks."

Blythe is somewhat startled at Annie's appearance here in the sunshine. She knows her daughter's beliefs about the harm done by too much exposure. Still, she is thrilled to have her close if only for a while. Instinctively, she realizes Annie has something important on her mind. She notices her daughter's body language, tighter, more earnest. Her work, perhaps, or maybe the book she's writing? Something. Blythe raises her eyebrows expectantly, hoping for an unsolicited response, but Annie merely supplies a weak smile. Not waiting any longer, Blythe offers, "Book going well, Honey?"

"Yes, so far. She's had quite a life." She wants…needs…to talk about Marie Curie. "I'm only up to when she's ten, yet she's gone through so much."

Her mother leans forward hoping for more. Annie doesn't elaborate.

"How so?" Blythe wonders, opening up her hands.

"Two deaths, in her family," Annie reveals, her lips tightening as she relives the details. "An older sister and then her mother."

"Oh, my," her mother responds, truly surprised. "And she was only ten at the time?"

Annie nods, appreciating the genuine empathy. By this time her father becomes interested in the conversation. He, too, senses his daughter has a need to discuss and process almost unimaginable losses.

"Sometimes life throws us impossible situations to deal with," he says, as he looks directly into Annie's eyes. "You look for explanations... reasons, but often there are none." He, too, now leans forward. "I lost my own father when I was only fifteen. One day he was with us and the next he was gone. All of a sudden just a memory."

He watches closely as Annie processes this information. Slowly, he adds, "My dad went from flesh and blood to just a memory in a moment."

This information is new to Annie. She is close with her mother's parents and her father's mother but strangely she's never thought about her other grandfather; he just was never there in the family she's grown up with. A chord is struck in her mind as a connection is made to what she needs to talk about.

"Will you tell me sometime what he was like?" she carefully asks, not wishing to possibly stir any sadness within her father.

"Of course," the reply comes easily. "He was quite a man." For now he leaves the story for another time. All he does is smile and nods as he remembers.

Blythe knows the moment is near. Sage and teacher, she waits expectantly for Annie to begin. There is no conflict in her mind; no fear or distress about what may be coming.

She decides to break the ice, to make her daughter feel comfortable with her questions. "Annie, Sweetie, it's all right. What is it you need to know?"

But Annie is still reticent, absurdly afraid she might hurt her parents in some way. She approaches the subject warily, as if by doing so no one will feel badly.

"It's just that you wonder sometimes about things," she begins. Pulling back her black hair, she smiles and grants herself a small respite.

But her mother jumps in, eager now to start this delicate conversation. "About what? Tell us? Ask us? Okay?"

At once, Annie realizes this is the point of no return. She looks at her mother with almost pleading eyes and begins. "Did you ever meet her?"

"Your mother, you mean?" Blythe answers quickly but firmly.

Suddenly, Annie feels she's hit a nerve within herself. She's looking at her mother but now there's this other person to acknowledge.

"Mom…"

"It's okay, Honey, really." Blythe glances towards her husband but realizes she has to deal with this on her own. "No. No, we never did."

"So, you have no idea what she was like?" Annie asks, already accepting the answer.

"No. The process…" she hates using the word but can find no other, "…was totally anonymous, usually in the dead of night."

"So, no records at all?" Annie ventures.

"No. That was the system back then. We assumed you were a second or third child – China only allowed one per family – and if they were too poor to be able to pay what was essentially a tax to keep the child they were forced to give that child up for adoption. It was the policy. No one's fault, really."

Annie digests this information but needs to know more. She asks, "How was it done? I mean, did men come and grab me and take me away?"

"No, nothing like that," her father answers kindly. "As we understood it the family would have dropped the child…" he quickly corrects himself, "…dropped you at the orphanage in the middle of the night and you were taken in. They cared for you for a while before you would have been transferred to a foster home."

Annie sees herself as a baby although she remembers nothing. She thinks how bewildering it must have been for a child to be suddenly uprooted from all it has ever known. She hears the cries in her head and imagines looking only at unfamiliar surroundings. She is grateful she cannot remember.

"So, how did you and Dad come to adopt me?" The question is asked with genuine puzzlement.

Blythe has been ready most of her adult life to answer this question. She welcomes the chance to finally explain everything to her daughter.

"When it became apparent I couldn't have children," she begins, the calmness in her voice soothing and meaningful, "we turned to adoption because your dad," she turns towards her husband and smiles, "and me desperately wanted to become parents."

"More than anything," he confirms, nodding at Annie.

"I understand that," Annie says, "but why a kid from China?"

"Oh, that was all down to your father. He'd been over there on business and saw first hand what was going on. So many children just needing a family to love them and give them a chance at a decent life." Blythe pauses and takes one of Annie's hands in her own. "He came home and told me, asked me what I thought about adoption. Truthfully, I didn't need much time and soon we were off and running.

"Of course, there was so much to do, so much red tape, but all the while we were both so... euphoric, I suppose, is the right word."

Annie's father jumps in. "Oh, you have no idea how excited we were. Must've bored our friends to death with the details." He laughs at the memory before continuing. "We spent three months in China, in a city called Nanchang. Lovely spot, right near a lake. And that's where we bonded with you and you with us." He smiles broadly and shakes his head at a memory still as fresh as all those years ago.

Annie sees her parents as they were then, holding her, talking to her, being as kind as they are now. They're thoughts that make her happy but she still wonders. Did this woman - her mother – care? Was she devastated or did she accept the practice as the norm in Chinese society?

Her mother reads Annie's puzzled expression and answers those questions for her.

"I cannot imagine what she went through…heartbreaking to say the least." She again grabs her daughter's hand. "I sometimes wish I could let her know how everything turned out for you. That her loss was our gain and what a wonderful young lady you've always been. That her giving birth to you was and will be a blessing for the world."

Annie accepts her mother's words as the only possible wise explanation. Her quick mind processes the whole situation and she finally manages to relax, to understand some things are just what they are and no amount of conjecture can alter anything.

But one thought continues bouncing around her head. *Does she ever think of me? Does she ever wonder?* Annie quickly realizes she will never know the answers. Instead, she takes comfort from knowing what she knows for sure; that she's been blessed with the life she has, and none of it would have been possible without her mother's supreme sacrifice.

Silently, Annie promises to honor that sacrifice by always being the best person she can be and by doing what she can to make the world a better place.

Suddenly, her mind feels fresh again, that she's already come to terms with what was. Smiling happily, Annie addresses her parents. "How lucky was I that you chose me?" she asks. "I mean, you guys are the best." She gently shakes her head. "You chose me. Me! Thank you. Thank you."

Leaving her place at the table, Annie hugs her parents. There are tears of joy but nothing more is said. There is no reason. And for however long they are together, for however long their lives may entwine, none of them will speak of this again, because there is no need.

CHAPTER FOUR

"Today," Annie began, standing in front of her mother's class of eager, excited learners, "we'll be making it rain." She let her remark hang for a few seconds as the children absorbed a seemingly impossible occurrence. As she had promised, Annie was bringing fun to her mother's third grade science lesson.

Annie and Blythe smiled at each other as they watched the looks on the kids' faces. They could almost hear their little minds asking themselves 'How can we make it rain in here?'

Soon, Annie put them out of their misery by arranging the students into groups of four and explaining the next steps. Before the kiddos arrived that morning Annie and Blythe brought from home all the necessary equipment and set it up on a large table at the back of the room.

"Now," Annie started confidently, feeling more comfortable talking in front of the class, "each of you, beginning with this group," she continued, pointing to four willing souls, "take a Mason jar to the sink where Mrs. Cavallaro will put some hot water in each one. Then carefully carry them back to the table, set them down and place one of those plates over the top. Then wait until the other groups join you with their jars."

Within three minutes all the groups were at the table with their jars. There was a lot of chatter about what might happen next but no one guessed correctly.

Retrieving a cooler full of ice cubes from behind her mother's desk,

Annie instructed one member from each group to pick out four or five chunks and place them carefully on the upturned plate.

Once that task was completed, Annie told the kiddos, "Now we wait and observe."

Eager, interested eyes focused solely on the jars and what was happening inside. As Annie watched these aspiring young scientists, her mind wandered to another time and place as she clearly saw Marie, at about the same age, participating in one of her father's research tests, possible one similar to the experiment she was now conducting.

She imagined a competent ten-year-old studying and learning everything her father could impart to her and her siblings. She saw Marie, perhaps in a dark blue pinafore dress, bustling around, assisting her father as he assembled and explained his latest scientific trial.

Marie's face, Annie pictured in her mind's eye, was a mask of absolute concentration and intense interest. She would want and need to know and understand each and every step her father showed them. Her questions would have been acute, to the point, never superfluous or lacking in clarity. Annie felt Marie, before leaving the lessons with her father, would completely understand the experiment from top to bottom. They would be lessons she would never forget; lessons she could carry with her as she, too, gradually began her pursuit of a scientific career.

"Miss Annie! Miss Annie," she heard one of the children call out, "look, it's raining inside the jars!"

Annie beamed, as did her mother, as they saw the excitement bubbling from the kiddos. And, indeed, it was 'raining' inside the jars.

"So," Mrs. Cavallaro asked, "what exactly is happening?"

The kids seemed unsure of an explanation until a young girl called Hannah offered an opinion.

"I think it might have something to do with the hot water and the ice cubes," she said, frowning, "but I'm not sure why."

Annie, pleased that this young lady had the courage to speak up, high-fived her.

"And you would be correct. Now, we need to think about those things – hot water and ice cubes. How many of you have a glass front door or a glass screen door in your house?"

A lot of hands went up.

"Okay. Now, how many of you have noticed in the winter, when it's cold outside but warm in your house, that the glass door gets all steamy wet and water drips down from the top to the bottom?"

Again, a lot of hands were raised. One boy, Austin, answered, "Yeah, it's all wet and cold and feels yucky."

Everyone laughed at Austin's description.

"Well," Annie jumped in, "that's called condensation and it occurs when cold air meets warm or hot air. That's why it rains because the warm or hot air from the ground rises and meets the colder air in the sky and the air condenses and forms water droplets or rain. Now, when the air above is really cold, the water droplets fall as snow or sleet. It's really as simple as that."

The kids listened intently to Annie's explanation and began to understand how their Mason jars, hot water and ice cubes were just like the outside.

"That is so neat!" Madison piped up. "I never knew any of this stuff."

Several other students joined in expressing their wonder at Annie's experiment before Mrs. Cavallaro had them take out their science notebooks and describe what they had learned.

"You did a great job, Annie," Blythe remarked proudly, as they cleaned up the table. "You're a natural at this."

"Well, I had a wonderful teacher, Mom," her daughter replied, smiling. "This school is lucky to have you."

As the weeks in her mother's class flew by and the school year dwindled down to the last two weeks, Annie spent a lot of time helping the still-eager learners with their biography writing and honing their math skills.

Their writing efforts actually benefited Annie in a way she hadn't imagined. While they thoroughly researched their subjects and found interesting facts to include in their reports, some of them inadvertently stumbled upon a different way of looking at their chosen people. What they asked was '*what if?*' What if this particular person hadn't done this, that and the other, or perhaps had been born at a different time and place? It was an observation Annie found relevant to her own biography of Marie Curie. What if she hadn't been born into a scientific and educational family? Would radium and polonium have been discovered and what consequences would have befallen the human race if they had not?

When all their reports had been completed, Mrs. Cavallaro invited the students' parents in one afternoon to hear the children present their biographies. It was a joyous occasion for all concerned and helped showcase the tremendous strides the kiddos had taken over the past school year. Annie, for her part, felt she had contributed in some small way by passing on some of the skills she, herself, had learned down the years. Just watching and hearing the kids speak so confidently filled her with such pride. Her two months in her mother's class certainly hadn't been wasted,

As a final piece of fun for the kiddos, Annie, in one of the last math classes, presented them with a thorny problem. It mostly centered on the addition and multiplication lessons they'd mastered throughout the year.

"All right," she began, smiling, "I have a question to ask you. Would you rather have one million dollars right now, or start with one cent which doubles in value every day for a month? That means, you have one cent on the first day, two cents on the second, four cents on the third, eight cents on the fourth and so on until you reach thirty-one days.

"Now, without thinking too much about your answer, raise your hand if you would take the one million dollars today."

Quickly, lots of hands were raised and Annie's mom counted them up.

"Okay, and who would take one cent now, which will double every day?"

Two hands shot up as the owners glanced warily around the room. Annie then asked her mother to read out the tally for each question.

"Million dollars…fourteen votes," she announced. "One cent now, two votes."

"All right," continued Annie, "now, I want each of you to use the math skills you've learned this year to figure out who will be richer after one month. Get going."

Towards the end of math class Annie called a halt to the students' intense calculations. Both she and her mother had walked among the children while they tried hard to figure out the answer to Annie's question. Both were impressed by the kiddos' level of understanding of the concept and the amount of concentration with which they worked. Annie told her mother those imparted skills were obviously a huge credit to her for the way she had taught them throughout the school year.

"Tell my principal that!" Blythe responded, with a laugh. "I could do with a raise."

"Pencils down," Annie instructed the children. "Now, does anyone want to change their mind about which deal to take – the million dollars now or the one cent that doubles every day?"

Lots of eager hands shot up.

Grinning, she said, "Yes, I thought that might be the case, but why? A million dollars now seems like a very good sum to have."

Many eager hands shot up again. Annie picked on Noah, one of the only two to have originally chosen the one cent double option, to explain the reason.

"I used multiplication," he said, proudly, "easy multiplication."

"How so?" asked Mrs. Cavallaro.

"You just multiply your answer by two every time. So, you start with one cent and multiply that by two to get two. Then you multiply that by two and you get four. Very simple, very easy," Noah explained.

"Who agrees with Noah?" Annie questioned.

Lots of hands went up.

"I have another way," a young lady in the back row offered.

"Oh, good," replied Annie, enthusiastically. "Let's hear it."

"You can get the same answer by using addition."

"All right. Can you explain that to the class?" Annie wanted to know.

The young lady, Ryleigh, stood up and confidently began.

"You start off with one cent and because that doubles all you have to do is add one more cent, so now you have two cents. The next day you add two more cents to the two cents you already have, so now you have four cents. Then you just have to carry on adding."

"Oh, I like that, too," Annie enthused. "Great job, Ryleigh. But here's the thing," she continued, addressing the class, "using either of those methods by day twenty-one, by my calculations, and you can tell me if you agree, you will only have ten thousand, four hundred, eighty-five dollars and seventy-six cents. Now I'm thinking I might want to take the million on day one," she said, looking very doubtful.

"No! No!" the kiddos called out.

"Oh, why not?" she queried, frowning. "Yes, Jackson?"

"Because, Miss Annie, the total *doubles* every day. So, the next day you'd have something like twenty thousand dollars."

"And nine hundred, seventy-one dollars and fifty-two cents, to be precise," she added. "But still nowhere near a million," she said, with a fake pout. "Oh, but then I see that amount only gets bigger and bigger every day, right?"

"Yes," agreed Noah. "That's right."

"So has anyone figured out exactly how much you'd have at the end of thirty-one days?"

Again, lots of hands shot up, which pleased the two teachers so much. Mrs. Cavallaro called on Holly to give everyone the answer.

Holly stood and proudly announced, "Ten million, seven hundred thirty-seven thousand, four hundred eighteen dollars and twenty-four cents."

Annie and her mother clapped Holly for providing the correct answer.

"Yes, Holly!" Annie almost exploded. "You are right. Who else came up with that number?"

All but two of the students raised their hands.

"So," Mrs. Cavallaro asked, "what's the moral of Miss Annie's little problem?"

"That you shouldn't always just jump right in," replied Nathan, "even when it sounds really, really good."

Annie nodded. "What else?"

"That you should use what you've learned to solve hard things," Marion said, firmly.

"Exactly!" Mrs. Cavallaro agreed. "And all of you have done that today, so, good job. Now, let's pack up and go outside for recess."

As the kiddos ran, swung, slid and kicked a soccer ball around, none of them realized that, in the years to come, they would proudly tell anyone who'd listen that they'd once had the now-famous Miss Annie Lee Cavallaro as a teacher.

CHAPTER FIVE

As much as she enjoyed her time helping teach her mother's third graders, Annie now switched her full attention to the week's long biotech conference at Harvard that Virginia West signed her up for back in May.

"Don't let the place intimidate you," advised her father, as he and Blythe helped Annie pack up and load her things for the trip. "You belong there," he continued, giving her a hug. "Never forget that."

Usually, Annie's confidence level hovered just below high, but she had to admit to herself Harvard was a totally different story. Not only that; now she had to mix, mingle and interact with others she presumed were out of her league in terms of intellect, personal achievements and career paths.

She also presumed Virginia had informed the conference's main speaker, Dr. Gail Stephens, a personal friend of hers, that Annie would be attending. Annie assumed that naturally meant Dr. Stephens might make it a point to personally speak with her, to perhaps discuss and get Annie's views on any number of relevant subjects. That prospect daunted her, too.

And yet, fresh challenges always excited Annie, making her think of where these numerous possibilities might lead. To properly put her fears and anxiety in perspective, she returned to the biography she was writing on Marie Curie, remembering how Marie, at the tender age of fifteen, suffering from possible depression, moved to the countryside home of some relatives.

After spending time tutoring, she and her sister, Bronislawa, who were unable to enroll in a higher learning facility because they were women, became involved with the Flying (or Floating) University. This clandestine organization was a Polish patriotic institution of higher learning that admitted women.

Annie not only despaired at the injustice they suffered for the crime of being female, but marveled at their indefatigable passion for craving an education. Surely, she concluded, if they could face such hardship and overcome it, then she, who was about to enter one of the world's foremost seats of learning, could do so without fear or trepidation.

Before Blythe said her final goodbyes she held Annie in a long, warm embrace. Tears of joy filled her eyes as she knew for sure this was the continuation of an amazing life. The prospects for her daughter were now limitless; the value she might bring to the world now boundless. It was a moment of profound pride.

"Enjoy every darn moment," she enthused. "Wish I was going with you. Any chance you can squeeze me into the trunk?"

They both laughed at Blythe's silliness, yet they both knew this was the beginning of a new chapter in the family's life. It wasn't that they'd be any different; it was just that none of them would be the same anymore. It was only a week but would seem like a lifetime.

The solitary drive took over three hours. Annie's mood, now upbeat and positive, augured well for the week to come. Virginia texted to wish her well, advising her to soak up the atmosphere and generally have a good time.

Mostly, listen and learn, the text read. *And don't be shy about asking questions and putting yourself out there. This is an opportunity not to be missed.*

Annie's GPS took her into the very heart of Boston, a city she'd been to twice before with her parents. She recalled the sights and sounds from all those years ago, remembering how alive and interesting a place it was. She felt comfortable going back and looked forward to doing a little sightseeing on her down time.

Her room for the week was located on the main campus in Cambridge, three miles west northwest of Boston, which she would be sharing with another attendee. This, in itself, pleased Annie because it would give her the chance to gauge somewhat the level of intellect and drive she most probably would be encountering.

On the other hand, it was also a little scary since, in her other academic world, she mostly kept to herself, usually only bouncing her ideas and theories off Virginia. She enjoyed working on her own but lately realized she needed to broaden her horizons to include other diverse, and perhaps, counter views if she was to test and find answers to the many problems swirling inside her head.

"Hi," the stranger said, as Annie entered her room, "I'm Kylie. Nice to meet you. Hope you don't mind but I've put my things on the bed in the corner."

"Annie Cavallaro," Annie replied, smiling. "And, no, not at all. That's fine."

She dumped her bags on the other bed, gazed around the Spartan surroundings and shrugged.

"Guess it'll do for a week," she offered, trying to break the ice.

"Own bathroom, though," Kylie responded, brightly. "At least that's a plus. Did you have a long journey?"

"A three hour drive. Not too bad. How about you?"

"Actually flew in this morning from West Virginia. I live a little outside Charleston, in a place called St. Albans."

"Sounds nice. You in school there?"

"It is nice. Not a coal mine or hillbilly in sight," she laughed. "And, yes, I'm in school - graduate school. How about you Annie?"

"Grad school, too, in New York. Fitzgerald."

"I'm impressed," Kylie responded. "Which area?"

"Biotech. Medical and chemistry. What about you?"

"Environmental. Someone's gotta save the planet," Kylie answered, with a smile. "Are you planning on going to the mixer tonight?"

"I don't know," Annie replied, diffidently. "I'm not much one for mixing."

"Drinks and free food. What could be better than that?"

"Think I'll catch an early night. It's a pretty full day tomorrow."

"Oh, c'mon, Annie. Part of coming to these get-togethers is to get-together. Make connections. Networking. See what other people are up to. I'm looking at it as a way of sizing up the competition."

Kylie's last remark hit Annie as strange. Even at Fitzgerald, she never thought of her fellow students as 'competition'. She always imagined they were all striving for the same thing – to in some way make the world a better place. But she did acknowledge it would be a golden chance to meet some of the other course participants and to perhaps assess where she fitted within their orbits.

"Okay, I'll come," she said, feigning enthusiasm. "Just don't leave me."

The mixer began promptly at seven-thirty and by the time Annie and her new friend arrived there must've been sixty or seventy people milling around, chatting, eating and drinking. Soon after, the facilitator of the course, Dr. Maurice Hawes, called for everyone's attention to say a few words.

"Welcome, one and all, to Harvard," he began, warmly. "Excellent turnout for what promises to be an outstanding conference. We have assembled some quite extraordinary guest speakers and presenters; all top people in their various fields.

"You are encouraged to attend as many seminars as you like and there will be ample time for questions – which I'm sure you will have. Tours have also be arranged of Harvard's extensive research facilities. Staff will be on hand to explain and answer any questions you undoubtedly will have.

"And, finally, this is a wonderful opportunity for all of you to talk and discuss amongst yourselves what each of you is currently working towards, to benefit from each other's knowledge and exchange views and opinions. I sincerely hope your week here at Harvard will inspire you to continue and expand the valuable work you have dedicated so much time and energy to. And without further ado please enjoy yourselves this evening."

Annie and Kylie quickly got themselves some food and a soda before settling down and learning more about how each of them had arrived at this point. Kylie did most of the talking since Annie was naturally diffident discussing even the remotest of personal information. She answered Kylie's questions as briefly as possible but after a while the conversation became stunted and awkward.

Fortunately, Annie seemed to be saved by two other participants who joined them and immediately took over the stage, touting their big ideas and ambitions for anyone to hear. Annie, who just wanted to leave and get a good night's sleep, left to use the restroom, vowing to go straight to her room afterwards.

As she started to exit the hall, she noticed a young woman sitting alone, seemingly anonymous and sad. Her head drooped and she constantly fidgeted with her glass. Annie, sensing a kindred spirit, quickly but calmly walked over to her, drew up a chair and introduced herself.

"Hi, Annie Cavallaro," she said, warmly, holding out her hand.

The young woman slowly raised her head, smiling weakly and clasping Annie's proffered hand.

"Mathilde Kizembouko and it is my pleasure to meet you."

An awkward silence gave way to more smiles before Annie asked, "Are you like me, not very comfortable with these things?"

"It is strange, yes," Mathilde replied, as Annie studied this young woman with intricate cornrow braids and bright, sparkling eyes. "I am certainly not used to such closeness except with my friends and family."

"May I join you for a while?" Annie asked. "I promise not to intrude, Mathilde."

Both women laughed as Mathilde answered, "I should like that very much. And most of my friends call me Matty, so I would like that also."

"Where are you going to school, Matty?"

"Right now, I am at Simpson-Bay University, but I am not happy there."

"Why, may I ask?" Annie gently inquired.

"They are trying to push me in a direction I do not wish to go."

"Oh, that's not good. What are you studying?"

"Biotechnology."

"Which area?"

"At this moment physics, but it is not what I want to do."

"Which is?"

"Medicine."

"Oh, me, too," Annie emphasized eagerly. "So, can't you just switch?"

Mathilde smiled ruefully.

"I do not wish to be disrespectful to those who have helped me get where I am."

Annie frowned, cocking her head.

"Matty, you have a choice. You can *always* change direction. I did myself, from med school to my current love – research."

"For you, maybe, but people would be disappointed in me if I wanted to do something else."

"Who? What people?"

"People who have sacrificed so much to send me here. You see, I come from the small African country of Norambuland. There, if they are lucky, only boys go to school because it is very expensive and not many families can afford the fees. Girls are expected to work in the fields, help the family, get married and have babies.

"But I have been very fortunate. I received a full scholarship through the G.L.O.B.E. to first attend my local high school and then pursue my dream of a university education."

"G.L.O.B.E., what is that?" Annie asked, intrigue that someone from such humble beginnings was now with her at Harvard.

"It stands for Girls Longing To Be Educated," Matty answered, her face now full of joy. "Some very fine people have put a lot of their money into seeing poor African girls receive a proper education. They hope we will return to our country and do good work. It is a fine program but they wanted me to study physics because our country is full of ores and metals. They hope I will be able to use what I learn to develop and enrich our resources.

"So far, I have done what they have asked but I think I can benefit my country by studying medical research. It is desperately needed."

"Will the funds you have been given continue even if you change majors?"

"I think so, yes, but I feel I will disappoint a lot of good people who have helped me."

"Have other girls from your country received this financial assistance?"

"Of course, yes."

"To study physics?"

"Yes."

"But not medical research?"

"I do not think so."

"Matty, your contribution to your country will be valuable no matter which discipline you choose. And, since other girls will be pursuing physics, you should follow the path you think will be of most use to your country. Also, doing what you love, what is your passion, will mean you will be able to give everything you have without feeling resentful. Always remember, being happy in what you do is half the battle."

Mathilde Kizembouko listened carefully to Annie's kind and thoughtful words of encouragement. She put her hands together and bowed her head.

"You are very wise for one so young. So, I thank you from the bottom of my heart for taking the time to speak with me."

"I'd be honored to spend some more time with you this week," Annie offered. "What you've achieved, what you are doing is special beyond words."

That night, before she went to bed, Annie called her professor and mentor, Virginia West, to ask a favor.

CHAPTER SIX

A NNIE WAKES EARLY, EAGER FOR the day to begin. As she quietly gets ready she remembers leaving the mixer with joy and anticipation. Mathilde, she recalls, finally agreed to Annie's suggestion they meet up as much as possible and attend as many seminars and workshops together. Mathilde's initial reluctance centered on her not wishing to impose herself or inconvenience Annie in any way. Annie smiles as she runs her response over in her mind.

"Matty, I'm very nervous about being here. You would be doing me a favor if you said yes. I already feel we are of like minds, that our passions are the same. Having someone like you to discuss and bounce ideas with would be amazing and so, so helpful. And I'm not taking no for an answer, so, tomorrow morning I will meet you for breakfast and we'll take it from there."

They meet up as planned, head for the campus cafeteria and over coffee and croissants discuss the day's program. Mathilde slowly begins coming out of her shell, feeling already that Annie is someone she can trust, even look up to.

"You are very kind to take me under your wing," she says, with a soft, warm smile. "I have been thinking what you have said to me yesterday and, yes, you are one hundred per cent right. I would very much like my studies to be in medical research. When I return to Simpson-Bay I will tell them of my decision. I hope I will not be expelled!"

The two young women laugh but Mathilde knows the threat may well exist. Annie immediately sees the fear and apprehension cloaking Mathilde's face. She reaches out and covers her new friend's hand with her own.

"Matty, on that front I might have some good news. Not promising anything but if you're willing to change schools we might be able to assist you."

Mathilde frowns.

"I do not understand. Change schools? Is that possible?"

"As I say, not promising anything but I talked with my professor last night and told her your situation. We have a small research group in my area at Fitzgerald and fitting you in, having you join us would not be such an adjustment. And the fact that you have a scholarship... well, that's just icing on the cake."

"I do not understand what that means," Mathilde chuckles, "but I am assuming it is something good."

Annie raises her eyebrows and nods. "One less barrier, let's put it that way. Now, all this is assuming you might be willing to come to us. Would you consider changing schools, Matty?"

"I would have to speak to people. To not do so would be disrespectful. But, yes, I would be very pleased to come to your fine school. And the great opportunity to study and learn with you and your professor will be something I should not miss."

"All right then," Annie answers. "I will do all I can to make this happen. Oh, wow, this is *so* exciting."

They spend the rest of breakfast talking more about themselves, becoming comfortable with each other, seemingly more like old friends than new ones. Then it's off to their first workshop with each of them feeling upbeat and cheerful.

The week's programs move inexorably through the days, exhausting most of the participants with just the sheer volume of information. Annie and Matty help bolster each other whenever the going gets too rough. But generally, they are enjoying the presentations and learning more than they ever thought possible.

On Thursday, just before Dr. Gail Stephens, Annie's professor's friend, is due to give her lecture, Matty tells Annie of a decision she has made.

"You and your college have been so kind to offer me a chance to study with you at Fitzgerald." Annie fears her new friend is about to tell her some bad news. She smiles a fake smile in anticipation. But Annie is wrong; the news is just what she wants to hear. "It would be an honor for me to accept. Thank you."

"Oh, Matty!" Annie exclaims. "Wow, this *is* great news. Wait until I tell Virginia. She was hoping for this as much I was. We'll get the ball rolling and make the transition as smooth as possible."

Looking at Matty, Annie suddenly realizes her unmitigated enthusiasm is not appropriate given the hard decision her friend had to make. She feels insensitive and tries quickly to apologize.

"Matty," she begins seriuosly, "I am so sorry for the way I reacted. This was so hard for you, I know. It's just that I am thrilled for you. You have made the right choice here."

"My family did not agree. They insisted I continue at my university to study how I can help my country with its natural resources. They do not want me to be disrespectful to those who have helped me." Matty then smiles. "We spoke some strong words to each other but they could not dissuade me. And, after I explained that my country also needs good medical people to help them find cures for the many diseases that are making us sick, they gave me their blessing."

Annie sits for a few seconds just staring at Matty, marveling at her young friend's resilience in the face of so much pressure. She has never known such a circumstance. She suddenly recalls her mother's profound proclamation to her from several years ago and recites the wisdom to Matty.

"My mother once told me what you become is more important than what you are. If your country is facing so much sickness and disease and you have a chance of perhaps finding cures, then you will become so much more valuable to your people than all the natural resources put together. Try thinking of your decision in that way, Matty."

Matty carefully considers Annie's kind and thoughtful words, quickly deciding they are not only encouraging but true.

"Your mother must be a very wise woman, too," she offers, her face lighting up with a huge grin. "I am very comfortable with my decision and knowing you will be supporting my efforts at Fitzgerald University only makes me feel excited and fortunate."

The two women break into smiles before Annie reminds them that Dr. Gail Stephens' lecture will begin in less than twenty minutes and they really should be on their way.

The lecture hall is full, bubbling with respectful chatter and anticipation. In fact, many of Harvard's summer-in-residence professors are also there, realizing this is a moment not to be missed.

Dr. Stephens is introduced by facilitator, Maurice Hawes, who jokes that even he is intimidated by the person standing next to him. He informs the audience of her level of academic achievements, in particular, her prestigious research career. "She is a Fellow of so many outstanding seats of learning even the fellows can't keep up!" he jokes again. "So, without further ado, please give a warm welcome to Dr. Gail Stephens."

Dr. Stephens, a tall, sharp-featured woman, steps confidently to the microphone. At nearly seventy, her disarming smile instantly warms her to the mostly young folk in the audience. She gives a brief chronology of her impressive academic life and achievements, with several self-deprecating remarks to illustrate how even she has struggled sometimes with various obstacles and disappointments.

She continues for over an hour highlighting four areas of medical research she considers vitally important to the benefit of mankind. Annie and Mathilde listen intently, rapt and astonished by the content of what they are hearing. Dr. Stephens gives, for the most part, an upbeat lecture, focusing mostly on the great strides medical research has made in the last fifteen years.

But she ends her presentation in the dark area of parasitic infections and diseases. On the huge screen she projects a fairly simple breakdown of the three main classes of parasites.

"I am assuming," she firmly states, pointing at the screen, "that all of you are aware, through your research progressions, of protozoa, helminths and ectoparasites?

"Protozoa can further be classified into four groups based on their mode of movement." Pointing again at the screen she highlights, in turn, the individual groups. "Sarcodina, Mastigophora, Ciliophora and Sporozoa. Now, can anyone tell me what is different about Sporozoa?" A few hands are raised, including Annie's. Dr. Stephens calls on her to answer.

"Sporozoa are organisms whose adult stage is not motile," Annie responds, confidently.

"Yes. Yes. Good. Absolutely correct." Next, her pointer moves onto Helminths. "There are three main groups of Helminths which, incidentally, is derived from the Greek word for worms." Some in the audience audibly groan. "Yes, I know," Dr. Stephens nods, "gross, right? But these are probably the most recognizable parasites folks are familiar with. Briefly, three main groups; flatworms, like tapeworms, some up to thirty-five centimeters in length; thorny-headed worms, mostly residing in the gut, and roundworms, found mostly in the intestinal tract, blood, lymphatic system or subcutaneous tissue.

"The last class, with which you all should be familiar, is ectoparasites. These, of course, are mostly the blood-sucking arthropods like mosquitoes, while others like ticks, fleas, lice and mites attach or burrow into the skin and can remain there for weeks or months. These arthropods are crucial to note because they are vectors or transmitters of many different diseases that can, and do, cause tremendous damage both in terms of morbidity and mortality."

Pausing briefly, Dr. Stephens brings up another chart. Dourly, she continues, "I want all of you to take a good look at these statistics. They are real and frightening. For instance, malaria kills more than four hundred thousand people each year, most of them young children in sub-Saharan Africa."

Mathilde leans forward, nodding her head in agreement.

"Now," Dr. Stephens asks, "why am I concentrating this last part of my lecture on parasites? You may wonder and I will tell you. It is because these Neglected Tropical Diseases get very little attention from the public health community. And," she emphasizes, "these NTDs cause devastation to over one billion...let me repeat that... over one billion people worldwide, mostly in rural areas of low-income countries.

"Most, not all, of the victims are children, who suffer in a number of far-reaching ways such as missing school, stunted growth and impairment of cognitive skills and general, healthy development.

"Which brings me to my main point of this important and imperative discussion. In Southern Africa right now and, in particular, the small country of Norambuland, there is widespread sickness and disease occurring to which we currently have no answers."

At the mention of her homeland, Mathilde rubs her eyes and shakes her head. Annie grabs her hand and tries to give her friend a reassuring smile. Now she is beginning to understand why Matty so desperately wanted to change her major.

Dr. Stephens continues, "This disease first reared its ugly head about five years ago. In the beginning, it was an endemic located within a small area. Fast forward to today and people are dying at an alarming rate. The disease is insidious and right now, despite our best efforts, no cure is in sight.

"It quite definitely is a parasite, but one that seems to have mutated to contain elements from all three spectrums. And, again, the reason I'm telling you all this is because *you* are the future solvers of not only this disease but many other similar ones around the globe that we still have no cures for."

The room is deathly quiet as Dr. Stephens' words resonate around the auditorium and into the minds of the attendees.

She continues, "What I would like you to do after you leave here tomorrow is to go back to your research centers and talk with your professors, mentors and whomever else you can rope in to see if there's a way to, at the very least, begin a dialogue about spending time and resources on solving some of these urgent problems. As I've said, *you* are now the solvers and saviors. Thank you for your time and your ears. Be well."

As a body, the audience rises and gives Dr. Stephens an almost five minute ovation. When she finally leaves the stage the atmosphere in the room has an aura of hope and responsibility. For a while, at least, everyone takes her message to heart.

Before they leave the auditorium, Annie and Matty are surprised to see Dr. Stephens walking towards them. Annie's heart pounds a little faster especially in the light of Virginia West's comments about this woman's accomplishments. But Virginia did warn Annie she would ask Dr. Stephens to speak to her and now they are almost face to face.

"Annie Cavallaro, I presume," Dr. Stephens says, offering her hand. "You answered my question about sporozoa so well. I was impressed."

Annie, diffident and awkward, offers her thanks.

"Virginia told me about you, that I should seek you out. And who is this?" Dr. Stephens asks, turning her attention to Matty.

"Oh, sorry. So rude of me. This is Mathilde Kizembouko. She's *actually* from Norambuland."

"I'm astonished," Dr. Stephens replies, as she pointedly stares at Matty. "So you've seen this strange disease first hand."

"I have not been in my country for five years. I have been here, in the United States, studying and learning, but I know from my family and friends about the sickness. It is very bad and getting worse every day." Her face, blank and serious, tells the other two all they need to know.

"Mathilde has decided to change majors and concentrate on medical research. I spoke to Virginia and she's offered her a place with me at Fitzgerald. Maybe we can do some work together on this disease to begin finding a cause and cure."

"There are a few people right now looking at it but so far all efforts have failed."

"How can that be?" Annie asks, a little too fervently; a little too angrily.

"Money, resources and priorities," Dr. Stephens answers firmly. "It's as simple as that. All I can do is highlight the problem in the hope that someone will recognize the urgency and do something about it. But, right now, I'm not holding my breath."

Annie seethes as she listens to what she feels are just excuses for doing nothing. Dr. Stephens quickly understands her frustration and offers some encouragement.

"Virginia has filled me in on the work you're doing at Fitzgerald. Very impressive. If I were you I'd speak with her. Perhaps there's a way to have you, and now Mathilde, concentrate some of your precious time on this. If you do, if you decide to look into this disease, you'll be doing pioneering work."

Annie is still dumbfounded that, despite the high number of deaths, no one thinks of this as urgent.

"Oh, yes, you can be sure I'll be talking with Virginia," Annie assures her. "This has to end."

Dr. Stephens covers some other topics with Annie and Mathilde before thanking them for their participation in the conference.

"You both have very bright futures. The world awaits."

"I had no idea," Annie tells Matty, as they walk through the quad. "Your country and your people," she continues, shaking her head, "I had no idea."

"Not many do. I am grateful for Dr. Stephens' concern. She is a very important lady and I know will try to help."

Annie is still upset that very little has been done to find a solution.

"This is ridiculous!" she rants, which for her is most un-Annie like. "It's almost as if no one cares because yours is a small, poor country in Africa. And there has to be a cure. There just has to be." Turning to Matty, she says, "If you are willing to help then I promise to dedicate all my research from now on to finding that cure. What d'you say?"

"I say you are a very determined woman and one I'd be honored to join."

Annie, calmer now, gives Matty a long, heartfelt hug before they head off for a well-earned dinner.

CHAPTER SEVEN

—————※ ※—————

I T WOULD BE A MONTH before Annie returned to Fitzgerald to
continue pursuit of her doctorate. At home, after relating her
Harvard experience to her proud parents, she decided to focus her
time on two fronts; Mathilde Kizembouko and Marie Curie. The
latter's biography had been neglected for some time and Annie was
eager to get back to, what she considered to be, another important
and personal project.

After leaving Mathilde at Harvard, she assured her new friend she
would work tirelessly to make her transition as seamless and painless as
possible. In this regard, she spoke often to Virginia to ensure Mathilde's
transfer suffered no glitches. And, indeed, by the week prior to their
return to Fitzgerald, all appropriate arrangements had been settled,
including financial and accommodation matters. Annie now breathed a
huge sigh of relief and could hardly wait for Mathilde to join her in the
research lab. Virginia, for all of her Herculean efforts, received a large
bouquet and a personal, heartfelt note of thanks, from Annie.

As she settled in the sun room to work on the next part of Marie
Curie's biography, Annie felt such a relief to be able to put all her other
projects aside for just a while. Whenever concentrating solely upon
Marie's life she always found herself immersed almost in another world.
The feeling was therapeutic, giving her the chance, if only for a while,
to be someone and someplace else.

Annie picked up Marie's story when she was in her late teens, still
struggling to become an educated young woman. Her determination

to pursue her studies, particularly her scientific ones, was remarkable in one so young. In order to make money and support her dreams, she first began tutoring younger students and then, for two years, became a governess with a wealthy family who were relatives of her father.

During this time, Marie fell in love with the son and both wanted to marry. The idea was firmly rejected by his family and Marie was devastated. Annie stopped writing, stared out the window and wondered. She wondered how Marie managed to cope with all the various emotions surrounding such a situation. First, falling in love at such a tender age and, then, having her wishes crushed at someone else's calling.

Annie sat back and pondered her own reaction. She, herself, had never experienced being in love; never felt the intensity of becoming attached to someone outside of her family. The moment jolted her, making her consider something she had never really thought about before. Here she was, at nearly twenty-six, wondering if she would ever feel the deep emotions Marie went through when she was much younger.

But it was a fleeting moment because what mattered to her right now, what consumed almost all her waking hours, was her education, her research and, most importantly, finding a way to help Mathilde's people in Norambuland.

Turning eagerly back to Marie's story, Annie described the next jarring chapter in her life when her close sister, Bronislawa, married and moved to Paris in 1890.

> *But you must come and join us, Bronislawa wrote in a warm, encouraging letter. We're in a large apartment on the Boulevard Saint-Michel. Lots of room and you could enroll at the University. Please say you will.*

Annie looked again at a copy of the letter and Marie's reply. Both copies were sent to Annie through her contact at The Curie Museum in Paris. Virginia helped secure Annie's introduction to the institution and now Annie was on first-name terms with its director, Renée Coutage.

> *It is impossible right now, Marie responded. I struggle with finances. Father cannot help me at this moment. You well*

*know his situation. So for the present I will continue my
education with my current tutor who is very understanding.
I am hoping to begin my serious scientific training soon by
practicing in one of the chemistry laboratories at the Museum
of Industry and Agriculture run by our cousin here in the
Old Town. I despair sometimes that I am losing so many
opportunities to advance and learn. But I am hopeful that
one day I will be able to join you in Paris and attend the
university there. Please know how much I miss and love you.*

Here, again, Annie realized how lucky she was, facing none of the
obstacles Marie found placed in her way. Marie was roughly the same age
yet struggled to find an easy path to her dreams and ambitions. When she
began thinking about writing Marie's biography, Annie knew only of her
scientific achievements and how revered she eventually became in that
orbit. But she hardly considered how that success was accomplished. She
merely assumed Marie had had a myriad of opportunities, and attainment
came easily and painlessly. How wrong that turned out to be as she
continued to research and delve deeper into Marie's astonishing life.

What struck her most of all, what affected her more than anything,
were the challenges Marie faced for simply being a woman. Among
other things, she had to deal with being raised in a society that shunned
educating girls and women; being refused admittance to higher learning
facilities and, later in life, not being easily accepted into the lofty, male
dominated, scientific fraternity despite her original discoveries that so
benefited society as a whole.

Annie sat back for a while and wondered what force, what drive kept
propelling Marie forward despite the odds. Her mother was dead, her
beloved sister now resided in Paris and her father apparently was not
yet in a position to assist her financially. And yet, Marie found a way to
continue her pursuit of a first-class education.

Looking back through her extensive notes, Annie realized Marie's
inspiration must have come from her parents, who always promoted
learning, being inquisitive and certainly to be of value to the world. Her
mother was a teacher and her father a scientist. They were the ones who
instilled in Marie the importance of always pushing forward despite any
challenges that came her way.

Annie left her room and sought out her mother. Blythe, in the kitchen, was delighted to see Annie, who, when writing, usually sequestered herself for hours at a time.

"There she is," Blythe exclaimed, opening her arms for a hug. "Hungry?"

"In a while, Mom, but first I have to tell you something."

Blythe motioned for them to sit at the table before smiling and giving Annie her full attention.

"It's the biography," Annie began. "I never imagined anyone having to overcome so many barriers and difficulties as Marie. I know it was a different time back then but, still, it just makes me feel so blessed and grateful to you and Dad and all my teachers for helping me so much." Taking one of her mother's hands in hers, Annie continued, "I just wanted you to know how much I appreciate all you've done for me."

Blythe began tearing up as Annie spoke, leaving the table and enfolding her daughter in her arms.

"Thank you, Sweetness but, honestly, we're the lucky ones. You've always worked hard, always done your best and, certainly, given us so much joy with your accomplishments. I'm sorry if her story is upsetting you but, as you say, it was a different time back then."

"No. No, I'm not upset just appreciative of what I have. I just needed to tell you that."

And then she was gone again after another warm hug.

Dearest Bronislawa,

I have just received a wonderful birthday present from father. As you know, his circumstances have improved recently and so he has offered to help me move to Paris! I am overjoyed, of course. Can I stay with you until I am settled? Please say yes! Oh, what a wonderful 24th birthday present this is. I will enroll at the University as soon as possible. Oh, Bronislawa, I am so very happy!

After beginning her next chapter with Marie's 1891 letter to her sister, Annie felt an uplifting emotional moment that took her, in her mind's eye, to far-off Poland as she watched an excited Marie begin what was to become the start of an historic journey. But the next two years were again difficult for Marie, and Annie marveled at this young woman's determination and indomitable spirit.

As soon as she was able, Marie rented a small apartment close to the University of Paris in the Latin Quarter. Just chronicling her new situation thrilled Annie so much she often found herself smiling as she entered the text. Here was a barely twenty-four year old young woman, in a hostile environment, experiencing a new and vibrant city. Right then and there, Annie vowed to visit Paris herself and, in particular, The Curie Museum.

> *But life was still a struggle for Marie, she wrote. She started her studies, physics, chemistry and mathematics, but being poor she had to exist on meager resources. In the cold winters she kept warm by wearing all the clothes she had. And so eager was she to learn she sometimes studied so hard and conscientiously she forgot to eat. She attended classes by day and tutored at night to earn enough money to keep her head above water. Hers was a tough, grueling life, but one she had chosen and welcomed with open arms.*

Again, this life that Annie described stopped her in her tracks as she tried to comprehend and come to terms with the hardships Marie faced every day. It made her self-conscious of all the times she had complained over too much homework or late night assignments. Never again would she grumble to Virginia about too tough a caseload.

But Marie's life, Annie discovered, to her great relief, improved considerably in the next two years. Being able to write about it, to see and feel the fruits of Marie's dedication and hard work, filled Annie with pure, unbridled joy.

> *In 1893, a little under two years since she'd left Poland for Paris, Marie earned her physics degree. This was a monumental achievement given all the odds against her, and one that made her proud beyond measure. Essentially, her life's work had finally been rewarded and recognized by such a prestigious seat of learning as the University of Paris.*
>
> *But still Marie was not satisfied. She began working*

at the industrial laboratory of Gabriel Lippman, while still continuing her studies at the university. With the help of a Fellowship to ease some of her financial burdens, Marie, less than a year later, earned a second degree. The future now seemed not only bright but full of so many possibilities. The time was ripe for her to begin her serious scientific career.

It was a satisfying moment for Annie to stop her writing for the day. The kinship she found with Marie brought her an amazing amount of personal satisfaction. Not only had she discovered a like-minded soul, an oddly contemporary fellow student, but she now looked upon Marie as a surrogate sister figure. It was a moment that mattered.

In another part of the house, Clive Cavallaro found his wife, Blythe, sitting grim-faced and ostensibly fighting back tears.

"Honey, are you all right?" he asked, genuinely concerned. Sitting down, he took her hand.

Blythe smiled weakly and nodded.

"Yeah, I'm okay, thanks."

"No, you're not. What's up?"

Blythe glanced out of the picture window, but the serenity of the beautiful garden failed to assuage her feelings.

Turning back to her husband, she confided softly, "There's a sadness in me that never goes away. And at times it overwhelms me."

"Sadness? About what?"

"About Annie. One day she'll be on her own, without me, without us. And the thought of that makes me sad."

"Oh, Honey," Clive responded, sympathetically, "that time is a long way off."

"I know. I know. But I look at her sometimes and remember. Remember how small she was, how happy and how the years have gone by so fast. I worry that she'll be on her own, that she won't have us to rely on, to give her comfort and support. I just feel sad sometimes when I think of those things."

"Well, she's still on the small side," Clive answered, with a grin, "and she's certainly happy. None of that is going to change. And what the years have done to her is turn her into a confident, amazingly talented, all-around good person. Honey, she's finding her way just like we all did.

She's okay, will be okay. She has sense, terrific empathy and passion in abundance for what she's doing. And I'm guessing she'll find someone, sometime, who will take her for who she is and be grateful beyond words they've found someone like her. She'll be all right, Sweetheart. You and I have made sure of that."

Blythe well knew Clive spoke nothing but the truth. She knew, too, Annie, her beloved Annie, would be okay. But she also realized that this sadness, however it diminished over the years to come, would never truly leave her.

CHAPTER EIGHT

L ATE AUGUST BROUGHT ANNIE AND Mathilde face to face again. The reunion was full of hugs, joy and endless chatter. In Annie's car, from the train station to Fitzgerald, this unlikely pair caught up with each other's lives whilst excitedly discussing the challenges both knew would be formidable, at times baffling, and yet critically urgent to Matty's people of Norambuland.

"Once we get you settled we'll go see Virginia. She's dying to finally meet you," Annie informed her. "But Matty," she continued, raising her eyebrows and grinning, "you should know beforehand she can sometimes be... well, most of the time, in fact...demanding."

"Oh," Matty answered, with an exaggerated frown, "and you are just telling me this now." Both young women laughed. "That is quite all right, I believe. I am used to teachers being strict. It is one way for pupils to pay attention and learn."

Virginia had secured a one-bedroom suite on campus for Mathilde in the block next to where Annie lived. After a couple of hours sorting out her things and grabbing lunch, Annie drove Mathilde to Virginia's office on the main campus.

"There you two are," she enthused, warmly. "I was beginning to worry." She gave Annie a huge hug before Annie introduced Mathilde. "Oh, this is so great, Mathilde," she gushed while hugging her, too. "I...we...are so happy and excited to have you with us on campus. Your previous school records and accomplishments are very impressive. I'd say we are lucky you chose us for your research doctorate. Now, sit yourselves down. We have lots to discuss."

Mathilde immediately warmed to Virginia, seeing a strong, positive woman who she felt would be demanding, as Annie had said, but fair.

"You are very kind to welcome me into your school, Dr. West. I hope I will not let you down."

"Okay, Mathilde, let's get one thing straight right away. You are here by virtue of one true fact, which is, in your academic career so far you have shown passion, intelligence, drive and a willingness to learn, adapt and be open to new ideas and theories. For us to be able to nurture and develop those traits with you is an honor and a huge responsibility. I hope we will not let *you* down. And, please, it's Virginia, not Dr. West. I only have Annie call me that when I'm upset with her!"

Everyone laughed as Virginia easily broke the ice. Mathilde bowed her head in thanks and a certain amount of relief.

"Now," Virginia continued, addressing both young women, "bring me up to speed with where you are and what you're thinking. Annie's told me quite a lot about the remarkable revelation Dr. Stephens presented at Harvard. So, let's hear your thoughts and plans."

For the next hour Annie and Mathilde convinced Virginia that their main research focus should be solely concentrated on the dire situation in Mathilde's African country of Norambuland.

"This is a no-brainer, Virginia," Annie asserted forcefully. "This disease is insidious and shows no sign of abating any time soon. We have to try and do something to figure this thing out.

"We know it's a parasite that's a combination of the three main types, which is scary in itself. It's attracted to the vitreous humor in the eyes. For some reason its main aim is to feed on the gel-like liquid, destroy a person's sight and move on and upward to attack the brain. Once there, it burrows deep, eventually causing massive bleeding and death. At the moment, despite some early work from African and European researchers, there is no known cure. What we need is a vaccine."

Virginia thought for a moment while Mathilde added some interesting information.

"The researchers in my country think the parasites are drawn to the vitreous humor because it's mostly made up of water but also contains glucose, proteins and collagen. But when it reaches the brain it feeds on blood. It has been impossible so far to stop it."

Virginia studied the two young women for a few seconds, marveling at the passion, intensity and selflessness they exuded. Annie's personality she knew well, but behind Mathilde's stoic countenance she saw sadness, a cry for help that was hard to dismiss.

"Well," she began, looking directly at Mathilde, "Fitzgerald certainly has the resources to help figure this out. But, obviously, it is no easy fix. You're talking about inventing a whole new vaccine, which normally can take years to develop, in a matter of months. They did it with Covid but the disease you're describing will have to be fought on many fronts. The vaccine needs to be so adaptable to treat its many different facets. Are you both willing to spend most of your waking hours on this?"

"Of course," Annie replied, for both of them. "It's urgent. It can't wait. We have to get on this right away."

"This is why I am here with you at your fine university," Mathilde responded, with a weak smile. "Under your guidance, with Annie for a partner, I will not rest until we have a solution. That is my firm promise."

Pride filled Virginia's heart at that moment as she listened to two twenty-somethings dedicate the next years of their lives to a higher cause. She gave each a hug before issuing a somber message of her own.

"This research, this journey you're about to embark upon, may necessitate you going to Africa, to Norambuland. Are you ready for that? Are you prepared to put your lives on the line?"

Annie turned, looked at Mathilde and waited.

"Matty?"

"To go back to my country and help them in any way I can, yes, yes I am willing to go."

"Well, that makes two of us," Annie confirmed. "That makes two of us."

The next month saw a hive of activity at the lab. Virginia, through a virologist she knew in South Africa, managed to have the head of the Norambuland research facility, such as it was, send her, after much reluctance, a number of different fluid samples from people in the area who either were stricken with the disease or had died from it. This, together with most of the data the researchers had accumulated so far, was immediately passed onto Annie and Mathilde to study, test and pore over. The work was exhausting and mystifying, like looking for a lost soul in the middle of the ocean.

While Annie took the lead, being the more experienced researcher, Mathilde was invaluable for the insights she provided with regard to the specifics of her country and its people. She gave Annie such an amazing in-depth analysis of culture, customs, geography, climate, demographics and a host of other relevant factors which might help them in their search for answers.

"Most of the areas in my country have experienced so many deaths from these parasites. We are a land of almost six million people," she explained to Annie as they took a mid-morning coffee break, "and I believe nearly three hundred thousand are gone."

Shaking her head in disbelief, Annie replied, "Matty, are there places, towns and cities that have been affected more than others?" She was trying hard to get a handle on the geographic make-up of Norambuland, to understand if certain spots were more susceptible than others.

Mathilde quickly pulled up a map of the country on her screen and went through each area and its climate with Annie.

"So you see, these places in red have been most affected." The map was almost entirely covered. "They are more inland so the climate is warmer. It is this that I think helps the parasites thrive. The other place, near or by the coast, is much wetter and cooler."

Annie studied the map, cocking her head and frowning.

"And in these towns and villages," she asked, pointing, "the cases are fewer?"

"Yes, that is correct. In fact, my whole family lives in that area and so far none of them have experienced what other people have. It is very strange, but I am so grateful."

Annie frowned again.

"It could be something or nothing, or just a weird coincidence. But I think we need to get in touch with the researchers out there in the field. Maybe they'd have some answers. Could be something to do with the climate, since you say it is particularly rainy there. I just don't know," Annie surmised, biting her finger, "but it certainly could be a factor. In the meantime, we'll just have to continue working with what we've got. How are you making out with analyzing the blood samples we've received so far? And do we have any from that area we've been discussing?"

Mathilde fetched the data printouts, handing them to Annie with a resigned shrug.

"I have discovered nothing that I would not expect to be there. Nothing extraordinary stands out. It is very frustrating. The parasites seem not to be discouraged by the normal immune system defenses. And, no, we have not yet received any samples from my area."

Annie saw how defeated Mathilde seemed by the lack of progress. To her, this was deeply personal; the lives of her countrymen and women hung in the balance. She left her seat and warmly hugged Mathilde.

"I know this is so difficult for you, Matty. But we've only just started the process. These things take time, sometimes years and years…"

"But we do not have years and years, Annie," Mathilde interrupted. "If we do not find a cure soon then…"

"I know. I know," Annie jumped in quickly. "And I'm going to talk to Virginia. This cannot wait. I agree with you. I think it's time we went to Africa."

CHAPTER NINE

"**Y**OU'RE GOING WHERE?"

"Africa, Mom, just as soon as Virginia can arrange it," Annie says excitedly.

"Oh, now, just hold on one minute, young lady!" Blythe responds, almost apoplectic. "Africa? I don't think so."

There is a brief silence as Annie considers her answer.

Finally, she says, "Mom, this is something I *have* to do. I already told you about the dire situation in Matty's country. We're going together to see if we can help figure this thing out."

"Yes, and from what you've told me people are dying in their thousands. Are you and she completely nuts?"

Annie begins to fume on the other end of the line. She expected push-back from her mother but not this outright objection. She tries again.

"It'll be very safe, Mom. Virginia will make sure of that. We'll be working from the research facility and they have protocols in place for whenever we'll venture out into the field. I'm really not worried."

But Blythe dismisses her daughter's defense and sees only the person she cares most about in her life putting herself in needless danger.

"Can't you do your work from here? I mean, is it really essential for you to go halfway around the world to do this?"

"We're drawing blanks so far and Matty has told me about a region where the people don't seem to be affected." Annie decides to concentrate on that aspect for an explanation. "Obviously, there's not much data in from there, so we need to be on site to check it out. Plus, their research facility needs help. They're thin on the ground. I'm sorry if this makes you upset."

"I'm not upset," Blythe responds strongly, "I'm scared to death."

The line again goes silent for a few seconds.

"Mom," Annie replies, softly, "thank you. I know you worry about me…will worry about me, but this is what I want to do. It's why I'm at Fitzgerald, trying my best to eventually make a difference somehow. This…going to Africa…seeing if I can help in some small way to come up with a cure, a vaccine…well…honestly, it's what I'm meant to be doing. I can't say no. I really can't and I don't want to."

Blythe listens carefully this time and what she hears makes her so proud of this daughter she's raised since a baby. She remembers. She remembers always telling her daughter, instilling it in her, in fact, that she could be anything she wanted to be. Well, now, she wants to travel to Africa to see if she can be of value there. It's nothing she didn't want for this precious child of hers.

"Oh, Annie, I so understand. I do. I do. It's just that…"

"I know, Mom, I know. But this is what I do, what I want to do. I'm sure it won't be the last time. I need you and dad to be happy for me, to give me your blessing. Honestly, I'm up late into the night sometimes trying to get some work done on the Curie book. She *really* put her life on the line. I can't be wrapped in cotton wool. And compared to what she put herself through, I'll…we'll…be okay, I promise."

"Can we at least see you before you go?" Blythe asks, hopefully.

"Well, yeah, of course. But it won't be for a little while yet. We need shots for some of the other diseases. You know I'd never go that far away without seeing you guys first. Virginia thinks it'll happen in maybe three weeks, so there's plenty of time."

"When you come, bring your friend. We'd like to meet her," Blythe offers, trying to be more positive. "She must be thrilled going back to her country?"

"She is, of course, but it'll be bittersweet, I'm sure. At least her family is okay so far. And, yes, I'll bring her, although she's quite shy."

The conversation continues with both mother and daughter saying only those things they know the other wants to hear. It ends with the usual sentiments of love, but as soon as Annie is gone the tears begin for Blythe.

"I'm really, really scared for her, Clive," Blythe tells her husband, as she relates Annie's earlier call. "Tell me something that will make me feel better."

Clive, the lawyer, used to dealing with emotionally fraught situations, puts those thoughts aside, concentrating only on being an understanding husband and father.

"Honey," he begins, with a warm smile, as he holds her hand, "of course you're worried. So am I. But, number one, we can't stop her going. She's an adult. Nor should we. This is who she is. This is what she's been working hard towards. Is it dangerous going to this hot spot in Africa? Of course, but this is her opportunity to put into practice everything she's learned at Fitzgerald.

"We've all taken chances in our lives," he continues, now touching his wife's cheek, "and we're all the better for them. She's right, we can't wrap her in cotton wool. That would be wrong for her and for us. She's on a path to who knows what. It's a journey and this is the first big step. I'm actually very happy for her and I know deep down you are, too."

Clive takes Blythe's head in his hands and kisses her forehead.

With a huge sigh she nods agreeably, as her eyes water with…what… sadness, fear, pride? All those emotions swirl around Blythe's head, but she now begins to feel better, more mindful, more understanding, but still not totally content.

"You're right, of course," she tells her husband, sniffing back a tear and bravely smiling. "This is the moment, isn't it," she proffers simply, "when everything changes, when we have to let her go and hope we did our job?"

"Oh, Babe, we did our job all right. Look at where she is and what she's about to do. Oh, yeah, we did our job all right. It's a moment, certainly. One that we all should cherish and enjoy."

"I think I'll feel better when we meet her friend," Blythe nods, as if trying to convince herself that her negative thoughts will hopefully disappear. "She'll look out for her, won't she?"

"Of course she will," Clive responds with a wide smile. "Honestly, love, everything will be fine." He hopes he sounds convincing because at this moment they're the only comforting words he can offer.

It's two o'clock in the morning. Annie sits at her laptop trying hard to complete the next chapter of Marie Curie's life. She knows time is now precious but she's anxious to chronicle the next important step in her biography. The years between 1894 and 1897, Annie discovers from her extensive research and help from Renée Coutage at The Curie Museum in Paris, are filled with stunning advancements and personal upheaval.

> *After earning her second degree, Marie began her scientific career proper by investigating the magnetic properties of various steels. This was not to be her life's work but a fortuitous stepping stone towards the monumental discoveries to come. It was at this time that she met a more experienced scientist. Pierre Curie, impressed with her credentials and work ethic, offered her laboratory space at The City of Paris Industrial Physics and Chemistry Higher Education Institute where he worked as an instructor.*

Annie stops in the quiet of her room, refills her coffee mug, all the while smiling at the irony of the passage she's just written and how it reflects her own journey. Up until she met Mathilde Kizembouko her research at Fitzgerald, under Virginia's guidance, concentrated mostly on extracting and understanding the properties of blood to expand on the many, as yet, unknown areas in which it might be used. But now, since attending the Harvard conference, she suddenly found herself thrust into the realm of searching for a solution to a deadly problem. How life changes, she thinks, as she sips her coffee and continues with Marie's extraordinary life.

> *Almost immediately, through their close working relationship, they began to develop strong feelings for each other. Pierre proposed marriage and was deeply disappointed when Marie did not at first accept. She still wanted to return to Poland to continue her education. In an effort to demonstrate his growing devotion, Pierre was willing to go with her even if it meant he would be reduced to teaching French.*

As she writes these words, Annie sees a conflicted twenty-six year old Marie struggling to balance opportunities and desires, both personal and professional. Her own journey so far had been devoid of conflict, except that now, with her decision to travel to Africa, she is more able to understand, in some small way, the hard choices Marie faced almost every day.

Annie, in her mind's eye, sees an independent woman, strong and determined to forge her own path. At once it is an inspiring moment for her; a moment to strengthen her own resolve as she moves into unknown areas and situations.

> *Shortly after rejecting, for now, Pierre's proposal, Marie, in the summer of 1894, returned to Warsaw to visit family and seek admittance to Krakow University. She was denied a place because of the rampant sexism in academia. She was a woman and, as such, did not seem worthy.*
>
> *Deeply disenchanted, she was convinced by Pierre to return to Paris to pursue her Ph.D.*

A smile returns to Annie's face as she rereads those precious words...*to pursue her Ph.D.* She silently thanks Pierre for persuading Marie to rejoin him in Paris. Obviously, without his steadfast belief and encouragement history most certainly would have taken a different course.

> *Although Pierre, in March of 1895, received his own doctorate for his extensive research on magnetism and was duly promoted to a professorship at the School, most people would readily admit that Marie was his 'biggest discovery'.*
>
> *Their professional and personal life together developed quickly. Their work was compatible, absorbing and important, while their relationship blossomed with bicycle rides and picnics in the magnificent countryside outside Paris. Pierre proposed again early that summer.*

Annie imagines the moment, delighted that this destined pair finally agreed to be together in love.

> *It was on a picnic when Pierre proposed.*
> *'My dear, sweet Marie,' he began, kneeling and holding*

her hand, 'would you do me the greatest honor of my life by becoming my wife?'

Annie sees them, sees them clearly on that summer's day. She hears Marie's voice accepting Pierre's proposal.

'I will, dearest Pierre, I will. You have made me so very happy. Thank you. Thank you.'

There was a chaste kiss and excited talk of when the marriage might take place. In fact, they were married on July 26, 1895, in a simple, non-religious ceremony. Marie wore a dark blue outfit instead of a bridal gown, which was to serve her for many years when she worked in the laboratory.

They continued their bicycle rides and liked taking trips abroad, which brought them even closer together. He was now someone on whom she could depend on both in her private and professional life.

The time is now three-thirty-five and Annie is tired but elated with the progress she's made on the biography. She rinses her mug, changes for bed, brushes her teeth and finally lays down under the covers, her mind still full of Marie and Pierre and the thrill of what it must have meant to them. Within ten minutes sleep overtakes her and, for a little while at least, she is floating free.

In her room not far away, Mathilde Kizembouko tosses and turns. She has none of Annie's peacefulness. None of her friend's certainty about the future. She frets and worries, mostly about the impending trip home to Norambuland. Her parents, indeed her whole family, she fears, will try their best to persuade her to remain with them. She knows it will be a huge problem and seeing them face to face will only make it worse.

On the other hand, and this is where Mathilde focuses on the positive side of her life, she is so looking forward to helping her people overcome the tragedy that currently surrounds them. Closing her eyes at this late hour, she finally drifts into sleep with feelings of resolve and tepid contentment.

CHAPTER TEN

Aᴏ FTER A HECTIC THREE WEEKS of preparation, coordination, finalizing the various flights to Africa and liaising with the small research team in Norambuland, Annie and Mathilde finally made their way to spend their last weekend with Annie's folks.

"Your parents are very gracious to receive me." Matty genuinely sounded humbled and grateful to be welcomed into a stranger's home. Of course, in her own country any outsider coming into a family's house would immediately become a member and treated accordingly. She hoped her experience with Annie's family would be similar.

"They're anxious to meet you, Matty," Annie answered, brightly, as they pulled into the driveway. "I'll try and stop them overwhelming you," she continued, with a laugh.

"And I promise to do the same with my family," Matty responded, with a huge grin, "but they are very expressive to say the least."

Blythe who had been keeping a sharp eye on the driveway for over half an hour, rushed outside when she saw the car pull in. Annie, soon engulfed in a huge embrace, managed to break free long enough to introduce Matty.

"Mom, this is Mathilde. Matty, actually."

Blythe hugged her, too. "So glad to finally meet you, Matty, I'm Blythe. Please call me that."

Matty half bowed her head. "If it is not disrespectful to you, then thank you, I will."

"C'mon. C'mon," Blythe said, ushering the young women into the house. "Your dad'll get your things in a while. You must be starving."

Annie mouthed the words *'See, what did I tell you?'* at Matty behind her mother's back, and both girls grinned broadly.

"Dad! Oh, Daddy, it's so good to see you!" Annie exclaimed, rushing into her father's arms. "This is my friend, Matty."

Matty bowed her head again, before being swept up in Clive's embrace.

"Hi, Matty, I'm Clive. It's great to have you here. How about a drink? Tea, coffee, soda?"

"I would very much like a glass of water if it is not too much trouble," Matty replied. "And I am so happy to be here, too."

Annie fetched herself a soda from the fridge before the group moved into the lounge.

"Make yourself at home, Matty," Blythe offered warmly. "We don't stand on ceremony around here."

Matty carefully folded herself into an easy chair but remained sitting on the edge of the seat.

"Annie tells me you are a teacher. That is a wonderful profession. I have benefited from many wonderful teachers myself."

"Third grade. Nearly thirty years now. And I'd like to think I've helped a few kids get a decent start."

Annie frowned before jumping in.

"Oh, she's just being modest, Matty. The kids adore her. I can attest to that. She makes more than a difference I can tell you."

Everyone laughed before Mathilde turned to Clive.

"And you are a lawyer, Mr. Cavallaro. Such a worthy profession, too. Annie is very fortunate having parents who are so accomplished."

Both parents smiled, hesitant to ask about Mathilde's family circumstances.

"You must miss home," Clive ventured, warily.

"My family is very important to me, yes. They have sacrificed so that I could receive an education. I am so thankful to them. But they wished for me to return home and use my education to help develop our country's natural resources. But I prefer working towards helping my country with its medical problems. I have resisted their wishes and it has caused some difficulties within the family. I am hoping when I return I can fully explain to them the importance of my decision."

Without wishing to place themselves in the middle of what appeared to be a delicate family situation, both Blythe and Clive hesitated before responding to Matty's heartfelt position. Finally, Clive, the father and lawyer, spoke for them both.

"Matty, we understand this has been very difficult and soul-searching for you, but in the end you are an adult with positive views and opinions as to where your future lies. I can promise you this will not be the last time in your life where you'll be faced with tough choices to make. We can only advise you to always do what you think is right for you in any given situation, however painful or conflicting that choice may be.

"We're sure, when you fully explain to your family your reasons for choosing this particular path, they will come to see and understand just what it is you are passionate about and how best you feel you can help your country. Please, don't be waylaid, sidetracked or in any way put off from doing what you know, for you, is right. Stay strong and resolute. All will eventually be well."

"Yes, Dad, you're right. That's exactly what I've been telling her," Annie jumped in excitedly.

Matty nodded. "She has indeed been saying those kind things to me. And now to hear them from someone so experienced in the world only makes me more sure that the decision I have made is the right one. Thank you. Thank you very much." She bowed her head in a grateful acknowledgment.

The rest of the afternoon and evening was spent eating, laughing and making plans for the weekend. Blythe wanted the time she and Clive had with the girls to be full of fun and meaningful moments.

As the weekend wound down a sudden thought occurred to Blythe as they all sat on the patio with dessert and coffee.

"Since you're not leaving for another day or two, I was wondering if you'd care to come into my class tomorrow."

"Well, sure, Mom, I'd love to. I had such a great time last May."

"Different set of kids now, Annie, but just a wonderful bunch. Matty, how about you? I'd love for you to come in."

Without hesitating, Matty answered, "It would be a great honor for me if I would not be in the way."

"Good, because what I was thinking was, and you can not do this if you'd prefer, is for you to tell the kids a little bit about where you're from and what life is like in Norambuland. We are actually studying parts of Africa in our social studies class, so to have someone like you from that part of the world come in and talk about your country would be unbelievably amazing. I mean, I'm sure some of the kids have never been too far out of town. Can I persuade you to do this for us?"

With a huge smile, Matty replied, "Oh, Mrs. Cavallaro...I am so sorry, I mean Blythe...that would be very special for me, too. If you think I would be able to assist your class in some way to learn more about Africa then I would be honored. Thank you for asking me to participate."

"You are going to love this, Matty!" Annie enthused. "And if no one asks any questions you can be sure I will!"

Everyone laughed and the scene was set for Monday morning.

"Girls and boys," Blythe began, as she stood before her class with Annie and Matty by her side, "I have a special treat for you this morning. I have two guests here with me who will be helping us with our lessons today." She turned, smiling, before saying, "This is my daughter, Annie...Miss Annie to all of you, and her very dear friend Matty...Miss Matty to you. Let's show them how we welcome guests into our classroom."

In a few seconds the whole room exploded with applause and loud cheers. Matty found it quite deafening.

"Now," Blythe continued, "this afternoon when we have social studies," she paused before asking, "by the way, can anyone remember what we're studying in social studies?"

A few eager hands shot up.

"Yes, Kyle?"

"Africa, Mrs. Cavallaro."

"Correct. And the big secret I have to tell you is that Miss Matty is from Africa!"

Gasps went around the room as the kiddos absorbed this information.

"And, she has kindly agreed to talk to you about the country in Africa where she comes from. It's called Norambuland. But first, we have a lot of other work to get to which Miss Annie and Miss Matty are going to help you with."

The morning passed by quickly with Annie and Matty assisting the kiddos with their math worksheets. Matty seemed amazed that the students were tackling quite advanced problems and she had to reach way back in her memory to provide the proper guidance. Annie, having been in her mother's class last school year, fell into the lesson quickly and effectively.

When it came to English and the kids' writing projects, both Annie and Matty were able to supply creative suggestions without doing the work for the children. Over lunch in the faculty room both young women, but in particular Matty, enthused about the high level of instruction.

"In my country," Matty offered a rapt audience, "this type of work would not be attempted for another two years. All your students are very lucky."

Eyebrows were raised at the comment and the gathering of teachers wondered how she'd managed to come so far so fast. Blythe spoke for them all.

"If that's the case then you are one amazing young lady. Here you are, a little over ten years from where my students are, and you're studying for your doctorate. That is so very impressive, Matty, and a credit to your dedication and hard work."

Julie Engel, another third grade teacher, echoed Blythe's words.

"Sometimes in this country we take education for granted," she began, nodding, "and sometimes we don't always appreciate the opportunities that come our way. But you, Matty, had none of those advantages. All you did was constantly work your butt off even when faced with what I'm assuming were tremendous obstacles. I wish you had more time so you could come and speak to my class."

Matty politely smiled, not really knowing how to respond to such high praise. It was true, all she'd done her entire life was work hard and then work even harder. That was the only path she'd known.

"You are all very kind to say these things about me. I know I have been very lucky to have been given the opportunities I have received. But no one can do these things alone. I have been very blessed with teachers just like you and many people who took me under their wings so that I might progress with my education."

"And she's here today," Annie jumped in, "because she had the courage to disagree with her family who wanted her to go in an entirely different direction. But Matty chose her own path, one that if we can start to figure things out in Norambuland when we get there, will hopefully save her country from this on-going deadly parasitic disease."

At this comment, Matty sniffed back a tear and was quickly consoled by Annie.

"I am certain I do not deserve all these kind words but thank you all so much. You are very special people and the children in this school are lucky to have you guiding them."

Blythe then glanced at the clock and suggested they return to the classroom to prepare for the afternoon's lessons.

During the morning session Annie and Matty roamed the classroom helping anyone who needed assistance with math, writing and science. This was a new experience for both the kiddos and Matty but, from the sound of animated chatter and giggles, everyone seemed to enjoy the interaction. Matty was surprised and fascinated by how much the children knew, while the girls and boys seemed enamored by a young lady with black skin who spoke so precisely.

When the time came for their social studies lesson the kiddos sat before Matty on a carpet in front of the smart board. Blythe made the appropriate introductions.

"All right everyone, now we come to the highlight of our day. Please pay attention because in tomorrow's lesson you will be expected to write at least a page on what Miss Matty is about to tell you. Now," she continued, turning towards Mathilde, "let's give Miss Matty one of our warmest welcomes."

In a second the whole class clapped and whooped for all it was worth. For Matty it was quite overwhelming. But, standing and smiling, she began confidently.

"Hello again, everyone, my name is Mathilde Kizembouko and I am from a small African country called Norambuland."

Annie pulled up a map of the world on the smart board and highlighted Norambuland.

"As I said, my country is small, with about six million people living there. Here in your country there are about three hundred, thirty million people. So, compared to the United States, Norambuland is very small indeed.

"I would like to tell you something about my growing up there. I was born in a small village called Tamopia. The house I lived in was not like anything you have in America. It was round, made of stone and had leaves from burkea trees as a roof. It was very warm and comfortable," she added, with a smile. "I lived in a house like this until I was about six years old. Then my parents, my sister and brother moved to a real house in the next town. I even had my own bedroom!" she exclaimed, with a wide grin.

"You are very lucky to have a school such as this one. My first school was another mud hut, where the children sat huddled together, without desks or books. But we always had fun and our teacher was the kindest lady ever.

"Later, when I was older, I moved to a bigger school which was only about two years old. Oh, my goodness, it was such a difference. Everything was so light. We even had our own desks and many, many teachers to help us learn."

A young girl, Pricilla, in the front row, raised her hand to ask a question.

"Did you have tests like we do?" she wanted to know, as she scrunched up her nose.

"Oh, yes, we did," confirmed Matty. "But that was a good thing because our teachers could see how well we were learning our lessons. Tests are very important as I'm sure Mrs. Cavallaro always tells you." Blythe nodded in agreement as she smiled a wicked smile. "Even now," Matty continued, "Miss Annie and me still have to take tests. But, if you have worked hard and paid attention to your teacher, it should not be too much of a problem."

"How did you come to be here?" Landon, a boy in the back row, asked.

Matty grinned. "I was very lucky. I was quite a good student and when I was in my high school my teachers heard of a person who was willing to give scholarships to deserving students."

"A scholarship, boys and girls," Annie jumped in to explain, "is like a present, where a generous person or organization pays for a student's education, usually when they go to college."

"Yes, so I was able to come to America to continue with my studies. Now I am in a research program with Miss Annie and I am very happy."

"And, girls and boys," Blythe interrupted, "both Miss Matty and Miss Annie will soon be going to Africa, to Norambuland, to see if they can help with a serious problem there. Now, since we are currently learning about Africa, I'd like Miss Matty to tell you about some of the important features in Norambuland. Miss Matty..."

"Oh, yes, I am so very happy to tell you about some of the wonderful things we have in my country. We have a sub-tropical climate. Lots of hot, sunny days, but also a rainy season where I come from in the northeast. This usually lasts from October to April or May and the amount of rain can be as much as forty to fifty inches. Yes," she acknowledged, as the kiddos' eyes opened wide, "that is a lot of rain, but it is needed to supply our wells and rivers with drinking water, and also water our crops.

"We grow almost all of our food which allows us to make delicious meals. Grains, fruits and vegetables are the main ingredients. Children learn from an early age how to cook, which is sometimes done on an open camp fire with an iron, three-legged pot. Using such a pot is very important to the taste of the food. Other times our meals are pan-fried in hot oil."

As she was talking, Matty noticed a boy's hand raised. She nodded for him to ask his question.

"What do you eat for breakfast? Do you have Rice Krispies?"

Some of the other kids giggled but to Matty it was a serious question.

"No," she answered, with a grin, "we do not have Rice Krispies. But we do have pap, which is a type of porridge usually made from pearl millet called mahanga." She turned and wrote the word on the board. "It is also served at dinner with fish, meat, cabbage and spinach.

"Another item we have for breakfast is veldt, which is a type of bread, made from wheat, flour, milk, salt, sugar and spices such as cinnamon and ginger. Baking powder is also added, which allows the dough to rise quickly. It is cooked over an open camp-fire and served hot with lots of delicious butter.

"Another treat our children enjoy is called a fat cake or oykyki." Again, on the smart board, she wrote the word. "The dough is deep fried into sweet, brown bread balls. The dough is usually prepared overnight before the sugar is added. It is then fried in hot oil until it is moist and fluffy. Our children like them as a snack. They are very delicious."

As the kiddos absorbed this interesting and mouth-watering information, Blythe asked Matty to speak about the wildlife and birds in Norambuland.

"As you can see from the pictures on the wall." she said, pointing to three large posters of lions, elephants and cheetahs, "we know about those, but what are some of the other ones?"

"Oh, we have many fine animals and lots of colorful birds," Matty confirmed, "as well as lots of reptiles and insects, which I do not like." She turned up her nose which elicited giggles from the class. "Some are poisonous but we learn from a very early age which ones are safe and which ones are dangerous."

"What happens if you get bitten?" Lola politely asked.

"That is a very good question. If you are near to a hospital you would go there. But unfortunately not everyone is close to one. So, when that happens, someone, usually an older person will treat you with our traditional medicines. These cures have been handed down in our country for many, many years. The medicines are made from a variety of herbs, leaves and ingredients such as berries we find all around us. And they are very effective. We don't lose many people to snake or insect bites in Norambuland."

"Now, some of the other animals we have are giraffes, wildebeest, the kudus antelopes, white and black rhinoceros, buffalo and plains zebras."

"What about tigers?" Chase wanted to know.

"No. No tigers, which sometimes surprises people. We also have lots of different kinds of birds. One important fact you should know is that the African fish eagle is our national bird, just like you have an eagle as yours. Just like it is in America, we have ducks, geese, guinea fowl, quail, partridges, pheasants, pigeons, doves, cuckoos, swifts, cranes, sandpipers, gulls and even flamingos.

"But two of the most interesting are jacanas and mousebirds. The jacana is a wader with very large feet and claws. This enables it to walk on floating vegetation in lakes. The mousebirds are grey with long tails and weave through leaves like rodents in search of food like berries, fruit and buds. This bird is very funny to watch as it can feed while it is upside down. Oh, I nearly forgot, we also have beautiful, colorful parrots."

Blythe could see, as excited as the kids still seemed, that they were beginning to fidget and look a little glassy-eyed at all the information they had to process. It was time, she knew, to wrap things up.

"All right," she began, clapping her hands, "I think Miss Matty has provided you with some wonderful and interesting facts about her country. We have time for just a few questions, so raise your hands if you have one."

Quickly, ten young hands were raised and shaken.

"Natalie, ask away."

"Miss Matty, what's your favorite food?"

"Oh, that is very easy to answer, Natalie. My mother always makes potjiekos...let me write that up for you...which is a rich meat and vegetable stew, cooked on an open fire in an iron three-legged pot. Having the correct pot is very important or the stew will not taste so good. That is my favorite dish for dinner."

"Nathan, what's your question?"

"Is there baseball in your country?"

"No, Nathan, we do not play baseball. Our national sport, indeed the whole of Africa's number one sport, is football, what you call soccer. Everyone plays it from an early age. I, myself played, and it was a lot of fun. The other big sport is athletics, particularly running. We all learn from a very early age that if we want to go somewhere we need to be good runners. It is nothing for our children to run two or three miles to the next village for supplies or to go to school. Running is very good for your heart. In my high school I used to run mile races. That seemed so easy," she added, with a laugh. "Also, African runners win a lot of marathons, like the Boston or New York City ones. They also do very well in the Olympics."

"Okay," Blythe advised, "last question for Miss Matty. Yes, Chloe, ask away."

"Were you sad having to leave your country? I know I would be."

"I was sad, yes, Chloe, of course. But some fine person gave me an opportunity to pursue my studies at a very well respected university in America. For me, it was the chance of a lifetime. I miss my family and my country but I am hoping when I have completed my education that I will be able to return and repay what others have sacrificed for me. So I am sad and happy at the same time."

"In fact," Annie jumped in, "as Mrs. Cavallaro has already mentioned, Miss Matty and I will be going to her country in the next few days to see if we can help with a big problem they are having right now. It'll be great for her to see her family again."

And with that, the kiddos went outside for recess without realizing that, in the years to come, they would proudly tell anyone who'd listen that they'd once had in their classroom for a day the now-famous Miss Annie Cavallaro and Miss Mathilde Kizembouko.

CHAPTER ELEVEN

B LYTHE IS OBLIVIOUS TO THE bustle and noise, the excited chatter from travelers saying their goodbyes and eager to be on their way. She sits, trying hard not to glance at the departure screen, holding onto her daughter's hand as though desperately hanging on to save herself from sinking. At this time, in this moment, Blythe knows only the feeling of dread. Her stomach flips repeatedly, her eyes never far from filling with overflowing tears. She looks forlorn, bereft of hope; an island in an island.

Annie, sensing her mother's angst, tries to keep the time they have left together light, filling the spaces with hopeful words and meaningful smiles.

"It's only for a month," she declares. "Really, no time at all. I'll call often, I promise."

Blythe pats her hand, nods and offers a forced grin.

"I know you will, Sweetie. I know you will. Thank you."

"I don't want you to be sad the whole time I'm gone," Annie says, looking directly into her mother's eyes. "I will be fine. The protocols are all in place. Promise me you and daddy will try and have some fun."

"Of course," nods Blythe, unconvincingly, still clasping Annie hand.

Annie feels the need to talk with her father, to make sure he fully understands her mother's anxiety.

"Daddy, can we get some coffee? Come with me?"

"Oh, sure, Honey. Be delighted."

As they move off, Mathilde sidles up close to Blythe.

"This is very hard for you, Blythe, yes?"

"So hard," agrees Blythe, sniffing back yet another tear.

"I and my family will take extra special care of her. We will treat her as one of our own. You do not need to worry although I know you will."

Blythe nods again.

"Kind. That's so kind and reassuring of you, Matty. She will be in good hands, I know that."

"May I tell you what my mother said to me the day I left Norambuland?"

"Of course," Blythe answers, leaning forward, intent on grasping any straw of comfort.

"My mother is a very strong-willed, opinionated and strict woman. She will always tell you what she is thinking; what is on her mind even if it is uncomfortable to hear. The night before I left she made me sit and listen to what she had to say. I was not prepared for her words but I have often remembered them. They have always been close to my heart and I am very grateful to her for her wisdom, love and caring for me."

Blythe raises her eyebrows and nods expectantly, eager now to hear what Matty has to reveal.

"She said to me, my dear child, nothing is more important than your education. And sometimes you will have to do what is necessary to be a good representative of our country and our culture. That means you must take nothing for granted. You always have to work hard no matter the obstacles placed in front of you.

"It is important, I so clearly remember her telling me, that you spend your time wisely just as we insisted you did as a child. Time to work; time to sleep and time just for yourself and your dreams. And that is what I have tried to do since I have become an adult.

"It is very clear to me you have raised your daughter very much as my mother raised me. She is now a responsible adult, making difficult decisions just as you and her father wished it to be.

"I deeply understand, Blythe, how much you and Clive will miss her and how worried you will be while she is away in Africa. But my mother trusted me to come to America knowing she had given me the correct upbringing to face whatever challenges that lay ahead. You have done the same with Annie and now you must trust her to face her challenges, too. That is all I have to say but I hope it will help you in some small way."

Blythe is momentarily stunned by Matty's words of wisdom. For one so young they are full of reason, sense and understanding.

Blythe hugs Matty before saying, "So wise beyond your years. Yes, you have helped me so much. I'll still worry but I now know she'll be safe if only because she'll have you there beside her. That's a great comfort to me. Thank you."

Over coffee, in a nearby airport café, Annie and her father sit close, each dancing around the delicate matters they know they have to address. Finally, Annie breaks the impasse.

"Dad," she begins, touching his hand, "I want your blessing, to tell me you understand."

Her father shifts uneasily but smiles and looks Annie in the eye.

"It's never been in question, Honey. I know this is something you have to do. You don't need my permission; you have my love."

"About Mom – you have to try and get her to relax about this trip. I can't be in Africa and thinking all the time she's crying her heart out. I will be okay, honest. See if you can get her to…"

"Annie, listen to me," Clive interrupts, "we both know your mom very well. I'm certainly not going to tell her how or what to feel. It's not a question of her approving or disapproving of the trip – that's settled. What she feels – what we both feel – is being powerless to help you if you need us, not just with this trip but for however many days we have left as your parents. That will never change. You will always be our child and it's our problem not yours.

"Parents always want to save their kids; that's just par for the course. And you have to accept that but not be tied down or limited by it. Both your mom and I trust you to make wise decisions now and going forward. We just hope we've done enough to guide you, to give you the strength and courage to pursue the life you want. Judging from the results so far I'd say we've done a pretty good job."

Annie nods, smiles and throws her arms around her father's shoulders.

"You have, Dad. You and Mom have been nothing but the best. And you know this leaving thing isn't all one way. I'm going to miss you guys like you wouldn't believe *and* I'll be worrying about you, too, until I get home. Just remember that!"

Blythe watches them saunter back from the coffee shop, rises, excuses herself to Matty, grabs Annie's arm and guides her to a quiet spot. Annie waits respectfully, unsure of what to expect but decides to speak first.

"Mom..."

Blythe, her palm insistently up, stops her.

"Baby, please, I just want you to listen to me for a few moments." Annie fears the worst but hopes for the best. "I have been," Blythe continues earnestly, "very selfish..."

"Mom, really..."

"Please, Sweetheart, just listen. I have been very selfish when I should have been immediately excited for you. You'll say that's okay, it's no big deal, but it is. I have behaved badly for someone who should know better...who knows you better. Although, naturally, I'll be anxious all the time you're away, I'm also so happy and proud of you for taking on this desperate problem. This is what you've worked so hard for, so I want you to know you have my blessing, thanks and love." Blythe takes Annie's head between her hands and kisses her forehead. "Find the cure, Sweetness. I know you will."

And then they are gone, these two young pioneers, these two young saviors. They are on their way.

As they settle in for the almost fifteen hour flight from JFK to the Oliver Reginald Tambo airport in Johannesburg, Annie and Matty experience very different emotions. Matty feels elated to be going home to see her family while simultaneously being apprehensive at the thought of dealing once more with demands she pursue her original studies. But as the plane winds its way down the Atlantic Ocean, mostly through the night, she manages to sleep remarkable well.

Annie doesn't sleep, deciding instead to spend her solitary time on the Curie biography. She well suspects the next month will probably afford her no time to work on it, so this is an opportunity to seize. Her laptop buzzes into life and she is soon immersing herself in Marie's life once more. She quickly reviews the last chapter she wrote before moving forward.

Now, she writes,

> *After Marie and Pierre's marriage, Marie decides the subject*
> *for her thesis will be researching uranium rays. Her colleague,*
> *Henri Becquerel, discovered that uranium salts emitted rays*

*that mirrored X-rays in their penetrating power without
depending on an external source of energy. They apparently
appeared directly from the uranium.*

Annie dwells on this information for a while, thinking how
fascinating this line of research must have been for Marie. She thinks
about her and Matty's impending journey to Africa to …what…discover
a cure or an antidote to the devastating parasitic disease spreading
rapidly there? Yes! This is exactly the blind path Marie undertook, and
now she and Matty are carrying a similar torch for others to follow.

Towards the end of the current chapter Annie explains how Marie
tries to prove her theory.

> *Using her husband's electrometer, which he had developed
> fifteen years earlier with his brother, she actually discovered
> uranium rays caused the air surrounding a sample to conduct
> electricity. From this Marie surmised that radiation must
> come from the atom itself.*
>
> *As much as this hypothesis thrilled and excited Marie
> another, more important, event thrust itself into the
> limelight. In 1897, Marie and Pierre's daughter, Irene, was
> born. This joyful happening was a blessing as well as a source
> of upheaval, particularly with regard to the family's delicate
> if not, precarious, financial situation. Irene was another
> mouth to feed so, to help support her growing family, Marie
> began teaching at the École Normale Superiéure.*

Again, Annie marvels at Marie's fierce determination to always
push forward even when she's tired and sometimes mentally exhausted.
Although teaching and caring for her infant daughter, Marie insisted
to Pierre that their research must continue.

> *"This breakthrough we've made on the uranium rays cannot
> be stalled or halted now," she tells her husband. "We must
> work and work to develop what we have begun."*

But they faced many practical problems, the least of which was
finding a suitable place to continue their research. After several

frustrating weeks they managed to secure an abandoned shed and soon turned it into their official, but rudimentary, laboratory. Unfortunately, it was poorly ventilated and not even totally waterproof, so they were oblivious to the harmful effects of any radiation exposure. But, it was their own facility, where they could continue to explore other possible elements that emitted radiation.

At this point Pierre was a part-time contributor to Marie's work. He had his own teaching and scientific duties to perform but when, in 1898, Marie found that the element thorium was an additional source that emitted radiation, Pierre became much more astonished and engrossed with her discoveries. By the middle of 1898 they both decided he should join in her research.

As Annie writes the next section she is thrilled to record Marie's response to her husband's offer of assistance.

> *Because Marie felt strongly that the majority of male scientists would find it hard to believe a woman was capable of producing original, progressive work and discoveries, she plainly told Pierre that while she would definitely seek his respected opinions, it was her, Marie, who owned the research.*

Just writing that paragraph fills Annie with such a feeling of empowerment, not just for Marie but for all the women scientists who have followed in her footsteps. She leans back in her seat, closes her eyes and lets the moment wash over her. She glances at Matty, wishing to share her...pleasure, but Matty is sound asleep. Annie notices the time, only four hours now until Johannesburg, and decides to put the Curie biography away. What she's written on the flight, what she's digested and taken to heart has buoyed her in ways she could never have imagined.

She stows her laptop, takes a drink, fluffs her pillow and carefully reclines her seat before trying hard to follow Matty's example. It works. Before she knows it the pilot announces their descent into Johannesburg.

CHAPTER TWELVE

T HE MOMENT ANNIE WALKED INTO the terminal in Johannesburg
only one thought entered her head – *OMG, I'm actually in Africa!*
It was six-twenty in the evening, a full twenty-four hours or more since
she and Matty had left New York. That world now seemed so far away
to Annie; the touching, heartfelt farewells to her parents; the long flight,
even the latest completed chapter of the Curie biography.

Their connecting flight to Cape Town wasn't set to depart for at least
another three hours, plenty of time to call her dad at his office, where the
time would be around noon. Her mom, unfortunately, would be in school,
but once ensconced in their Cape Town hotel for the night, she would
make sure she spoke to Blythe, who she knew would be worried stiff.

When they finally found a quiet spot to relax with their drinks,
Matty beamed broadly at Annie.

"I want to officially welcome you to Africa. I hope you are as happy
as I am?"

"Oh, Matty, you have no idea. Never in my wildest dreams, but
that's the beauty of being in research, you never know what's around
the next corner."

"Yes," Matty agreed enthusiastically, "as a young girl growing up in
Norambuland I did not believe I would ever leave my village. But here
I am studying for my doctorate and joining someone as learned as you
as we try to help my people. For me, my life has been amazing."

"And it's only the beginning remember," Annie enthused. "I know
you are destined to do some great, innovative work."

At seven, Annie took out her phone, pulled up in her father's office number and waited, hopefully, for the connection to go through. When it did she could hardly contain herself.

"Dad! Dad, hi, it's Annie! Can you hear me okay?"

"If you'd stop shouting," he joked, "we'd be just fine."

"Oh, sorry, but I was just pleased it went through."

"It's all right, Sweetheart. Now, where are you?"

"Johannesburg. Landed about forty-five minutes ago."

"Good flight?"

"Yes, great. Even managed to get some work done on the Curie bio. How are you, Dad?"

"Up to my eyes in paperwork as usual. But we're fine...missing you already."

"She okay?"

"Sure. We actually took in a dinner and a movie last night. That helped."

"I'll call her when I get to the hotel in Cape Town."

"You'd better or else." Clive joked again. "How's Matty, pleased to be nearly home?"

"She is, but I keep having to remind her this is not a vacation trip. Tomorrow is when all the fun starts."

For a brief moment there was a lull in the conversation until Clive spoke from the heart.

"Do what you do best, Sweetheart. There is nothing you can't figure out. Those folks are lucky to have you along for the ride. I'm very proud of you. Never forget that."

"Oh, Daddy, thank you. Thank you. I'll do what I can."

After briefly putting Matty on the line, Annie said goodbye to her father's familiar, upbeat voice. It was not sadness she felt now but absence.

The two hour flight by South African Airways to Cape Town went by in a flash. They were met at the airport by a member of the Norambuland research team and driven the short distance to their hotel. Once ensconced, Annie called her mother while Matty, in another room, called her parents.

Blythe picked up immediately, just grateful to hear her daughter's voice again.

"Sweetheart, hi. Oh, thanks for calling again. Dad told me you'd spoken to him earlier. How are things?"

"Safely here. Tired but raring to go." After a pause, Annie asked, "And how are you doing, Mom?"

"Good, Sweetheart. Really, I'm okay. Missing you of course, but staying busy at school and looking after your dad, as usual."

They both giggled at that remark.

"Yeah," agreed Annie, "he's a handful all right."

"So," continued Blythe, "you're finally in Africa. What now?"

"We head out tomorrow with the guy from the research center up the coast to Norambuland. Matty says it'll be like a mini safari. Only problem is, it's the rainy season so there won't be a lot to see."

"Will the rain hamper your research? I mean, getting out into the field and that."

"No, actually, Mom, it's a good thing because the parasites will not be out and active. We'll be able to travel around in relative safety."

Blythe blew out a silent breath in relief at that piece of news.

"And Matty? She must be overjoyed to be going home again."

"She is, but I think she's apprehensive. She still thinks her parents will try and persuade her to go back to her original studies. I'm going to try my best to help her there, but I guess her mom is very strict and stuck in her ways."

"Then be the peacemaker and make her see sense, that Matty's calling is with you and trying to find a cure for that dreadful disease."

"Oh, don't worry about that, Mom, I'm way ahead of you already," Annie said, with a laugh.

"Atta girl!"

"Well, Mom, I gotta sign off for now, long journey tomorrow. Need to get a good night's rest. Give yourself a big hug and one to Daddy, too. I'll call again as soon as we're settled at the center. And don't worry, I'm fine, really."

"I know, Sweetie, but a mom's a mom, you know and always will be."

"Love you. Bye."

"Bye, Sweetheart. Bye."

And then she was gone again.

The over three hundred mile journey to Norambuland began for Annie and Matty early the next morning in the company of their guide and driver from the research center, Philippe Drombasso. An excitable man, Philippe described how the other members of the small research team were anxiously awaiting their arrival.

"My colleagues are very honored to have such distinguished scientists come all the way from America to help solve the very bad disease we are experiencing. They have studied your careers and feel they are in very good hands. And to have our sister, Mathilde, back is just so joyful for all of us."

Annie was anxious to dispel any false hopes for a quick solution.

"We will, of course, do what we can to assist you and your colleagues, but I have to tell you, Mr. Drombasso, there is so much detailed work ahead of us that will take months if not years to complete. But we are happy to take this journey with you and the team."

Matty nodded her agreement while adding, "In the month we will be here I am sure, under Annie's leadership, we will be able to make a significant start. But our work will not be done. It will continue in America."

"Yes. Yes, I understand completely what you have said," Philippe answered. "It is just that the situation is dire and we are hoping for a miracle."

Annie, as a practical and now seasoned researcher, replied, "Unfortunately, there are no sudden miracles, Mr. Drombasso. All Matty and I can promise you is to put all of our knowledge at your disposal."

"Yes. Yes, thank you. We will be patient."

By this time they had covered almost one hundred miles and were now driving along a stretch of road parallel to the Atlantic Ocean. Annie was immediately fascinated by a myriad of birds peppering the sand and dunes or diving into the sea from great heights.

"What are some of those, Matty?' she asked.

"The big ones are the African fish eagles – our national bird - as I told your mother's class. Then there are sandpipers, gulls, ducks and mostly swifts."

As they turned again inland the landscape changed dramatically. Now the land was generally flat, dotted liberally with a variety of trees.

"Those are beautiful," Annie commented, to no one in particular, "and so tall."

"They are leadwoods," explained Philippe. "Yes, they are very tall. Some even grow to be sixty-five feet or more. As you can see they are growing by the edge of that river. These trees are highly respected here for their spiritual and cultural value. In times past, the ash from dead, burned trees was used to make toothpaste or mixed with milk to form white-wash paint for the huts."

Also along the river Annie noticed what seemed to be a palm tree. She asked Philippe about it.

"That is called a maharani. Again, very important to our people. The leaves provide fiber for weaving mats, hats or baskets and are very strong. And the tall leaf stalks are used to make fencing. Again, very strong. The nuts are quite hard but can be processed and eaten. Our traditional drink called ombike is made from the palm fruits. And since tourism is one of our main industries, the nuts, which some people call vegetable ivory, are often carved into small ornaments and trinkets and sold to tourists as key-chains, necklaces or charms. So, you see, nothing is wasted here in Norambuland."

As they made their way farther north the rain began in earnest. Before long it lashed against the windshield and then cleared up almost as quickly. Annie noticed the amazing sapphire sky which filled her eyes with its deep blue/purple canopy. It was, she thought, the most vibrant, beautiful color she'd ever seen.

As if that moment of magic wasn't enough, as they scaled a steep hill and descended the other side, what should greet them but a herd of bush elephants wallowing in a large, muddy water hole.

"Oh! Oh!" she gasped, before grabbing Matty's arm.

"Yes, it is truly amazing when you see them so close for the first time. But you will get used to it," Matty joked.

Philippe stopped so that Annie could take pictures. They weren't the last ones she would take on this trek. Before long they encountered zebras, giraffes, hundreds of wildebeests and even a few buffalo. Annie felt she had slipped back to second grade again and was watching an African wildlife program in class, except that this was real and almost unbelievable.

As they left the rural landscape, the last fifty miles of their trip again astounded Annie. Gone were the mud-hut villages, the vast farmlands and the abundance of wildlife. Now, as they neared Timsotto, the capital of Norambuland, a relatively modern city greeted her eyes. It was as if she'd suddenly stepped off the moon into the streets of New York City.

Well-kept apartment blocks, glass-sided office buildings and bustling streets stretched for miles. But in this northeast area the rain was still plentiful and, as they travelled through Timsotto on their way to the research center twenty miles away, it lashed down once more. Philippe continued to do an excellent job of navigating the sometimes flooded roads and within another half-hour they arrived in Natalville where the center was located.

Inside they were warmly greeted by the small staff, headed by Dr. Desmond Amdao, a seemingly nervous man who smiled and nodded at every opportunity.

"Welcome," he began, shaking hands with Annie and Matty, "welcome," he repeated nervously, "we are very pleased to have you join us at our modest facility. Please, let me introduce everyone here."

The other five members of the research team bowed and shook hands before respectfully stepping back in deference to their boss.

"I am sure," he continued, "you are tired after your journey, so please, go with Philippe to your hotel and we will all meet back here tomorrow morning at nine o'clock."

Annie frowned. She hadn't come all this way to delay her mission by even a few hours.

"If you don't mind," she offered, pleasantly, "we would like to get a feeling for your facility and its capabilities. As you know our time with you is short so a quick tour would help us enormously gauge how we might proceed." She waited, with eyebrows raised, in expectation.

Dr. Amdao stared at Annie and Matty for what seemed an age, a deep frown creasing his brow.

Finally, he answered, "We are not as prepared as we would like but I will show you the most important areas. Please come with me."

For the next half-hour he walked Annie and Matty through some of the labs and clinician areas and, with the help of his assistants, explained in brief terms where they were with respect to gathering data, samples and field reports.

As Annie listened carefully she was dismayed to learn that generally speaking not much positive progress had been made in the eighteen months this facility had been functioning. When she posed several pertinent questions to some of his fellow researchers, Annie received generalized answers, evasiveness and in some cases a reluctance to discuss important topics involving the supposed data that had been collected.

Overall, Annie came away from the tour with a sense that this group, under the direction of Dr. Amdao, was doing nothing more than treading water. It left both she and Matty with empty feelings and worries that their intended help would be dismissed once their time in Africa was over.

In an effort to show Dr. Amdao her imperative intention of finding a long-term solution most probably with the formulation of a vaccine, and to also impress upon him that the status quo at his laboratory could not be allowed to continue, she issued a veiled threat which she hoped he would take to heart.

"This evening, Dr. Amdao, Ms. Kizembouko and I will go over the data you and your staff have so far collected which, as far as I can tell from a cursory review, is not nearly extensive enough to provide the basis for a full controlled study, and we will provide you tomorrow with our thoughts on a pathway to remedy the situation."

Dr. Amdao frowned and immediately began to protest at this apparent up-start American's attitude and disrespect.

"I will excuse you your discourtesy, but I will not allow your unkind words to besmirch what we have tried to do here. Further…"

"Dr. Amdao," Annie interrupted, "forgive me, but we don't really care about your hurt feelings. All we care about is finding a relatively quick solution to a devastating disease that has, I might remind you, already killed in excess of four-hundred thousand of your people and several hundred thousand in other parts of Africa.

"Now, we are here at the request of the Norambuland government. We have their full authority, as I'm sure you know, to do whatever it takes to help solve this dire problem. You should know I will not hesitate to contact the Health Minister should any road-blocks be placed in our way. Am I making myself clear?"

Matty's eyes opened wide while Annie's forceful oration was in full swing. She could hardly believe her friend was speaking in such a direct manner to the head of the facility, but was so proud of her for saying what needed to be said. Her head swiveled towards Dr. Amdao, awaiting his response.

After a few seconds, he curtly replied, "Very well. You will, of course, have our full cooperation." And with that he turned on his heels and walked away.

Later that evening in their hotel room, Matty reiterated what she had felt earlier about Annie's passionate and required speech to Dr. Amdao.

"I have to tell you how very brave I thought you were when addressing Dr. Amdao. Those were things that definitely needed to be said but I do not think I could have done what you did."

Annie, while pleased to hear the praise, felt a little dismayed by Matty's words.

"I understand completely," she replied, warmly yet firmly, "but one of the lessons I've learned being in research and you have to, too, is that you can never, ever, take 'no' for an answer.

"I also understand how you were raised, Matty, that you may not have been encouraged to question those people in authority positions. That was your culture but now you're an adult and fully involved in a field that requires questioning everything, even your own research, in order to hopefully discover the necessary solutions. Believe me, it took me quite a long time to figure this out for myself. I was terrified of Virginia at Fitzgerald when I first met her and began under her tutorship. But she gave me the exact advice I'm passing onto you; question; question and then question some more. Took me quite a while to feel comfortable with that but it worked and I'm a much better researcher now."

When she finished speaking, Annie hoped she hadn't compromised a growing friendship, but she was also convinced what she had to say needed to be said. She needn't have worried because Matty's response came with a warm, receptive smile.

"I am very fortunate you came into my life, Annie, when you did. You have already taught me some many wonderful things I did not know or understand before. I will take your words and advice very seriously. It will make me not only a better researcher but also a better person. Thank you. Thank you."

Later, after dinner, they settled down to a long night of sifting through the data Dr. Amdao's team had accumulated, and formulating their own comprehensive plans for moving forward with or without his help.

While deep into the figures and information they were disturbed by someone knocking on their door. Cautiously, Matty opened it to find one of Dr. Amdao's researchers standing diffidently outside. Matty recognized the young woman and invited her in.

"I am so sorry to disturb two such important people," she began, almost in a whisper, "but there are some things I think you ought to know."

Annie invited the young woman to sit down before asking her to continue.

"My name is Joyce Obuna and I am one of Dr. Amdao's researchers."

"Oh, yes, we met you earlier at the lab," Annie confirmed. "How can we help you?"

"I heard what you said to Dr. Amdao about the studies we have so far conducted and you are quite correct. We have made little positive progress despite being well funded by the government. I should not be telling you this. I should not even be here but my people are still dying in the thousands and Dr. Amdao doesn't seem to …to…care. All he seems to care about is continuing to receive the government grant money. I cannot stay long for fear of being seen but I wanted you to know what is really going on at our facility."

Both Annie and Matty were shocked to hear what Joyce revealed, shaking their heads in almost disbelief.

"How can you be so sure?" Matty asked, pointedly. "We understand he is highly respected in his field."

"That is true but he does not seem to like or listen to any opinions but his own. We researchers have to follow his directions without question or we are no longer employed at the facility. As you have seen our equipment is not very modern despite the fact that the government gives us adequate funds. It is all very disturbing.

"But I must not stay any longer," Joyce said, as she made her way out. "I just wanted you to be aware of our desperate situation. Thank you both for taking the time to listen."

"No, thank *you*," Annie answered, shaking Joyce's retreating hand. "You can be sure we will act on this information. Go now and be safe."

After Joyce's departure Annie and Matty considered their options for dealing with Dr. Amdao. Matty had no idea how to proceed but Annie knew exactly what she would do.

"We are here at the request of the government. That is our authorization. Dr. Amdao can either help or hinder our research but he will not stop it. Tomorrow," she continued, smiling, "I will tell him I am taking charge for the month we are here. After all, we haven't come all this way to be defeated by someone's ego and greed."

CHAPTER THIRTEEN

B Y TWO O'CLOCK THE NEXT morning Annie and Matty had pored over what little data and information Dr. Amdao's team managed to accumulate in the eighteen months of its existence. Considering the vast number of deaths and the large, on-going contingent of hospital cases battling this parasitic disease, there seemed to be a dearth of basic, critical studies one would normally expect. There were very few in-detail autopsy reports; blood samples lacked in-depth analysis; tissue samples seemed to have been haphazardly taken, broken down inconsistently and with insufficient classification; mutations of the parasite and their different effects on the body's immune system had barely been monitored and much, much more. For Annie and Matty the result of their late night review session was depressing to say the least.

Despite these revelations Annie put together a comprehensive plan of action to address most of the shortcomings. At breakfast she presented Matty with the list.

"We only have five assistants at the facility so manpower is short. Nevertheless, we will assign each to a specific task. I'm putting you in charge of Joyce and Philippe and I'll manage the rest including our friend, Dr. Amdao.

"Here are the protocols and systems I want you to work on with Joyce and Philippe. You know these well but you can adjust, modify or use your initiative as you see fit in order to get to the bottom of what we need to find out. These are crucial, Matty, but I know you can handle them."

Looking carefully over the pages, Matty seemed surprised and grateful Annie had entrusted her with some vital investigative work. For a moment her pulse beat faster as she just hoped she'd be able to deliver on Annie's visions.

"This is an honor for me. That you would think I am capable of managing this task makes me feel grateful beyond anything I can put into words. So, thank you, Annie. Thank you."

Annie gave her a friendly frown in return.

"Do not, ever, doubt your abilities, Matty. Being here with me proves you are more than up to the job. Now, any questions about your list?"

"No. You have made everything very clear for me. I could never have produced such guidance in the short time you've had."

"But now you can, so, I say let's eat up and wait for Philippe."

Annie's expectation of Dr. Amdao's reaction to her insistence of taking charge of the research operation for the month she and Matty were to be in Africa was well founded. It did not go well and ended abruptly when the doctor stormed from the facility promising repercussions from the Ministry of Health. Fortunately, Annie had foreseen his predictable threats, contacted the Ministry herself and received assurances that she and Matty's positions would be honored and that Dr. Amdao would be told to stand down for the duration of their visit. After an hour of unpleasantness Annie and Matty were able to proceed with their plans to begin combating the deadly parasitic disease.

Addressing the five remaining members of the team, Annie began positively by complimenting them on the work they had managed to carry out under difficult circumstances. That being said, she went on to describe the intense work schedule she expected them to carry out. Her pointed comments were met, not with dread, but rather with palpable excitement. At last, one member quietly offered, they were actually going to do the work they'd been trained for.

It was an intense but productive day. Matty, Joyce and Philippe worked on reanalyzing the few blood and tissue samples already collected. The lab equipment, Matty soon realized, was totally inadequate to provide any sort of meaningful results. She quickly informed Annie who, after an urgent call to her contact at the Health Ministry, received assurances fresh, up to date machines, would be dispatched to her overnight from South Africa.

In the meantime, Matty and her team would begin cataloging deaths and hospitalizations from the six divided areas making up Norambuland. Annie wanted to confirm what Matty previously told her, that one area had produced very few infections or deaths than the others, or if that was just an anomaly.

While Matty concentrated her efforts on the geography of the parasite, Annie needed to get a first-hand look at the scale of the disease. With the help of another assistant at the facility, Kip Grieno, as her guide, she toured a dozen specially built cemeteries where over three hundred thousand bodies were buried.

Astonished by what she saw, Annie shook her head, saying, "This is unbelievable. When you see all these graves on this scale...it's just... just..."

"It is indeed a very sad sight. We have tried to be respectful to the dead and their families," he offered, pointing to the numerous small crosses, pots of flowers, headstones and memorials dotting the fields as far as the eye could see, "but sometimes the sheer volume is overwhelming."

Annie nodded her agreement, saying sadly, "That a parasite caused all this is totally unacceptable. We *have* to solve this problem before another four hundred thousand of your people die."

Walking slowly and sadly back to the jeep, she added, "I will need you, Kip, to get the team some fresh tissue and blood samples from the recently deceased. I'll let you know exactly what I want when we get back. Do you think the families will cooperate with that request?"

"Of course. Most are willing to do anything to stop what is happening. I will contact the necessary authorities immediately."

Their next stop took them to the largest hospital where multiple patients were being treated at various stages of the disease. Again, this was a sobering experience for Annie to see the catastrophic damage caused by a simple parasite. Suitably masked, gowned and gloved, she and Kip toured ward after ward of patients, some as young as six and as old as ninety-four, staring down on people with little or no hope.

Doctors were on hand to educate Annie on the onset, path and ultimate destination of the parasite. It always began with an eye infection, traveled through the sinuses and ended in the brain. It feasted on the gel-like vitreous humor until it rendered the person blind before moving upward at a relentless rate, finally settling in to eat away and eventually destroy the brain.

As she walked through the lines of beds filled with patients blankly staring at the ceiling, comatose and without hope, Annie finally came face to face with the actual stark reality of the disease. It was hard for her not to break down at the sight of this devastation but she managed to remain strong while thinking all the time, *Oh my god, I have to do whatever it takes to fight this monster.*

Outside, the darkened sky and showers perfectly matched her mood. Kip explained that the patients they'd just seen represented the cases from last summer, six months ago.

"That is the only silver lining here," he offered. "The parasite seems to die or become dormant during the rainy season from October to March or April. Otherwise our deaths would be much higher. People then become complacent and continue with their normal lives, forgetting when the summer returns to take the necessary precautions. This is a cycle that needs to be broken."

Annie thought that information interesting and possibly useful, certainly in terms of educating the population on the cyclical nature of the disease. But it did not solve the continuing underlying problem of prevention once the parasite had entered the body. For that there was only one answer; there needed to be a vaccine.

"We're going to need blood and tissue samples from a wide range of patients who are still alive. I will also need to know the geographical area where each lived, as well as their sex and age."

"It will be done," Kip quickly assured her. "The doctors at the hospitals will be eager to assist you."

"All right, thank you, Kip. Now let's head back to the facility."

Later that afternoon, in the quiet of her makeshift office, she and Matty talked over the day's events. Naturally, Annie began with descriptions of her visits to the cemeteries and hospital.

"Oh, Matty," she almost whispered, "some of the worst moments of my life. So sad and horrifying. I've never felt so helpless or inadequate."

"Sometimes there are no words," agreed Matty. "But it is good that you have seen for yourself what I could only describe before. There is no one in my country who has not lost someone close to them."

"And the awful way people with the disease are suffering. It's not a quick or painless death. In particular, I will never forget the very young children. They've never had a chance to really live."

"And also, so very tragic for an older person to end their days in such a grim and frightening way," Matty added, solemnly.

After expressing more regret Annie asked how her reviews had gone with Joyce and Philippe.

"As we suspected, the analysis the facility has done of the little blood and tissue samples they had collected is incomplete and lacking any sort of functional reliability."

"In other words," Annie interrupted, "it's useless."

"I would have to agree. It is very disappointing when you consider how much funding they have received from the government. But I also have a little good news to report," Matty continued. "You asked for a geographical breakdown of how the disease has affected each of the six regions of the country."

"Yes, and?"

"We have noticed five of the six have rates of infection that are high and consistent with each other."

"And the other one?" Annie asked expectantly.

"Mostly non-existent," Matty replied, pointing to the area highlighted on her screen.

"What's the population?" Annie asked, increasingly interested.

"Small – perhaps six or seven thousand people – living in scattered villages by the River Ballooka."

"And none of the residents have come down with the disease?"

"Only those who appear to have lived outside the area for a while. It is very strange." Matty added, with a frown.

"Could be something or nothing," Annie surmised, "but at some point I think we should pay them a visit. All right…moving on, we know the pathology of the three main classes of parasites. But what we don't know, unless you, Joyce and Philippe gathered the information from Dr. Amdao's collected data, is why they seem to mutate and contain elements from all three spectrums?"

"No," confirmed Matty, "there is apparently nothing in the facility's information to address that issue. It is very disappointing."

"So, tomorrow, use some of the lab samples from the various parasites and try and figure out an answer. Cross mutation is extremely rare and I want to know why it's happening here. I am going to set up and calibrate the new equipment when it arrives first thing in the morning. That'll probably take most of the day and then I'll have to train the staff on how to use the various machines. I'll need you to do a run-through with Joyce and Philippe when I'm done, if that's okay?"

"Yes, thanks to you and the equipment at Fitzgerald, I am very comfortable being able to pass on what I have learned. So far, they have been very happy to receive my guidance."

"All right, Matty, I think we are done here for the day. Let's get back to the hotel and eat dinner, then I need to call my folks. You should do the same."

Blythe is ecstatic when Annie's face appears almost out of nowhere at five o'clock in the afternoon. She stares at her phone's screen hardly believing she can actually see her daughter in Africa.

"Oh! Oh, Sweetie, hi, hi."

"Hi, Mom, can you see me okay?"

"Yes! It's amazing, like you're right beside me. How's my darling girl?"

"Tired. Been a long couple of days, but things are slowly moving forward."

"Good, good, that's good, Honey. Where are you now?"

"In the hotel near the facility. It's about eleven here so I can't stay on long but I wanted you and Dad to know we're okay and working hard."

"That's sweet of you to take the time, Can you bring me up to speed?"

"Well," Annie hesitates, wondering just how much to share, "I guess I'm running the show while we're here. The place was a mess, Mom. Not much progress had been made in eighteen months, so I got the okay from the Health Ministry to kick out the guy who's been in charge. And when we leave he won't be back."

"Oh, my god, Annie, so you caused quite a stir?"

"It needed to be done. The guy seems to have been using the funds for his own purposes."

"Just be careful, Honey. You don't need too many enemies in Africa."

"I will. There's a lot of good people here who've got my back."

"Are things as bad with the disease as they told you before you left?"

"Worse. Oh, Mom, I visited some of the graves of those who didn't make it and also toured a hospital. Devastating and very sad. All ages, some as young as six. Blind and comatose. It's heartbreaking to actually see this disease up close and personal. But, that's why we're here…to see if we can make a difference. Now, how about you and Dad? You guys all right?"

"Sure. Missing you like crazy but keeping busy. Daddy's involved in some big fraud case so I don't see much of him. And I'm in school most days 'til four so not much time to sit around moping."

"Class going well?" Annie asks, remembering the time she and Matty went in and helped out with the kids.

"It is. As a matter of fact we talk about you and Matty a lot."

"You do?"

"Yes. We followed your trip on the map and also your journey up the coast. They were so excited to learn what you'd seen. So, you see, I'm never far away from you."

"Oh, Mom, that's great. I'll try and carry some souvenirs back with me to bring in as a sort of 'show and tell'. Please give them my best and let them know I'm thinking about them."

"Is Matty doing all right? Has she seen her folks yet?"

"Not yet. Weekend after next we're planning a short trip. Should be fun," she adds, slightly skeptically.

"Just support her, Sweetheart. As I said, try and be the peacemaker."

"I'll do my best but I gather her mom's not the easiest person to get along with."

"If anyone can smooth the waters it's you."

"Different culture, Mom, so we'll have to see how it goes, but Matty's determined to stay with me at Fitzgerald."

"Just having you there to support her will make all the difference."

"I hope so. Look, Mom, I'm sorry but I have to go now. It's late here and we've a full day tomorrow with new machines supposedly showing up. Give my love to Daddy and give yourself a big hug. I miss you so much."

"Right back at you, Sweetheart. Stay safe and thanks so much for calling. Bye."

And then they are gone – a world apart again.

In another room, Matty is having a delicate conversation with her mother. It is only the second time they have spoken since Matty arrived in Africa.

"I want to know when you will be coming home, my child. Papa and I have many things we wish to discuss with you and, of course, our family will want to see you after you have been away for so long."

Matty knows all of this and is beginning to dread the encounter. She quickly thinks of the right words to say to keep her mother from talking right now about her schooling, her apparent duty to her country and her need to be of service to her family.

"Maman," she uses her favorite name for her mother, a holdover from the time Norambuland was part of colonized French West Africa, "I am so looking forward to seeing you, Papa and everyone. Yes, it has been a long time but I have always held you all close in my heart. If all goes well, Annie and I will be visiting the Saturday after next, if that is all right with you, Maman?"

"That will be very fine, child. We will have much to speak about."

Matty regards the last remark as ominous. She decides to ignore the inference and instead asks if everyone in the family is well.

"We are so far. There have been very few casualties of the disease you are studying in this area, so I am sure the worst is past."

Again, Matty ignores her mother's pointed comment. She knows the disease is cyclical but trying to explain that now would be of no use. At least she's aware of what lies ahead when she visits.

"That is good, Maman. I am so looking forward to introducing my friend and colleague, Annie, to you and Papa. She is teaching me so much."

This time it is Matty's mother who dismisses what she has clearly heard. She knows her time for speaking her mind will come in due course.

"She will, of course, be very welcome in our home, as well you know, child."

"I do, Maman. You and Papa are always very kind to strangers."

After several more awkward moments Matty tells her mother it's time for her to go.

"We will arrive by mid-day, Maman, but until I see you I send you and Papa my love."

"Thank you, child, and may you be safe on your journey."

And then they are gone, leaving both to consider what the visit would bring.

CHAPTER FOURTEEN

$$\longrightarrow\!\!\text{*}\;\text{*}\!\longleftarrow$$

T HE NEW EQUIPMENT ARRIVED BEFORE eight o'clock the following morning. When Annie and Matty began opening the crates and boxes they were immediately astonished by the up-to-date quality of the machines. She texted the Ministry with her grateful thanks.

"This is awesome," she announced, as the pieces were carefully removed. "Now we can get some serious work done."

"As modern as anything at Fitzgerald," agreed Matty, smiling, as she began assembling the various components under Annie's guidance.

The equipment included a hematology analyzer, a blood gas analyzer, two incubators, an important immunoassay analyzer, a flow cytometer, a CO_2 incubator and an ultra-low temperature freezer. In addition, there was some general equipment and supplies which the facility would desperately need going forward when Annie and Matty had left. All in all, the delivery from the Ministry of Health far exceeded anything Annie could have wished for.

Joyce and Philippe, under Matty's guidance, began clearing the necessary lab space to accommodate the machines and supplies. They eagerly participated, telling Matty how they could hardly wait to begin their instruction and use of the equipment. They concentrated on getting the hematology analyzer up and running to be ready when Kip produced the blood and tissue samples he'd promised Annie. The ultra-low temperature freezer was next to be utilized so that some of the samples could be frozen at minus sixty degrees Celsius for future use.

Annie, meanwhile, busied herself with the more sensitive,

complicated machines, calibrating and fine-tuning them until she was satisfied they were performing as intended. The arduous task took most of the day but by six o'clock they were running and performing perfectly. Tomorrow, if Kip delivered the blood and tissue samples, she and Matty would be ready to start the long journey of discovery.

As promised, the next morning Kip and another staff member brought in a treasure trove of samples. Immediately, Annie and Matty separated them into their relevant categories which included geographical location, gender and age, and current or deceased blood and tissue samples, which comprised, among other things, eye and brain pathology. Some of this valuable human material was quickly placed in the low-temperature freezer to be transported later back to Annie's lab at Fitzgerald.

Over the next week the painstaking, delicate work of preparing samples, running them through the various machines and instruments, collecting and analyzing the results and entering the subsequent data into the main computer system began in earnest.

"Finally," Annie announced to the team, "we will now be able to start the process of discovery. While this is an awesome responsibility, it is also an exciting moment to be part of a possible solution. I want to thank you all again for basically putting your lives on hold. Let's hope your efforts will not be in vain."

Joyce spoke for the team when she replied, "No, it is us who have to thank you and Matty for giving us this great opportunity to serve our country. We will work very hard until we have found the answer."

A quick round of applause greeted Joyce's comments before a diffident Annie told everyone it was time to get back to their tasks.

Two days before Matty and Annie's visit to Matty's parents, Annie along with Kip took a tour of what was known as Area 5, one of the six individual parts comprising the whole of Norambuland. Ever since Matty had informed Annie that this particular part of the country had, for the most part, experienced very few infections, Annie wondered why and how such a phenomenon could exist when all the other areas had been devastated.

The location, in the north-east corner of the country, was rural, with villages full of simple mud hut homes with cement block rooms, surrounded by mahangu fields, maharani, leadwood and kiaat trees growing tall along the banks of the River Ballooka. According to Kip, the swift running river provided the village people with all the water necessary for daily life.

The villages comprised six to seven thousand people, who were mostly self-sufficient, using agriculture as their main source of food, and wood as the main material for any number of projects from fencing to carving trinkets to sell to the tourists.

Annie thought the area a breath of fresh air after being cooped up in the research facility for over a week. As Kip drove her around she noticed the people seemed happy with their simple lives, smiling and waving as the jeep passed by.

"What are they doing differently," she asked Kip, "to be almost immune from the disease? I mean, they're basically farmers, so they're outside most of the day. Why haven't they come down with this parasite? Can we stop at the next village and talk to some of these people?"

"It is a mystery for sure," Kip replied. "And, yes, we will stop in Mughana and speak with some villagers."

"Will you translate for me?" Annie asked.

"There will be no need. All of our children from an early age have to learn English. You will have no problem understanding them."

For Annie, that was a relief. Hearing explanations directly rather than through an interpreter would make her questions easier to ask and the answers easier to understand.

As Kip brought the jeep to a halt a group of excited children soon ringed the vehicle. Kip's appearance they were used to, but Annie's dark hair and strange, to them, facial features made them stare and giggle.

"Sorry for that," Kip offered, as a way of apologizing for what he thought was their bad behavior, "but they do not see…"

"Many people who look like me," Annie interrupted, with a huge smile. "It's all right, Kip, I've been doing quite a bit of staring of my own since I arrived in the country."

Soon several adults joined the children, who ushered them back to the playground of the small, one story school. A tall woman addressed Kip with a warm, friendly smile.

"And how can we help two such fine looking people today?"

Kip made the appropriate introduction.

"This good lady here is a scientist from America who has come all this way to help us with our disease."

"Annie Cavallaro," Annie jumped in, holding out her hand, "so pleased to meet you. And I'm sorry if we have disturbed your class."

"No apologies necessary. Mrs. Tamouso. I am the schoolteacher here."

"Do you have time to talk with us?" Annie asked. "We're seeking information that might help us defeat this disease."

"Indeed, I will assist you in any way I can."

"We've noticed," Annie began to explain, "that this area in Norambuland has seen very few infections, hospitalizations or deaths. We are trying to find out why."

"That is very true. The people around here and our children are very healthy. And we behave as everyone else does."

"We'll be looking into diet, occupations, hygiene and a host of other factors to see if something is different here than in all the other areas. Perhaps, as the first possible volunteer," Annie asked, with a huge smile, "you might be willing to answer a few questions and let Kip take a sample of your blood?"

"That would be a very small price to pay, so please, ask your questions."

"Thank you. Now, would you say you are typical of the adults around here?"

"Of course. We are all neighbors and follow traditional ways."

"How about your diet? What kinds of things do you eat?"

"Mostly food that is grown right here. Grains, fruits, meat, chicken and fish. It is all very nutritious."

"And what do you drink?"

"All of our water comes from the river. It is very clean, fed by our long rainy season, which I'm sure you have experienced."

Annie nodded before saying, "Yes, we've been caught once or twice in a downpour. And from that water you make all your drinks?"

"Yes. Mostly tea and coffee. It is also used in our cooking process and a lot of other things."

After asking a few more questions, Annie directed Kip to take a blood sample from Mrs. Tamouso. Then it was off to interview more of the villagers. On the way, they took a route along the river and Annie asked Kip about the low-hanging trees with almost black leaves, dotting the banks on either side.

"They're new to me. I don't think I've seen that type before. What are they?"

Kip responded, "That is because they are only found in this particular area. They are called pampousas and seem to thrive by this river. Unlike most of our country's other trees they do not have much value now except to adorn the banks of the river."

"You said 'now'. What did you mean by that, Kip?"

"In the past, the leaves have been used in various ways by our elders as a medicine to soothe some aches, pains and minor infections. But since the villagers now have access to modern pharmaceuticals the practice has largely died out."

"Are they always in leaf?" Annie wanted to know.

"Yes, they are not deciduous. They provide lots of cover for the birds and other animals."

Annie seemed interested but content with Kip's answer.

"Before we leave I'd like you to take river water samples and soil samples. They might tell us something. Oh, and cut me a few of those leaves."

Kip nodded although he failed to understand what use they could possibly be.

For the next few hours Annie and Kip toured some of the other villages in the area, speaking and asking questions of the townspeople, and taking blood samples from young and old alike. Even the elderly folk, whose immune systems had declined over the years, seemed not to have been infected with the disease. The whole scenario was a mystery to Annie.

As they made their way back to the facility along the banks of the river the rain began again in torrents. As if by magic, scores of villagers appeared along the banks with containers and bottles, setting them down under the pampousa trees, collecting the rain.

Annie, bemused, asked, "What are they doing, Kip?"

"Collecting fresh rainwater for their use. They set the containers under the trees because the leaves are funnel shaped and the water runs easily into the bottles or whatever container they have. It is very efficient and provides the villages with their necessary water."

She asked Kip to stop the car, retrieved a sterilized bottle from the trunk and made her way, through the rain, to the nearby bank. For the next three minutes she held the bottle under the funnel-shaped leaves until it was full. She replaced the seal and returned to the jeep.

Kip seemed amused by her strange antics, pointing to the bottle and asking, "You think this will help our research?"

Annie raised her eyebrows and shrugged, saying hopefully, "Who knows, Kip, perhaps the answer to our prayers is in this bottle of rain."

The research center now began accumulating a vast array of samples from the field, which certainly hadn't been the case before. With the new analyzing equipment in place and functioning well, the team started the arduous task of preparing and running them through the various machines to provide foundational data on which to ultimately build a comprehensive understanding of the disease, its pathology and, hopefully, its ultimate demise.

While the other team members, under Matty's guidance, concentrated on blood and tissue samples taken from both alive and deceased folk, Annie spent her time on actual parasitic specimens, along with soil, water, vegetation samples and people's personal medical and day-to-day histories.

This whole concerted effort was crucial and urgent considering Annie and Matty's time in Africa was only to last another ten days. But the assembled team was dedicated and determined to do whatever was necessary to find a solution. They diligently and happily worked twelve to fifteen hour days, never complaining whilst obviously sacrificing their precious personal time and relationships. For Annie and Matty to witness such unselfishness filled them with an awe-inspiring respect they would never forget.

As the weekend of Matty and Annie's visit to Matty's parents neared, they felt comfortable leaving the research team in the capable hands of Joyce and Philippe. Their level of understanding the techniques and procedures Matty had so patiently instilled in them left the two leaders confident the facility was not only in good hands, but able to possibly make some major strides forward. In one way, it was a test to see what might happen once Annie and Matty had departed for good. Come Monday morning they would find out.

CHAPTER FIFTEEN

They left their hotel early on Saturday morning with Matty driving a borrowed jeep from the facility. The trip to her parents' bungalow in the city of Brannisville would take two hours, part of it along the coast road and the final fifty miles inland. Matty, of course, knew the area well so she acted as tour guide for a still wide-eyed Annie.

As they neared their destination Annie asked Matty how she was feeling about seeing her family again after being away for so long.

With her eyes firmly on the road, Matty answered, "We will have so much to say to each other. They will want to know many things about me. I hope I will be forgiven for going against their wishes."

Annie cocked her head at the last remark.

"Matty, there is no need for you to apologize for any of the decisions you've made."

"No, no, I am sorry but you do not understand." She paused before saying, "In my culture we are taught to honor our mother and father and to try our best to follow their wishes. I fear I have disrespected them for not doing what they wanted me to do."

"Matty," Annie replied firmly, "in most cultures children are taught to honor their parents. That is a given. I certainly did and do. But at some point children become adults themselves and that means breaking free from their parents' shadow and making their own decisions. Yes, sometimes we disappoint our parents but in the end we have to live our own lives."

Matty listened patiently, ever respectful of her friend, but she knew Annie would always find it difficult to understand the deeply different cultural bonds in their respective societies. Yes, both teach honor and even reverence towards their parents, but in Africa it went deeper than that; obedience, it seemed, mattered more.

Finally, Matty answered, "When you have been raised to believe your parents always know what is best for you, when you feel their knowledge and history will always be your guiding light, it is very hard to break away from that position.

"I am sure there must have been times with you and your parents when there was conflict because your way was not their way. And even though you may have chosen your path I expect there was pain in your heart for forgoing their wishes. It is now the same for me. I do not wish to disappoint my parents by doing what I know is right for me but it still leaves a pain in my heart."

Annie touched her friend's arm, finally realizing the predicament Matty faced. All she could do was be supportive, try not to interfere and assure Matty that despite everything her parents would never disown her.

Matty managed a brave smile as she responded with, "Oh, I know they would never do that, Annie. It is just that I hope they will still be proud of me no matter what."

As Annie thought about her own parents, how they always gave her their best advice then left it up to her to make her own decisions, she thought how sad it was for Matty not to have the same choice. Right there and then she decided to speak her mind if given the chance.

The Kizemboukos' bungalow was situated on a quiet street just within the city limits of Brannisville. The house, now twenty years old, sported fresh paint courtesy of Mr. Kizembouko and an extensive garden the pride of Mrs. Kizembouko. As Matty drove closer, past familiar roads, buildings and local landmarks, she couldn't help remembering all the good times spent on the street. It had been a strict childhood but one full of joy and happiness surrounded by great friends and neighbors.

As soon as Matty pulled the car up to the house Mr. and Mrs. Kizembouko emerged and hurried towards their daughter. Matty quickly got out, meeting them halfway on the grass and throwing her arms around their necks. Annie watched the touching scene, patiently waiting until the family had finished its tender reunion. As she left the jeep Matty brought her parents over for the introduction.

"Maman, Papa, this is my very good friend and mentor, Annie Cavallaro."

"We are very honored to welcome you into our home, Miss Annie. Mathilde has told us so much about you." She offered her hand which Annie grasped in both of hers.

"Thank you so much for allowing me to accompany Matty," Annie answered, respectfully. "I've been so looking forward to meeting you both." She spoke genuinely but also with an awareness of how crucial it would be to get off on the right foot with Matty's parents.

"We do not stand on ceremony here," Mr. Kizembouko offered. "We hope you will feel very much at home."

While he spoke Annie carefully looked at the couple. Mrs. Kizembouko held herself very straight, her sharp, attractive features surrounded by jet black hair interwoven with colorful beads. It was as if her whole head shimmered in the faint sunlight. Matty's father, on the other hand, looked somewhat conservative, his small, stout stature blending in rather than standing out.

"You're very gracious," Annie responded. "I'm sure I will be."

"Let us go inside so we may offer you some refreshment after your journey," Mrs. Kizembouko suggested.

As they sat around the light-filled living room drinking tea and ombike, a traditional alcoholic beverage made from the palm fruits of the maharani tree, Annie did, indeed, feel at home. The house had an aura of warmth about it, with its pastel colors, bright drapes and comfortable furniture. The conversation, light and superficial, only briefly touched upon the disease and Annie and Matty's roles in trying to stem the devastation.

"It is very kind of you to come from America to help with this problem," Mrs. Kizembouko said, plainly. "Has there been any progress?"

Annie thought quickly for a few seconds about how to answer the question. She wanted to be positive, to offer their presence in Norambuland, and Matty's in particular, as an integral part of solving the puzzle, but she also needed to be careful about giving non-researchers false hope.

"Yes, I'm pleased to say we have managed to lay the foundations for this on-going fight. The team at the facility, which," she emphasized, "has largely been trained by your daughter, is now operating with confidence and purpose. We have new equipment which is already providing some early data and results. I am very encouraged by the way things are going."

"Good. That is very good," Mr. Kizembouko replied, hugging his daughter. "We are pleased Mathilde is being of assistance."

Annie could have left the comment to die on the air but instead answered, "Well, Mr. Kizembouko, Matty is not just being of *assistance*. She is," looking straight at her friend, "so much more. Her contributions have been extraordinary and I know she is going to be with me on this entire journey until we have a solution. You and Mrs. Kizembouko should be very proud of her." She made her comments with a big smile hoping her words might have some beneficial effect on what she knew promised to be some difficult conversations between Matty and her parents.

Mrs. Kizembouko decided not to respond to Annie's pointed remarks, preferring instead to save her opinion until she and her daughter were alone.

"Of course we are proud of her, as we are of our other children. We have always taught them how important it is to contribute to our country."

Her response was crisp and without warmth. Annie decided to change the subject.

"Matty's tells me she has a brother and a sister. What do they do?"

"Our other daughter, Sasso, is training to be a nurse. Right now she is away on a probationary trip at a hospital in the south. And our son is following in his father's footsteps. He is helping with our country's mining output, which is very important for our economy."

Annie noticed the emphasis Matty's mother put on her son's contribution. It did not bode well for her eventual 'talk' with her daughter.

The rest of the afternoon was taken up with small talk and a brief tour of the neighborhood, ending up at another relative's house where an outside traditional dinner was cooked in Annie's honor. To make the moment extra special the younger children celebrated Matty's homecoming with a native dance they had been practicing for a week.

For a while Annie was able to forget about the tension between Mrs. Kizembouko and her daughter, enjoying the food and festivities, as well as the warm and honest hospitality from her hosts. She went to bed that night feeling satisfied but wary of what tomorrow might bring.

"Oh, Mrs. Kizembouko, this bread is so delicious!" Annie exclaimed at breakfast, as she devoured another slice of fresh, hot, buttered veldt, a dense bread made of whole wheat flour, milk, salt, sugar and spices such as cinnamon or ginger. "You are a wonderful baker."

"Thank you. I baked it this morning over our open fire. But before you are too full I would like you to try an oshikwiila." She brought over a hot pan to where Annie sat and slid a millet pancake onto her plate. "Please try this with some fruit."

Annie duly obliged but before she finished Mrs. Kizembouko deposited a round, hot, fluffy bread ball onto her plate.

"These are called oykyki or fat cakes. Our children like to eat them for snacks." She stood close by as Annie sampled the treats.

"Mmm. Mmm. Oh, yes, these are so good. But if I eat too much of your good cooking, Mrs. Kizembouko, I'll weigh a ton!"

Everyone laughed at Annie's comment.

"It is simple food but it is what the land provides us. We are very grateful," Mrs. Kizenbouko offered.

After breakfast, where Annie helped wash and clean the pans and dishes, Mrs. Kizembouko took her daughter to a quiet, secluded part of the garden. Annie and Matty's father remained in the house.

Outside, Mrs. Kizembouko sat across from Matty and prepared to speak her mind.

"Maman…"

Quickly, Mrs. Kizembouko interrupted her daughter.

"Mathilde, no, you must let me speak. I have waited a long time. You must hear my words, what I have to say."

Respectfully, Matty nodded, sitting straight-backed, paying immediate attention.

"To say your father and I are disappointed with the choices you have made would not be accurate. We have sacrificed so that you could receive a good education, which resulted in you being awarded a GLOBE scholarship to study physics. Now you have suddenly decided, without consulting your father or me, to take a different path."

"But Maman…"

"No, child, please let me finish. This country was built on its ability to provide metals and ores for the whole world. Now uranium is in high demand and the country has the opportunity to help the world with its needs. This is where our future lies. This is where your future lies, not in medical research."

As Mrs. Kizembouko spoke her mind to Matty, Annie, inside the bungalow, was having a crucial conversation with Matty's father.

"It has been just so great meeting and becoming friends with Matty," she began, lightly. "You must be so proud of her."

"Most certainly, but we are disappointed she has chosen to change her focus of studies. We had high hopes she would contribute to our economy by continuing with physics."

Annie waited a few seconds before replying, trying hard to form the appropriate response in her head.

Finally, she answered, "Mr. Kizembouko, can I tell you what it has been like for me to work beside Matty for these past few months?" Without waiting for an acknowledgment to her rhetorical question, Annie continued, "The level of understanding and dedication she has brought to the difficult and, for her, unfamiliar tasks both me and our professor have set her, has been truly amazing to witness.

"It is so clearly obvious that she has such an affinity for medical research. I understand you wish her to go in another direction, but, Mr. Kizembouko, *this* is her calling. And honestly," Annie pressed, "it's not as though she will be lost to Norambuland forever. I know she will return at some point in the future to continue helping to solve some serious medical issues that are bound to arise in the years to come.

"I know it is not my place to interfere in family matters, so please forgive my rudeness. It was not intentional. Yet, I need you and Mrs. Kizembouko to see what wonderful potential your daughter has and that with your continued encouragement she will be able to achieve great things for the world." Stopping, Annie shrugged and said, "That's all I have to say. Thank you for listening."

Mr. Kizembouko, expressionless, stared at Annie for a few seconds. She feared the worst, that his response would be a condemnation of her. She was completely wrong.

With a broad smile and a nod, he answered, "I can understand now why Mathilde regards you in such high esteem. You are wise beyond your years." Annie, surprised, looked at Mr. Kizembouko with wide eyes, listening diffidently as he continued. "Your parents have raised you well. They have given you the ability to speak fearlessly which, in my culture, is not the preferred way for our children. But it is plainly clear to me that the choice Mathilde has made with regard to her studies is the correct one. You have now convinced me of that fact.

"My wife is strong-willed and a traditionalist when it comes to our culture, so it is not easy for her to accept any other way except her own. But we also have to be realistic and to acknowledge that the world around us is changing. We must change with it. Please do not worry. Mathilde will be able to study those subjects she feels are best for her and our country. I will see to that."

Annie, thrilled by Mr. Kizenbouko's words, thanked him profusely.

"Hopefully, we will be able to solve the parasite disease now plaguing your country. And Matty will be a huge part of that. Thank you. Thank you."

While Annie was speaking with Mr. Kizembouko, Matty and her mother were carrying on their conversation about her future plans. Already Mrs. Kizembouko had expressed her still-strong objection to Matty changing her major.

She finished her disapproval by saying, "Your behavior will be looked upon by those who have supported your studies since you were a child as disrespectful not only to the family but to all who know you. Now, my hope is that it is not too late for you to rejoin your previous university."

As her mother lectured her she remembered the support and yes, love, shown to her by Annie, Virginia and the rest of the small research faculty at Fitzgerald. Sad to say, they felt more like family to her right now than her mother did. She also recalled Annie's constant words of encouragement to pursue her own path and dreams. For Matty, this was a pivotal moment in her life, one unlike any other she had faced before.

Calmly, Matty answered, "Maman, all I have ever done is to try and please you and Papa. And I know I have been very fortunate in having such caring parents as you. But that was when I was a child and now I am an adult. It is time for me to make my own decisions, for what is in the best interests of my country and me.

"Right now, that means concentrating all my efforts on solving our dreaded disease. Fitzgerald and Professor Virginia have been kind enough to provide a pathway for me to obtain my doctorate. And Annie…" at the mention of Annie's name Mrs. Kizembouko frowned and looked away, "…and Annie has promised to be my mentor and friend so that I may be able to realize my dreams.

"I am sorry, Maman, if I have disappointed you," she continued, pleasantly, as her father approached from the house, "but this is the life I wish to live."

Mr. Kizembouko caught the tail-end of Matty's heartfelt comments and immediately hugged his daughter.

To his wife, he said, "This will be an end to this nonsense, Mother. Our daughter has never disappointed us. She will have our blessing to do whatever she wishes to do with her life." Directly to Matty, he offered, "Mathilde, dear, sweet child, continue with the important work of discovery you and Miss Annie have begun. It will be a great savior for our country. Now, come back into the house both of you. We need to celebrate this joy before you leave."

They did leave two hours later with relief in their hearts. Matty and her mother had a brief, private conversation in which Mrs. Kizembouko also gave her blessing to her daughter's future career. It was a genuine moment, full of tears and apologies; smiles and love.

CHAPTER SIXTEEN

With Matty's family situation now resolved, the journey back to the facility took on a celebratory air for the two young women. Riding happily along they heaped praise on each other for managing to bring Matty's parents over to their point of view.

"I do not know what you said to my father," Matty began, "but whatever words you used certainly persuaded him to support me and my new area of studies. Thank you."

"Matty, I only told him the truth," Annie responded. "That this is where your future lies, doing important medical research which will ultimately benefit the people of Norambuland. I also told him this is what makes you happy and fulfilled; that this is where you feel you are most valuable. Now, what did you say to your mother?" Annie asked, with a grin.

"It was not an easy conversation. She still clings to the fact that, as I am her child, I should behave in a certain way. Respectfully, I told her that now I am an adult and should make my own decisions about my future. It was still not going well," she continued, with a laugh, "until my father came to us with the news that he and she must now support my wishes and dreams. But I know he would not have done that without your kind intervention. In the end, my mother gave me her blessing, too."

The rest of the two-hour trip was spent reviewing what they needed to accomplish before they left for America next Saturday.

"It'll be interesting to see what Joyce, Philippe and the team have discovered since we've been away," Annie remarked. "I'm hoping for good things."

Annie was relieved to be able to relax for the rest of the evening in her hotel room. The weekend with Matty's parents, although finishing on a high note, had been fraught with tension. In an effort to return to a semblance of normality she called her parents, spending a joyful half-hour bringing them up to date on the latest developments.

After the call ended, she retrieved her laptop and a fresh bottle of water before settling down to do a little work on the *Curie* biography to take her mind off current events. Within seconds, her phone buzzed. On the line was the familiar voice of her agent, Peter Corbett.

"Annie," he exclaimed, "glad to finally get a hold of you. You're in Africa?"

"Hi, Peter. Yes…Africa. Trying to solve a serious problem out here."

"Oh, wow. I'm impressed. When are you planning on coming home?"

"Next weekend, all being well."

"Good. That's good, because I've heard from the publisher. They need an update on the biography. I've already sent them the chapters you sent me and they are very excited."

"Well, that's a relief, Peter," Annie answered, cheerfully. "I'm doing my best."

"Yeah, I know, but the thing is you've only got six months to finish. I can ask for an extension…say three months, but after that they'll be looking to cancel and then you'd have to return your ten grand advance."

Annie, with everything else going on, had forgotten about the strict timeline. She was taken aback by the news.

"Oh, yes, Peter, I might need that extra three months, but don't worry, I'll have the thing finished on time."

"Good. Good, Annie, because I really feel you've got a winner here from what I've seen so far. And, not to get your hopes up, but I think her life story has the makings of an interesting movie, given the right director, script and actors. I've got quite a few Hollywood connections, so you never know."

That information stunned Annie and for a few seconds she remained speechless.

"You're kidding me, right, Peter, a movie? Really?"

"As I say, don't get your hopes up and I probably shouldn't have said anything, but stranger things have happened. Anyway, it's gotta be really late where you are so I'll sign off for now. Just remember…six months…tops. Okay?"

"Got it," Annie replied, still in shock. "You'll have your book on time. Bye."

And then he was gone leaving his client still dumbstruck.

After rereading the last chapter she'd written on the plane to South Africa, Annie consulted her notes and the vast array of critical information supplied to her by her contact at The Curie Museum in Paris, Renée Coutage. The material continued to amaze Annie, particularly with regards to Marie's fierce independent nature in the face of on-going sexism. So far, hers had not been an easy life to live.

Picking up Marie's story where she'd left off on the plane, she began to write…

> *'After finding, in the middle of 1898, that the element thorium was an additional source that emitted radiation, Marie, to protect her discovery, published a brief, simple paper which was presented on her behalf by her former professor and mentor, Gabriel Lippmann, to the Academy. Unfortunately, two months earlier in Berlin, Gerhardt Carl Schmidt had published his own findings that thorium gives off rays in the same way as uranium.*
>
> *However, one crucial, different fact Marie recorded was that two of uranium's minerals – pitchblende and chalcolite – were more active than actual uranium itself and may contain some element that causes that reaction.'*

Annie thought about Marie's supposition, imagining how difficult it must have been back in 1898 to verify it. Modern equipment and instruments were not available, so Marie and Pierre resorted to more basic methods.

> *'To prove her theory, Marie and Pierre ground, by hand, huge quantities of pitchblende using a pestle and mortar, because the element was only present in minute amounts.*

But all their hard, tiring work proved worthwhile and in July of 1898 they published a paper announcing the existence of this new element, which they named polonium in honor of her native Poland.'

Annie read and reread the paragraph she'd just written, feeling how elated the pair must have been by their new discovery. Even all these years later Annie, too, reacted with stunned excitement that such a moment had been possible.

'Throughout the rest of 1898 the Curies continued their research into the composition of uranium and in December they remarkably discovered a second element which they named radium, from the Latin word for 'ray'. Surprising as this was, the Curies faced another problem.

"Pierre," Annie imagined Marie saying, "these discoveries are all well and good but we really need to prove them by isolating in pure form."

They knew pitchblende contained both elements, polonium and radium, but it was difficult to obtain pure samples. To do so required tedious, time-consuming work and took four years. Between 1898 and 1902 they published thirty-two scientific papers on their discovered elements, including one amazing pronouncement that, when exposed to radium, diseased tumor-forming cells were destroyed much faster than healthy cells.'

Again, Annie reread her words, realizing at once the significance of such a moment. Immediately she understood how the Curies' then supposition would eventually come to benefit the whole world of medicine through radiation therapy. For Annie, it was a staggering discovery and one that gave her hope in the search for a solution to Africa's parasitic disease problem.

Returning to the biography, she wrote...

'It took the Curies over four years to separate out radium salt by a process of crystallization from a ton of pitchblende. From that vast amount they were only able to isolate one

tenth of a gram. And, in fact, they never managed to isolate polonium.

Such was the magnitude of her discoveries that in 1900 Marie was appointed to the faculty at the École Normale Superiéure as its first woman member, a monumental and life-changing achievement.

But not all of 1902 was triumphant. In that same year, she returned to her native Poland upon the death of her beloved father. The sadness she experienced was compounded by the fact that it was his tutoring and encouragement from an early age that set her on her scientific path. Without his passion that all of his children be exposed to a first class education which, at the time, only sons could be expected to receive, Marie, along with her three sisters, would not have had the chance to fulfill their destinies and dreams.

In June of the following year, under the guidance of her mentor and professor, Gabriel Lippmann, Marie Curie, at the age of thirty-five, received her doctorate from the University of Paris. This high honor recognized the nearly twenty years' hard, tireless work to which she had dedicated her life. It was to be the first of many prestigious awards she was to receive throughout her lifetime.'

Annie closed her laptop for the night at two in the morning, exhausted yet elated by the events she'd recorded. As she lay in bed her thoughts continued to be with Marie, marveling at what this young woman had achieved through sheer will and determination. To say the message was inspirational for Annie would be like saying the mighty Atlantic Ocean was just a teeny-tiny pond.

Both Annie and Matty were eager to return to the research facility on Monday morning to see what the team had accomplished in their absence. Joyce met them in the main lab with some encouraging news.

"We have two pieces of good information to tell you about," she began, cheerfully. "We think we now know why this parasite is so lethal."

Annie and Matty both looked astonished that such a fact maybe had been discovered.

"Oh, wow! Tell us more," Annie demanded, pleasantly.

"We have processed a few hundred of the blood samples, both from the deceased and those currently in hospital with the disease. From our preliminary analysis we think we have determined that, indeed, all three classes of this parasite are present and apparently are able to mutate into one organism and that one organism can replicate itself on its journey to the brain."

"So," Annie interrupted, "you're saying you have found that protozoa, helminths and ectoparasites have basically joined together to form one free-living organism capable of infecting, blood-sucking and being visible sometimes to the naked eye, like flat or round worms."

"Yes," Joyce replied confidently, "that is what our analysis shows."

"But helminths cannot multiply in humans," Matty said, confused. "How is this possible?"

"That mystery we have not yet determined. But it is quite clear from the histology we have conducted on the human tissue samples all three are present in one organism. And we have proved that by the dissection of many of the parasitic samples we collected. Yes, it is quite clear," Joyce emphasized.

"Oh, wow, Joyce, this *is* fantastic news. Congratulations."

"But that is not all," Joyce continued. "Philippe has been very busy analyzing the blood samples you and he collected on your recent journey to Area five."

"The one with villages along the river where there have been no reported cases?" Annie asked.

"Yes, that is the one. Well his blood analysis – and again, these are preliminary results – shows none of the subjects with any of the parasitic markers. This is important, of course, because we conducted tests on the blood samples of those, few lucky people who survived the disease and found lingering evidence of the infection. None of Area five people have this marker which suggests no one there has ever contracted the disease."

"In other words,' Annie responded, excitedly, "they appear to be immune."

"Yes, exactly. That is what the evidence is pointing to."

"But why and how is this possible?' Matty wanted to know.

Joyce laughed a little and raised her eyebrows.

"That is what we are all wondering, Matty. How is this possible?"

Annie frowned while still considering Joyce's news.

"Let's not get ahead of ourselves here," she cautioned. "Yes, this is certainly very interesting but it could be something or nothing or even a weird coincidence. Let's think about this for a while. In the meantime, we also need to concentrate on why and how this parasite mutates so easily and why is its main focus or point of entry the human eye?"

They all agreed that finding the answers to those crucial questions might go a long way to better understand the whole trajectory of the disease.

As the week wore on and Annie and Matty's time in Norambuland wound down, the team continued working hard to understand and breakdown all the complexities of the disease. Annie, still very interested in the results from Area five, asked Kip to revisit it and secure a lot more River Ballooka water samples, as well as several pounds of leaves from the pampousa trees along the river bank and more soil samples. When he returned, she had him place them all in the ultra-low temperature freezer until they were frozen to minus sixty degrees. Later, she would have the facility package them up and sent to her and Matty at Fitzgerald.

On the day before they left, Annie took Joyce aside and gave her some good news.

"I've been in contact with the Health Ministry and they have agreed to my recommendation that for this particular project you should be in charge here when we return to America. I'll still be in overall charge but I need someone I can rely on to coordinate the research from this end.

"Since you are only a few months away from your doctorate like me, you are the obvious and perfect choice, Joyce. Will you take on this assignment for us?"

Joyce, momentarily speechless, finally broke into a wide smile.

"That would be such an honor for me. Are you sure?"

"Yes, absolutely. You are the right person to lead things from over here."

"Then I gratefully accept and I hope I will not let you down."

"I know that won't happen, so thank you for doing this for us. It's very important work."

On their final evening in Norambuland, Annie and Matty were

treated to a simple, but delicious, dinner at Philippe's house. It was both a joyous and a somber occasion given the circumstances of their visit and departure. There were many hugs and warm speeches, with everyone present feeling they were now in the presence of a close-knit family.

The rest of the night was spent with packing and checking flight arrangements. By ten o'clock the next morning they were on their way back to Fitzgerald with hope and fear in their hearts.

CHAPTER SEVENTEEN

U PON THEIR RETURN TO FITZGERALD, Virginia gives them a couple of days off to unwind. They spend the two days with Annie's parents relating the most important parts of their trip and catching up with laundry and sleep. Blythe and Clive are overjoyed to see them return safe and sound, as well as hearing how much progress has already been made with the parasitic disease.

"Honestly," Blythe gushes, "I'm in awe of what you've achieved in so short a time. At this rate it won't be too long before you have a solution."

Annie frowns at her mother's optimism. She well knows the journey has just begun.

"Mom, thanks, but this is a marathon not a sprint. I'm not even sure we're ever going to find all the answers. All I know is, Matty and I are going to give it our best shot."

"That is correct, Mrs. Cavallaro...Blythe... we will not rest until we cannot fight any more."

"And I can't think of anyone else but you two to do that," Clive jumps in.

There are grateful smiles from the young women who still have no idea how this journey will end.

"The only real, long-tern solution," Annie confides, "is a vaccine of some sort. And to even think about that is daunting."

"Then don't," insists Blythe. "As you've said, it's a marathon not a sprint. No one is expecting a miracle. I'm sure it took Salk more than a month to come up with the polio vaccine," she adds, grinning and nodding.

"Just do what you can when you can. Besides, you both have doctorates to work on, too. So, you're going to have pretty full schedules one way and another. Take things one day at a time. No burn out, promise?"

"This is why I respect your mother so much, Annie," Matty offers, before turning back to Blythe. "You always speak words of wisdom. Thank you. I will always try and remember your advice."

"Yeah," Annie agrees, "thanks, Mom, always the voice of reason around here. Oops, sorry, Dad," she adds quickly, with a giggle. "You've also been known to tell it like it is sometimes."

Everyone laughs at Annie's attempt at damage control. It was a precious family moment which, thankfully, Matty takes pride and delight in sharing.

Back at Fitzgerald, Virginia greets the two would-be pioneers with a down-to-earth reality check.

"Annie," she begins, in a voice her student knows well, "you have three applied science classes to pass and a dissertation to write for presentation before the board of examiners. May will be here before you know it, so…?

Annie nods as her mouth tightens.

"I know, Virginia. I know. You've always told me Fitzgerald's doctorate program is one of the most demanding in the country."

"The botany class is led by Jim Plother. Great professor. Detail oriented. He'll probably be able to point you in the right direction with the parasitic disease, particularly with regards to your theory about leaves, rain and river water. The class includes both the physiological and structural functions and compositions of plants to a degree you never knew existed. I've signed you up beginning next week. The other two will follow shortly after. Get these done and out of the way. Then we can work on your dissertation. Okay?"

"Yes, thanks, Virginia. I'm actually looking forward to the classes. Can't miss May now, can I?"

"Not after all the hard work you've put in these past two years, no." Virginia next turns to Matty and says, "Now, Matty, you've got a little over eighteen months. I'll guide you through the rest of this academic year and then I'll ask Annie to take over for your last year. Having someone who's been there helps a lot, I find. I have a revised class schedule for you to keep you on track. Any questions?"

"Only… when do we get time to sleep, Virginia?" Annie asks, with her eyes and hands wide open.

"Welcome to academia, girls. Welcome to academia. Now, as long as you fulfill your academic obligations, you are free to concentrate your other time working on the parasitic dilemma. You can use every resource available to you here at Fitzgerald, as well as tapping into any of our expert personnel you think may be able to assist. They have already been alerted and are willing to take the ride with you. Okay?"

"We are very grateful to you, Virginia," Matty offers, bowing her head. "We will try not to let you down both with our studies and our parasitic research. Thank you."

"And that's seconded by me," Annie adds.

"Good. Good. And never forget, I'm always available, too."

Wise time management now becomes the order of the day for Annie and Matty. There is so much to do and accomplish and only a certain number of hours available.

"It is now as my mother always told me," Matty confides, with a huge smile. "Your time is divided into three parts; studying, eating and sleeping. I do not like to say she was correct."

Annie grins, too.

"My mother said something similar except she added that you should always take a little time just for yourself. And we will."

For the first few days back Annie suggests a complete review of all the data so far collected, as well as adding in any new information Joyce has sent over from Africa.

"I'd like you to continue concentrating on the blood and tissue samples," Annie tells Matty, "as well as analyzing and breaking down the make up of the vitreous humor. We know it's mostly water but there's also glucose, proteins and collagen. We need to know what types all three contain and if there are any other substances present. For some reason the parasite is attracted to the vitreous humor. We need to find out why.

"While you're doing that I'll begin dissecting a couple of the parasites we have. There must be something in their genetic make up that attracts them specifically to the vitreous humor and eventually to the brain matter. None of this will be easy because, as we now know, we're dealing with all three classes of parasites that seem to have evolved or mutated into one entity."

The next two weeks produce impressive amounts of new data, particularly with regard to the blood and tissue samples Matty has been analyzing.

"I have discovered one protein that is present in the blood of those who have not had the disease but not in those who have," she offers. "And, also, there is an amino acid in that protein that follows the same pattern."

"That is very interesting, Matty, because while analyzing the tissue samples from the parasites, I've found something similar. The physiology of the parasites taken from the brains of those who've died show a very interesting internal structure, specifically, their digestive organs. There are enzymes and hormones in their bodily fluids that may be attracted to the vitreous humor of the eye, which could be why they enter the body that way.

"Now, the 'clean' parasites that I've analyzed, the ones that did not invade the body but were captured as control specimens, they do not seem to possess these enzymes or hormones."

"So, that might mean," Matty surmises, "there are two different types of this parasite. But how can that be?"

Annie shrugs before saying, "Perhaps their physiological make up has been compromised or altered in some way, either by geographical or biological circumstances. Whatever the reason, it's another path for us to walk down and all we can do is to follow it wherever it goes."

Two days later, Annie is ecstatic to receive the sub-frozen leaves, river water and bottles of rain samples from Kip. She immediately transfers the majority to her own lab's zero freezer while gently thawing a half dozen for her next analysis project.

Annie is doubly excited because she still hears Virginia's voice of reason ringing in her ears concerning her need to complete the last three classes for her doctorate. One of those classes is applied botany with Professor Jim Plother who, as Virginia assured her, will help lead her in the right direction and hopefully supply her with the necessary investigative skills to perhaps uncover the secrets hidden in the leaves, rain and river water.

She skips along to Plother's office and finds him with his feet up on his desk reading a scientific printout from one of his students. He sees her approach and beckons her in.

"Come. Come," he orders, as he sets his reading material aside. "You must be the one Virginia warned me about," he offers, with a grin. "Annie, is it?"

"Yes. Annie Cavallaro," she responds, also with a grin, although hers is more nervous.

"Sit yourself down and spill the beans," he continues, still smiling. "You need botany, right, to finish?"

"Yes, that's right. And two others, but your class will be the icing on the cake."

"You've got that right," he counters. "No free rides here. But Virginia tells me you may have some interesting theories to pursue. Something about leaves and rain water. Sounds intriguing. Tell me more."

Annie looks at the man who now could hold her future in his hands, taking in his unruly mop of long, gray hair and half-rimmed glasses that, indeed, make him seem professorial and perhaps mad at the same time. She hopes for a little of both; predictability and eccentricity; feet on the ground and head in the clouds.

"Has Virginia told you about my trip to Africa with Mathilde Kizembouko?"

"Mentioned it, yes. Something about research into a parasitic outbreak, yes?"

"Yes. In Norambuland there have been over four hundred thousand deaths from this disease caused by a parasite. We went over for a month to see if we could help figure out a solution."

"Parasites, eh? Affect plants, too, you know. Very destructive. So, what did you learn?"

"That they enter through the eye and end up destroying the brain. Horrible death."

"And I assume you're proceeding with all the normal analyses? Blood and tissue samples etcetera?"

"Of course. Some of the work is beginning to look promising. But there is an anomaly in one of the geographic areas we call Area five."

"Oh," Plother exclaims, "sounds mysterious…Area five…something from sci-fi maybe?"

Annie frowns, disappointed with Plother's apparent flippancy. She ignores his hollow reference.

"Actually, Area five is where there have been no reported cases. We are wondering why. The people work in the fields. The children play outside. Life goes on very much the same as in other parts of the country. And yet, no cases and no deaths."

Plother leans forward, looks at Annie over his half-rims and asks, "And you suspect…what?"

"All the villages are served by the River Ballooka and along the banks are trees called pampousa."

"Not familiar with the name," Plother interrupts.

"I had the lab over there send me a few pounds of leaves so we can break down their makeup to see if we can come up with any indication that those trees are somehow connected to the apparent immunity of the region. I also have river, rain water and soil samples for the same reason."

"Well, this is beginning to sound very interesting from a botanical point of view," Plother offers. "There may well be an ecological side to this, even a pollution one, too. You did well requesting those samples. Our equipment is very sophisticated, of course, but there's a lot of extensive, detailed preparatory work to also get through. I will guide you but I will not presume to lead you in any particular direction. That will be for you to decide and pursue as appropriate. There will be trial and error…lots of error, I can assure you, but by the time you've finished I am confident you will have a reasonable explanation for the anomaly. You will also, I'm sure, satisfy my requirements for passing you in this class. Any questions, Ms. Cavallaro?"

Annie is surprised by Plother's enthusiasm for her suppositions, and she realizes any assistance he can give her may actually significantly cut down on the time-line for a solution to the whole parasitic problem.

"Only two, Professor. How soon can I begin and can I involve my classmate, Mathilde Kizembouko, in the research?"

Plother smiles, genuinely pleased at her eagerness to get started.

"Bring your samples in tomorrow. I'm particularly interested in the pampousa leaves, so let's begin there. And, yes, I would welcome Ms. Kizembouko also. She definitely needs to be a part of this process of potential discovery. Alas," he adds, with a wide grin, "her participation will not relieve her of the need to take my class next year."

"Matty! Matty!" Annie almost screams at her friend. "You're officially part of the Area five investigation. We start tomorrow. Plother's really up for it. Oh, I'm so excited!"

"That you would include me in such an important part of the research makes me very humble. I hope I will be of assistance."

"Matty, for the last time, will you stop apologizing. You belong here alongside me. Jeez, you're the whole reason I got hooked in the first place. Oh, this is going to be so much fun!

"I've decided this is going to be the basis for my dissertation. I've already talked with Virginia and she feels the same. She also suggested your eventual dissertation could also be concentrated on the disease but, obviously and hopefully, based on the formulation of some sort of future vaccine. What do you think?"

"I think it is like it would be made for me. But you must promise to be my guide for I am still not certain I have the ability to do this by myself."

Annie stands in front of Matty, her hands on her shoulders, her eyes laser focused on her friend's face.

"One more time," she begins, firmly. "Never, never, never underestimate yourself. This is just the beginning. And, now, repeat after me...I am worthy..."

"I am worthy..."

"...and capable..."

"...and capable..."

"...of great things..."

"...of great things."

"Okay, that's better," she offers, with a huge grin. "Now, let's go celebrate."

CHAPTER EIGHTEEN

───※ ※───

I N THE RUN-UP TO THE Christmas break Annie and Matty's hectic schedules did not abate for one second. Matty was either assisting her friend in Professor Plother's class, catching up with some of her own required classes or continuing to analyze the vast array of blood and tissue samples from the parasitic patients. It was exhausting work but so rewarding and, to her credit, she never complained.

Annie, for her part, now likened her life to a perpetual whirlwind, twisting, turning and blowing in a dozen directions at once. Yet she, too, was not complaining but, rather, adjusting and enjoying life as it should be lived; to the fullest.

Apart from Plother's applied botany class, she also found time to squeeze in a few more chapters on her Curie biography. Now well aware of the tight deadline for submitting her manuscript, she spent at least two very late nights drinking coffee, munching on snacks and filling the 'pages' on her laptop with thousands of critical, insightful words. Now, on night three, she reviewed those chapters, reading;

'Sexism raised its ugly head again for Marie shortly after she had earned her doctorate from the University of Paris. She and Pierre were invited to the Royal Institution in London to give an important, groundbreaking address on radioactivity. However, being a woman, Marie was not allowed to speak, so only Pierre presented their findings.'

Again, Annie stopped reading and tried to understand the prevailing norms of the day. Despite now being acknowledged an esteemed scientist who had made some groundbreaking discoveries, Marie was still not allowed to represent herself just because she was a woman. And this was just over one hundred years ago. On the one hand, Annie felt nothing but loathing for the institutions back then which denied someone of Marie's proven credentials of receiving her just rewards. Conversely, she was also proud of the great strides her gender has made since those dark days of denial and misogyny. She, herself, in her relatively short academic career, had never experienced even the slightest implication that she was not worthy of taking her place beside men in the scientific world.

Picking up the biography once more, Annie read the next painful episode in Marie's war against sexism she had chronicled.

'In December 1903 it was announced by the Royal Swedish Academy of Sciences that Pierre Curie and Henri Becquerel were to be the recipients of the Nobel Prize in Physics. Incredibly, Marie was not included in this great honor despite the overwhelming evidence that it was mostly her research, passion and indefatigable drive that unearthed the ultimate discovery of radium.

Fortunately, one member of the Academy's committee, mathematician Magnus Leffler, alerted Pierre to the biased, unforgivable sexist slight. To his credit, Pierre immediately complained to the Academy and Marie's name was quickly added, making her the first woman in history to receive a Nobel Prize.

Neither she nor her husband travelled to Stockholm for the ceremony. Pierre intensely disliked ceremonies and Marie felt they were too busy to interrupt their scientific research to make such a long and arduous trip.'

Again, Annie read and reread this passage, experiencing a myriad of feelings. The first emotion was one of amazement at Marie's incredible achievement. Here she was, a month past her thirty-sixth birthday, receiving perhaps the most prestigious award in the scientific world. Not only that, but how groundbreaking was she for being the first woman to have that esteemed honor bestowed upon her? Shaking her head and just trying to assimilate the information filled Annie with such joy and pride.

But as much as she felt elated by Marie's award, she still was horrified by the fact that Pierre found it necessary to step forward and inform the committee about Marie's major contribution to the discovery of radium. That the Academy was prepared to overlook, indeed dismiss, her leading scientific investigative skills, appalled Annie almost beyond words. To her, it was a stunning example of pure, unadulterated bigotry.

But her feelings were definitely mitigated somewhat by the action Pierre took on his wife's behalf. His insistence that Marie share in the prize was an example and a credit to him and, perhaps, in some small way, laid the foundation for future amply qualified women to be not only recognized but accepted equally as men in their respective fields. Annie's respect for Pierre, upon learning of his action, took on a whole new dimension.

Her other deep admiration for Marie's award centered on the fact that she did not have the advantage of a formal education in her early, formative years. Only by her sheer determination and iron will did she forge her own path. Of course, her father and mother set the foundations in place, but only through her own discipline, drive and vision for herself did she finally come to attain the status of Nobel Laureate.

Continuing with Marie's story, Annie, full of enthusiasm, read the next phase;

> *'Although Marie and Pierre did not travel to Sweden for the award ceremony they did accept the monetary prize which enabled them to employ, for the first time, a laboratory assistant, which helped alleviate somewhat their ever growing research responsibilities in light of Pierre's recent appointment to a professorship at the University of Paris. It also took them a lot closer to their dream of running their own laboratory, which they began in earnest and was finally completed in 1906.*
>
> *The next year, although the Curies were still heavily committed to their continuing radium research, they were blessed with a second daughter, Eve. It was a moment of pure joy for them as well as a strong reminder that their lives did not wholly revolve around scientific matters.*

Marie, coming from a large family, knew the importance of roots and the sense of belonging. To ensure her two daughters always understood their Polish heritage, she quickly employed governesses to teach them the Polish language. To further cement the children's knowledge of their ancestry, Marie and Pierre took them on many visits to Poland, during which time Marie celebrated with them her own family beginnings. These trips were to become a highlight of her daughters' early lives.'

At two-thirty in the morning Annie decided to call a halt to writing and reviewing any more that night. Although late, she still needed time to assimilate in her mind the importance of what she'd written. First and foremost, the words 'Nobel Prize winner' kept flashing across Annie's brain as a constant reminder of such an astounding and breathtaking feat. Here was Marie, barely thirty-six and already the recipient of one of the world's most respected and treasured awards. For some people, at such a young age, the honor might have inflated their ego to an extent whereby they considered themselves superior to their colleagues and studies alike. But Marie, Annie knew from her extensive research into her life, almost certainly was aware that the award was merely a stepping stone to future discoveries. That is why she and Pierre invested the prize money in hiring an assistant and began building their own laboratory. It was an important lesson for Annie to learn and take to heart; do not be sidelined by flattery or accolades; continue doing the work that needs to be done. This is what Marie did, fearlessly in the face of prejudice and personal obstacles.

Annie downed the last dregs of her cold coffee, stretched out her tired arms and yawned. It had been a long night but a productive one. She needed to sleep but Marie's voice continued speaking to her. This time she heard her celebrate the importance of having a life outside of the scientific one, in particular in Marie's case, a family. Not only was she now a world renowned scientist but she was also a wife, mother and sister. Her joy at being a mother and teacher to her daughters manifested itself by her determination to ensure they fully understood their Polish heritage. Although they never knew a life in Poland, Marie made certain that part of *her* life would not be lost on her girls.

Although late, Annie immediately called her mother. Blythe answered, worried, seeing her daughter's number appear on her screen.

"Honey! What? What is it? Is everything all right?"

"Yes, Mom," Annie replied, in a reassuring tone. "Sorry to wake you and Dad but there's something I need to tell you and it can't wait."

"Oh, all right, Sweetie. Your dad's still zonked out so give me a minute to take this in the other room," she whispered.

"Okay," Blythe continued, from a couch in the living room, "I'm all ears and, Honey, just so you know, it is *never* too late to call me any time. Now, what's up?"

"Nothing's up, Mom, but I just needed to thank you and Dad for always making me aware of my roots...you know...in China. I've just finished a section of the Curie bio where she'd just had a second daughter and she went to extraordinary lengths to make sure her kids knew about and understood their heritage and where their mother came from. Mom, she hired governesses to teach them Polish and took them on numerous trips back to Poland to explore her and, obviously, their roots.

"And it got me thinking about how you've done the same for me in many different ways. I know I'm an American through and through but I also have Chinese blood in me and you've always made it a point to make me aware of that. I know if I ever have kids I will make sure they know and understand all that. I'd even take them there, if you'd come with me, to show them all the places it started for me. Anyway, I just wanted you to know how grateful I am that you never swept anything under the carpet, that you always answered my questions and never made me feel ashamed for the difficult beginning I had."

Blythe didn't respond for a few seconds, letting Annie's words wash over her like a pleasant shower.

"Oh, Honey, just to hear you say those things...well...no, it's nothing that you don't deserve. Just because you had a different journey than most doesn't mean where you came from should be forgotten. Yes, I hope you will go back with maybe your kids. That would be so cool. You will always be part Chinese and you should cherish that part of you. I think Marie would have loved meeting you," she continued, with a laugh. "And I know you would've loved meeting her."

"Oh, Mom, you have no idea. She's already taught me so much, so many good lessons to remember, and this from someone who lived over a hundred years ago. Amazing. I'm totally blown away by her sometimes. I can hardly wait until I let you and Dad read the book when it's done. Which reminds me, my agent called to let me know I only have a few more months to finish it…which I will, of course…"

"…Of course," Blythe butts in.

"…*and*…

"…and," Blythe interrupts again.

"…*and*…guess what? There might be a movie deal, too!"

"What? A movie of your book?"

"That's what he said. Apparently he knows some people in Hollywood who might…and he stressed the word *might*…be interested in turning it into a movie. How about that? Wouldn't that be so cool?"

"Oh, my god, it would, but first things first. Finish it and go from there."

"Well, a girl can dream, can't she?"

"Indeed. And on that note I think it's time for both of us to get to bed. Thanks again, Honey, for your kind words. I'll pass them onto dad, and sweet dreams, Baby, sweet dreams."

CHAPTER NINETEEN

———⟡ ⟡———

P ROFESSOR JIM PLOTHER'S APPLIED BOTANY class had only two
participants this morning, one week ahead of the Christmas
break. Plother had decided from the moment Annie told him about
the mysterious pampousa tree leaves that she and Matty would have
this particular class to themselves.

Over the first two weeks of the sessions he instructed them on the
two fundamental areas he knew would benefit them most; physiological
and structural botany. Physiological dealt with the organic functions of
plants while structural focused on the structure and composition. Of
course, both young women had some prior knowledge of these areas but
not to the deep extent into which Plother delved.

They already knew, for example, that plant leaves contained, among
other substances, sodium, potassium, calcium, magnesium, iron,
manganese, silica, phosphorus, ash, carbon, nitrogen, organic acids,
non-structural carbohydrates, various mineral substances and soluble
and polymeric sugars. But Plother extended their understanding by
conducting intense analysis of how each substance interacted with
the others.

After satisfying himself that they fully grasped the importance of
his molecular reasoning and explanations, he then allowed them to
concentrate their time on examining the make-up of the pampousa
leaves. To this end, he decided to leave them to their own devices, so
that their discoveries, if any, would be theirs alone and he would review
their findings at the appropriate time. Of course, he would always

be available for advice but he made it clear that their work should be regarded as groundbreaking and, as such, would certainly satisfy his requirements for passing his class.

"Professor Plother," Matty commented, as she prepared a thawed pampousa leaf for analysis, "has been very gracious in allowing us so much freedom to pursue our investigations. And his botany lessons so far have taught me so much that I never knew existed in the world. I am so grateful he is allowing me to participate in this class with you."

"Matty, I'm sure after he reviewed your transcripts with Virginia he realized, like all of us, the potential you bring to the table. Plother's not a fool. He invited you because he knows your value in eventually solving this problem. But you're right, what he's taught us so far has been eye-opening. The depth and detail he went into blew me away, too. But now comes the hard part; living up to his expectations."

Matty smiled, before saying, "With you as a partner, I know we will not let him down."

"And, right back at you with that," Annie countered. "Couldn't ask for anyone better."

Although Annie exuded confidence, she also knew their path would be long, winding and hopefully, not a one-way street. Within herself, she pinned a lot of hope that somehow the answer to defeating this deadly parasite lay somewhere in the pampousa tree or its leaves. But she also entertained thoughts that that idea might just be a desperate stab in the dark. Just as quickly she dismissed that negative thinking, confident that she and Matty, as well as the staff at the facility in Norambuland, would sooner or later have a solution.

While Matty worked on breaking down the components of the pampousa leaf, Annie began the arduous task of analyzing the river and rain water samples. But it was interesting, revealing work and she was soon engrossed in the whole process. River water, she soon found, was a difficult nut to crack simply because it obviously contained so many different substances and minerals from so many different sources. Annie had a good idea of what she was looking for, a component exclusive to this river, but finding it might be like seeking a needle in a haystack.

After a week, she'd managed to identify ninety-five percent of the particulates. The rain water proved to be an easier task but there were still some annoyingly few soluble substances and particles she needed to uncover. The day before they left for their Christmas break, the two young women and Professor Plother met in his office to bring him up to speed with what they'd learned so far.

"I've read your preliminary reports but it's so much better hearing things from the horse's mouth, so to speak," he began, a wide grin spreading across his face. "Matty, give me where you are right now please."

Matty, still not as comfortable as Annie when it came to addressing the professor, shuffled her papers and cleared her throat.

"I will do my best to explain what I have found, Professor Plother. The examinations and analysis I have conducted so far reveal some very interesting findings." Plother nodded encouragingly. "First of all, the pampousa leaves are very absorbent."

"Which means?" Plother pointedly asked.

"Which means, Professor, they allow, in particular, water and its constituents to be assimilated within them."

"Nothing strange about that," remarked Plother. "All leaves suck up a variety of different substances, as well as light and air."

"Yes, I agree, Professor, but I have also found that pampousa leaves are very porous, allowing such water and its constituents to pass easily through its membranes, but only when fully saturated."

Plother considered Matty's findings for a few seconds. With a frown, he commented, "Okay, that is strange. A leaf that is both absorbent and porous. So, what's your hypothesis?"

"Well, my findings are very preliminary, Professor, but my best supposition is that, by storing such substances for a fairly long period of time, the leaf allows those substances the chance to metabolize and change their characteristics into something completely different. Once that is achieved, the leaf then expels the matter, mostly in the form of water, and it falls into the river or onto the ground."

Annie listened, fascinated by what Matty had explained and added, "Matty, didn't you, or maybe it was Kip or Philippe, tell me while we were in Norambuland, how in the past grandmothers and mothers used the pampousa leaves as a remedy for all sorts of aches, pains and minor cuts and bruises?"

"Yes, that is most certainly true. I, myself, can remember my own grandmother treating me with a leaf when I once had a stomach sickness. It was very effective," she added, with a smile.

Annie, intrigued with Matty's recollection, asked for more information.

"Exactly what did they do with the leaves?"

"Sometimes they would gather a large potful and then boil them over a big fire. Once the mixture had cooled, they would remove the leaves and pour the liquid into jars or cans. It was this liquid that was used for internal aches and pains. My stomach problem went away almost at once when my grandmother made me drink some. I was very grateful.

"At other times the leaves would again be boiled and then they would be mashed into a sort of paste. It was this that was then applied to problems outside of the body, like bruises, cuts and animal bites. It was very effective."

"So interesting, Matty," Annie answered, fascinated, "and information that might be quite valuable. We'll talk more about this later."

"All right," Plother replied, "I'm also starting to get intrigued. Of course, Matty, your findings are, as you say, very preliminary. Lots of work left to do, but an excellent beginning. Congratulations, now, Annie, tell me about your water analysis."

"Very arduous and, at times, frustrating..."

"Welcome to my world," Plother interrupted, with a grin.

"...but I have managed to narrow down the percentages I haven't been able to identify."

"To what?"

"About five percent of the particulates."

"Excellent but what seems to be the problem there?"

"Cannot identify certain of the constituents," Annie replied, frowning. "Maybe if you took a peek, Professor, they'd jump right out at you?"

"And spoil your fun," Plother offered, with a bigger grin this time.

"Oh, wow, you really mean for me to earn a pass in your class, don't you?" Annie responded, with a sarcastic shrug.

"You do the work, you get the pass. That's the way it goes. But more importantly," Plother continued seriously, "I want you to make the breakthrough so that when it comes time to present your dissertation, you can honestly say the work was all yours. Trust me, I'm correct here."

"What if I keep drawing blanks? I could be running down a dead-end."

"No. Sooner or later you will find the reason, the explanation. Just don't give up. But I will give you one suggestion. After listening to Matty's report on the leaves, I'd seriously look at that angle. To me it sounds promising and the most likely.

"Now, so far I'm very pleased with your industry and dedication. Come back after the Christmas break refreshed, and then finish the job. But I will warn you, I'm a very harsh critic and taskmaster. No fudging allowed here. Okay?"

"Okay," both women answered.

"Off you go then. Have a great break and I'll see you in the New Year."

"It's *so* good to be home again," Annie gushed to her parents, as she and Matty unloaded their bags on a cold and snowy winter afternoon.

"Let's get you into the warm," Clive offered, now busily gathering up their things and ushering them into the house.

Blythe walked arm in arm with the two girls, a smile on her face bigger than the proverbial Grand Canyon. Once inside, she took a long look at each of them.

"Beautiful, just beautiful," she exclaimed, as she gave each a huge hug.

"Mom," Annie expressed, faking embarrassment, "it's only been a few months!"

"I know. I know," Blythe answered, nodding, "but just to have you both here is…is…well amazing."

"Hope you still think that way after a week," Annie playfully countered.

"You are very gracious to invite me to your home for Christmas," Matty said, smiling broadly at Blythe and Clive.

"Nonsense," Clive responded kindly. "We now regard you as part of the family. We just hope you won't find it too boring."

Matty shook her head, saying, "I am sure that is the last thing it will be."

And she was right. The next day, Christmas Eve, was spent decorating the huge tree, preparing food, visiting friends and neighbors, and enjoying a family dinner at Annie's grandmother's house. It was a time for laughter, closeness and not a little love.

"I hope this is not too overwhelming for you?" Gwen, Annie's grandmother, asked Matty as they sat quietly enjoying each other's company. "Do you have a big family?"

"I do, so I am very used to happy, noisy celebrations," Matty answered, grinning.

"Well, I hope in some small way we can make you less homesick. Being away from family at holidays is always hard. I miss Annie's grandfather every day, but especially around good times like these. If you ever feel sad just come see me and I will cheer you up." She squeezed Matty's hand as if to emphasize the point.

"You are very kind and Annie, I can tell, is so fortunate to have you as a grandmother."

As the evening drew to a close Matty did, in fact, begin to feel she had not only made new friends but gained a precious family, too.

Christmas Day brought new traditions into Matty's life. There was Clive, complete with a Santa hat, making breakfast for the family. With Annie's help, he included in the fare some of Matty's favorite Norambuland treats. Veldt, a dense whole wheat, milk, salt, sugar and cinnamon bread, as well as a reasonable stab at oykyki or 'fat cakes', were presented to her in a mock ceremonial fashion. She was so overwhelmed by the kind gesture that it took several minutes and quite a few tissues to dry her happy tears.

After breakfast the family settled around the tree, opening presents, laughing, talking a-mile-a-minute and comforting Matty again when she became emotional at the Cavallaros' generosity. Her presents included clothes, electronics and a hefty check to help with the rest of her school needs.

Finally, Blythe gave Annie and Matty each a tiny box, explaining that this had been a tradition since her daughter's first Christmas. After carefully removing the wrapping the two young women each found an exquisite gold charm; Annie's was a book, symbolizing her biography of Marie Curie, Blythe explained, while Matty's was a tiny heart to constantly let her know how much she was loved. This time it took a lot longer for the tears to subside.

The rest of the day was spent with a walk in the local snow-covered park, a game or two of Annie's favorite Scrabble and a family dinner. Before bed, Matty addressed the family.

"I will never be able to thank you enough for you kindness in including me in your Christmas celebrations. Meeting Annie at Harvard has turned out to be one of the best things that has ever happened to me. Now with all of you…well…it just seems as if I have been fortunate and blessed to now call you my friends and yes, my other family. Thank you so much. So very, very much."

There were more tears and hugs which brought this Christmas Day to its happy, joyful conclusion.

CHAPTER TWENTY

ANNIE EXCUSED HERSELF FROM FAMILY obligations two days before she and Matty were set to return to Fitzgerald, dedicating the day to catching up on her Marie Curie biography.

Matty, too, was grateful for some personal time, which enabled her to sit down and write a long, expressive email to her parents, as well as grappling with some long overdue school work.

Blythe also took the opportunity to prepare for her 3rd grade class resumption, while Clive had to actually return to his law office to consult with a client in an important case involving possible fraud and embezzlement.

In the quiet of her room, Annie reviewed the last few chapters she'd written on Marie before concentrating on getting a lot more serious work done. Before she could write one word an email came in from Renée Coutage, Director of The Curie Museum in Paris.

> *Ma chère, I am wondering how the biography is progressing? I hope you now have all the documents and records you need from the museum. If not, let me know. Your recent text amazed me…Africa? Magnifique! Very interested in your theory about the rain you have collected in a bottle. You MUST come to Paris and visit me here at the museum. I will show you something few people have seen in Marie's collection of artifacts we have here. You will be amazed that this coincidence happened over a hundred years ago. I will*

say no more. You must come see for yourself when you have the time. The chapters you have sent me so far are beautifully written and certainly capture and convey the very essence of who and what Marie was. If these are any indication of what is to come then the book will be extraordinary! I cannot wait to read it, ma chère. Adieu, Renée.

Annie could hardly believe what she read. To receive such high praise from *the* director of The Curie Museum…well…unbelievable and humbling. In reply, she wrote…

Renée, thank you so much for your kind, inspiring words. I'm sure I'm not yet worthy but I will do my best to live up to your expectations. The book, I hope, will be finished in about four months. I will continue sending you the chapters for review and criticism. Your input is so valuable and helps me enormously. I am intrigue about the Marie artifact you mentioned. I will definitely come to Paris as soon as I can but please understand I am in the middle of trying to solve a devastating disease in Africa. We are making progress and as soon as I am free I will visit. Seeing the museum will be such a highlight for me, as will finally meeting the person who has done so much to guide me through writing Marie's biography. Thank you so much again for all you have done to help me and for your friendship, which I appreciate more than you can know. Fondly, Annie.

Taking a few minutes to digest Renée's email, Annie suddenly believed she could now really finish not only a book, but one that might make some small difference in the lives of those who read it. Such praise from Renée also gave Annie a renewed, fresh impetus to press on and complete the biography as soon as possible. But this promise to herself was easier said than done considering the much more important work she had undertaken with the parasitic disease. She worried about burning the candle at both ends, of failing at both enterprises while achieving nothing in the end.

She then remembered Marie's story, one she now knew so intimately and admiringly. There were real hardships, disappointments, family misfortunes, but also great achievements in the face of all those obstacles. Through it all, Annie remembered, as she passed Marie's whole life through her mind's eye, this brave woman continued to make extraordinary, groundbreaking discoveries that certainly changed and benefitted the world then and now. If she, Annie, could manage to produce only a sliver of the accomplishments Marie created virtually out of nothing, then that, most certainly, would be satisfaction enough.

Settling down, she began to write…

'On the 19th of April, 1906, Marie's world suffered a catastrophic hammer blow. While walking on a Paris street, Pierre was struck by a horse-drawn vehicle, fell under its wheels, fractured his skull and was killed. Marie, devastated by the loss, had to first deal with the almost impossible task of telling her two young daughters. She turned, in desperation, to their fellow Nobel Prize winner, Henri Becquerel, for advice.

"You must be honest with them, my dear. They most certainly will not grasp the full meaning of their father's death but in time, with your love and comfort, they will come to accept what has happened."

Marie felt her eldest daughter, Irene, being nine years old would certainly understand what had happened and the resulting consequences of her father's death, but two year old Eve would need much more comfort, patience and, above all, love.

"It's Papa," she began, quietly, as the girls sat before her wondering why they had been summoned to Maman's bedroom. She gathered Eve onto her lap, ran her fingers through her fair hair and glumly continued to speak in a voice both low and kind. "As you know, Papa loves to walk the streets of Paris and this morning, while on his way to work, he had an accident."

Irene frowned before asking the obvious question.

"Is Papa all right, Maman?"

Fighting back tears, Marie replied, "Oh, my beloved

children, no, he's not. He fell under the wheels of a horse-drawn cart and hurt his head very badly."

"I can kiss it better for him," Eve answered, innocently. "He does that for me all the time when I hurt myself."

"Yes, he does, my sweetness, but Papa hurt his head so badly that…that…he's gone to be with the angels."

"You mean Papa died?" Irene asked, staring wide-eyed.

"Yes. Yes," Marie managed to whisper before holding both girls close to her. "I'm sorry. I'm so sorry. Papa is gone."

Eve, still not grasping the significance of her mother's words, asked, "So, when will Papa be back so I can kiss him better?"

"Oh, Eve, my sweet, Papa will not be back for a long, long time. But we should think about him every day for he loves you both forever."

The scene, heartbreaking and almost unbearable, left three people without the light of their lives; without the man who loved them all beyond measure.

As the weeks slowly passed and the family tried to heal and accept the reality of Pierre's passing, life for the Curies returned, somewhat, to normal. The children continued with their educations through the governesses Marie had engaged and she, reluctantly, returned to her work, determined that her husband's massive contribution to the scientific world would not be lost.

To her surprise, the University of Paris offered her the Chair of its Physics department. This was indeed an honor considering she would be the first woman professor at the university. Marie accepted the position in the hope that the university would help her create a first-class laboratory as a tribute to Pierre.

Unfortunately, the University of Paris initially failed to provide her with such a world-class facility, so upon hearing the news, the director of The Pasteur Institute, Pierre Paul Emile Roux, suggested to Marie that she move to them to fulfill the Curies' dream of operating their own laboratory.

Only then did the University of Paris reconsider its position, suggesting it collaborate with The Pasteur Institute to create for Marie what was to become The Radium Institute or The Curie Pavilion.

This huge step forward provided Marie with the impetus she needed to continue her important research into isolating radium, a journey she had begun with Pierre and one she wanted to finish as a tribute to him.

That road proved to be long, sometimes frustrating and, without her realization, dangerous. In the early 1900s little was known or understood about radium's possible affects on humans. Because of this ignorance, obviously no safety precautions were taken when handling any of these materials.

After several years of painstaking work, experiments and analysis, in September, 1910, Marie Curie and Andre Louis Debierne, her collaborator since Pierre's death, succeeded in isolating radium in its pure metallic form through electrolysis of radium chloride. At the same time, they also defined the new international standard for radioactive emissions which eventually became known the 'curie'.

Despite Marie's major achievements in physics and chemistry - the discovery of the elements polonium and radium, as well coining the word 'radioactivity' to describe the rays emitted from these elements - she again faced in the following year the harsh world of feminine discrimination and xenophobia. The French Academy of Sciences, by one or two votes, failed to elect her into its membership. In fact, it would take another fifty-one years before a doctoral student named Marguerite Perey became the first woman member of the Académie Francqise.

At the time of Marie's consideration for membership of the Academy, the French public's attitude towards foreigners still tended to be one of distrust, bordering on hatred of strangers. During the French Academy of Sciences elections, this xenophobia was fuelled by a false speculation that Marie was Jewish. The right wing press took up the gauntlet, vilifying her for being a foreigner and an atheist. It was hardly surprising then that her application for membership was refused.'

Annie stopped writing, again stunned by the injustice served on Marie. Although well acquainted with the details through her extensive research into Marie's life, Annie still found it difficult to comprehend how just being a foreigner or believing in another religion could prevent anyone, let alone someone of Marie's world renowned scientific stature, from being accepted into a society in which they were, ostensibly, an integral part.

From her own experience of being born in another country, of which she had no memory, Annie reflected that, while she looked different from the average American, she had never felt discriminated against because of those very looks. And certainly she had never known any form of bias in her academic world from grade school through to Fitzgerald.

Unfortunately, as Annie settled down to continue with the next chapter, she had to record another harrowing episode for Marie, which also occurred during the turbulent year of 1911.

'For about a year, Marie had been conducting an affair with one of Pierre's former students, the physicist Paul Langerin. He was married but estranged from his wife. He was in his late thirties while Marie was five years older.

Again, when the news of the affair broke open publically, the press bitterly condemned and smeared her character, calling her a foreign, Jewish home-wrecker. At the time the scandal was revealed Marie was away at a scientific conference in Belgium. Upon her return, she found angry, hostile mobs at her house, which forced her to take her family to the safety of a friend's house. She worried most about her two daughters, only returning home when the local authorities assured her the danger was over.

The double standard in France at that time was staggeringly unfair. Marie was the accused, the guilty party, while very little in the way of condemnation was directed towards her lover, Paul Langerin. Of course, the affair ended, but the damage to Marie's character remained for a long time.

Despite the major setbacks in her personal life, Marie, determined as ever, continued with her important scientific work at The Radium Institute. After managing finally to isolate the element of radium, she diligently worked on ways to expand its usefulness. This proved to be extremely challenging since metallic radium existed only in very small quantities.

The tempestuous year of 1911 still held unexpected surprises for Marie. Almost single-handedly she had managed to advance the world of chemistry by the discoveries of the elements polonium and radium, as well as by isolating radium and furthering the study of the nature and compounds of this extraordinary element.

To honor and acknowledge her remarkable scientific achievements, The Royal Swedish Academy of Sciences awarded her the Nobel Prize in chemistry. Marie Curie thus became the first person to win or share two Nobel Prizes, and stands alongside only Linus Pauling as a Nobel Laureate in two different disciplines.'

Again, Annie stopped writing to consider the magnitude of Marie's accomplishments. Here she was, at forty-four years of age, the recipient of two Nobel Prizes as well as having discovered, or helped discover, two new elements. Annie could only imagine, with awe, the depth of Marie's intelligence and scientific knowledge at a still relatively young age.

She considered her own field of study and wondered if she would ever reach the heights Marie had climbed, not in terms of success for success sake, but rather, like Marie, to be of some sort of value to the world with her work and career. Annie, modestly and honestly, only hoped for a tiny part of Marie's magic to rub off on herself.

Although tired from absorbing once again Marie's incredible story, Annie needed to finish her current chapter before ending for the day.

'After receiving confirmation of her Nobel Prize, Marie heard that the chairman of the Nobel Committee did not want her to attend the award ceremony due to her questionable moral standing. She, however, insisted she would be present since the Prize was awarded to her for her discovery of polonium

and radium, and there was no correlation between her
scientific work and her private life.'

Annie smiled as she wrote this paragraph, silently thanking Marie not only for standing up for herself, but for demonstrating how strong women behave in the face of discrimination. She finally went to bed that night feeling she had learned an important lesson, one that she was determined to retain and practice for the rest of her life.

CHAPTER TWENTY-ONE

THE RETURN TO FITZGERALD AFTER the welcome Christmas break meant Annie and Matty were immediately plunged back into a world of critical work, hard study and very little sleep. But this was cheerfully accepted and, indeed, looked forward to. Both young women realized how precious time now was, that the next few months would prove whether or not they could come up with a solution to the devastating parasitic disease.

The two main areas of research were now clearly concentrated upon the pampousa leaves and the river and rain water samples. Matty's priority was to isolate any substance within the leaf's composition that may provide some sort of resistance or deterrent to the parasites themselves.

She well knew from past experience and handed-down family lore that the pampousa leaf contained something that had in the past proven to be very effective against certain ailments. The fact that the pampousa trees grew almost exclusively along the River Ballooka in Area 5, and that the residents of the villages served by the river had suffered no ill effects from the parasite, strongly suggested an almost certain connection between the two.

Annie's main purpose now was also to isolate, from the remaining five percent of the particulates not yet identified from the river and rain water samples, the compound, substance or material responsible for probably protecting the residents in Area 5 from catching the disease.

Holding up a thawed bottle of rain, collected while dripping off the pampousa leaves, Annie excitedly exclaimed to Matty, "The answer is in here! I'm convinced of that. Here, and in the leaves you have analyzed. Nothing else makes sense."

It was now well into February and the long days and nights they had willingly endured finally brought them to this seminal moment of belief in their own scientific conclusion; the answer lay with the pampousa tree.

"Yes, I agree one hundred per cent," Matty offered, nodding and smiling, "but we still have the problem of isolating whatever substance is responsible. There are five compounds within the leaf's structure, but they are made up of many different components. So far I have identified twenty that are present in many, but not all, of the other trees in Africa. Those we can eliminate from our search. That now leaves me with five which I am continuing to work on."

"Yes, I understand your frustration, Matty," Annie sympathized. "I'm having the same problem with the rain and river water samples. But, like you, I have now narrowed down the list of possible responsible particulates. I only have three but they're proving tough nuts to crack."

Matty thought over the problem for a few seconds before making a suggestion.

"Forgive my rudeness in making this observation but…"

"Matty, for goodness sake," Annie interrupted, "you don't need to keep apologizing. We are a team here. I *always* want to know what you are thinking or if you have any insights you feel might be useful. The last few chapters of the Curie bio I've been writing have certainly taught me that we should never be afraid to speak up. Okay?"

Matty nodded before replying, "Yes, I do know that by now, but sometimes my old habits are hard to overcome. But thank you, Annie, I will no longer be scared to say what I think."

Annie went over and hugged her friend, then, looking her in the face, said, "I am not more important than you on this project. In fact, I can't do this without you. Okay?" Matty smiled and nodded again before Annie continued, asking, "Now, what is your suggestion?"

"One way to perhaps solve both our problems, of identifying the particular substance or particulate responsible for apparently providing immunity to my people in Area five, would be to test all the ones we both have left against the three types of parasites. That way, we would find the one common to the pampousa leaf and the rain and river water."

"Of course!" Annie exclaimed, excitedly. "Genius, Matty! I'll get in touch right away with Joyce or Kip at the Norambuland facility and get them to immediately send us a bunch of samples from the three parasitic spectrums." Then, she added, "I don't know for sure but I suddenly feel we are now at the beginning of the end of our search."

Joyce Obuna, whom Annie placed in charge of the Norambuland facility after Dr. Amdao's financial misdeeds came to light, promised Annie the samples she requested would be in her hands by the end of February, two weeks away.

Since they now had some relatively 'free' time on their hands, Annie suggested it would be a great opportunity to make up the two remaining classes they needed to complete their doctorates.

Since Matty had become so closely involved with Annie in trying to solve the parasitic disease disaster in Norambuland, Virginia had accelerated her course work so as to bring it in line with Annie's. This was not easy since Matty was basically a year behind where she needed to be. But with Virginia and Annie's help she had managed to cover most of the required courses and was now on track to receive her doctorate, alongside Annie, in May.

The two outstanding classes were Applied Molecular Interpretation and Advanced Cellular Identification, both taught over a four week period by Dr. Michelle Sanders. Of course, Dr. Sanders was well versed in Annie and Matty's involvement with the African parasitic fight, and welcomed the opportunity to be of assistance in any way she could.

"However," she began, as the young women sat before her on their first morning, "just as Jim Plother told you with his botany class, I will also only point you in the right direction and leave you to make whatever discoveries you can. You need to do this important work yourselves, which I know you appreciate and completely understand."

"We do," Annie agreed, "and we thank you for having so much faith in us to figure things out."

"Yes," Matty added, "we have found that Dr. Plother's way of teaching has been so very beneficial to us."

"Well, that's not to say I will be an innocent bystander. I will require frequent detailed reports on your findings as well as the evidence to back up those findings. I am fair but I am also a hard taskmaster...or mistress..." she added, with a smile. "Now, our first three days together will be spent reviewing what you should already know and moving on to the crucial business of interpretation and identification, which you are so desperately going to need if you are to solve the problem as you have explained it to me. So, let's get started."

The next two weeks did indeed provide Annie and Matty with some of the additional tools needed to confront, analyze and form firm, sound judgments when they came to experiment with the actual parasite samples Joyce was sending them. Dr. Sanders, impressed and encouraged by their immediate grasp of complicated concepts, quickly shifted her focus to those areas she well knew would be most beneficial to their parasite examination; in other words, from the theoretical to the practical.

The parasite samples arrived in the first week of March. It was decided Matty would take the protozoa, while Annie concentrated on the helminths. The four classifications of protozoa, which Matty well knew by heart now, would each have to be broken down and subjected to multiple experiments to see if any reacted to any of the remaining unidentified particulates in the pampousa leaves.

Similarly, the three main groups of helminths consisting of flatworms, thorny-headed worms and roundworms would provide Annie with days of intricate and painstakingly controlled tests with, again, the five per cent of the rain and river water particulates she had yet to identify.

The work was exhilarating but exhausting. The two young women had hardly any time to themselves since their evenings were spent with Professor Sanders, who brought them close to completing their requirements with her.

Annie became really anxious about the Curie biography. It had been quite a while since she'd written anything and, so, she decided to take her agent up on his offer of extending her deadline for delivery of the manuscript by three months. That gave her breathing space. She was also sure she could complete the book by September. He texted that the publisher had granted her request which, of course, removed a huge burden from her back.

By the end of March both Annie and Matty were at a point of comparing notes on what they had found and observed so far.

"It appears," Matty started, eager to share her news on the

experiments with the four groups that made up the protozoa spectrum, "that there has been a negative reaction when immersed in a solution made from the chlorophyll of the pampousa leaves. So I isolated each particulate and tested each of the four groups against them in turn. It was very time consuming considering the number of different substances in the chlorophyll."

"I'm sure," Annie sympathized, knowing what she had gone through herself. "And?"

"And, I found one constituent of the chlorophyll – one, incidentally, that seems to be only present in pampousa leaves, that repelled the protozoa every single time. So I then went to Professor Plother and asked if he would check my work to make sure I was correct in my analysis."

"And?"

"He did and he also found one constituent of the chlorophyll of the pampousa leaf – the same one I found - that he did not know what it was, but that it certainly did repel each of the four protozoa groups. He said he checked many times and the results were always the same."

Annie was not totally surprised by Matty's findings since she had a similar experience with the bottles of rain water and the river water.

"I also finally managed to separate the remaining five percent particulates I hadn't yet identified," she offered, excitedly, holding out her hands in front of her, "and I found one, too, that had an amazingly negative effect on every single helminth I introduced it to.

"Now, we need to do the molecular interpretation and the cellular identification individually on the particulates we have both found to be effective against the protozoa and the helminths, and then we need to test the same particulate on the ectoparasite samples we have, which I think are mostly ticks and mosquitoes."

Annie noticed Matty's almost subdued demeanor as she described her findings. Puzzled and frowning, she asked, "Matty, what's wrong? These are significant breakthroughs we just might have made. I'm about ready to start jumping for joy."

Matty's lips tensed and her eyes began tearing up.

"No, it's not that I'm not very happy about our results. It's just that if our theory is correct then the answer to this terrible disease has been right under our noses for years. How could so many people have missed it?"

"I know. I know," Annie replied, sympathetically, "but this is such a new disease and these things take time and lots and lots of research. I mean, it took Jonas Salk six or seven years to develop the polio vaccine. Honestly, Matty, no one could have known about the value of the pampousa leaves besides its use years ago to treat simple ailments. We only found out…or think we've found out…because we did the research on a new disease and carefully considered every aspect of life in your country. It was only because Area five had no cases that we took a closer look. Sometimes, I guess, these diseases are solved by luck. But there is absolutely no reason to beat yourself up on this. You've done so well. We've done so well. But there's still a long way to go."

Matty well knew the truth of Annie's wise words.

Smiling again, she answered, "You are correct, Annie. I realize I am so fortunate being even a tiny part of solving this problem for my country. You always make me feel better. Thank you."

"Not so much 'a tiny' part, Ms Kizembouko," Annie nodded, her voice serious. "You have done some amazing analytical detective work on this. So don't ever forget that. Couldn't have accomplished any of this without you. Okay?"

"All right, Ms. Cavallaro," Matty teased back.

"Now," Annie said, bringing them back to their continuing research, "before we set off on a wild goose chase I think we should get our two professors together and bring them up to speed on where we are. Perhaps they'll suggest some ways to short-cut what we have left to do."

The meeting with Plother and Dr. Sanders took place two days later. Both professors were intrigue to be consulted, fully expecting to receive a lot of positive news about their students' research. They were not disappointed.

"All right," Plother began pleasantly, "we're all ears. Take your time."

Annie and Matty were well prepared, knowing full well the professors would ask demanding questions, while expecting substantial and in depth reasoning of the answers.

The session lasted over two hours, with both professors astounded with the young women's grasp and execution of the complex nature of the experiments they had conducted to arrive at their stunning conclusion about the pampousa leaves.

"We are suitably impressed," Plother offered, generously. "You have indeed found and proved your hypothesis. But now the real work begins."

"That's correct," Dr. Sanders jumped in. "How to transform it into a safe vaccine suitable for all age groups? How long will one dose last? Oh, so many as yet unanswered questions. You are still at the beginning of this amazing discovery but I, for one, am now prepared to pass you through my class."

"I concur," agreed Plother. "Course work more than satisfactory completed. Write up your notes, et cetera, in presentable form and we will have them published in the appropriate journals. Congratulations. Outstanding work."

Both Annie and Matty were truly surprised by their professors' reaction and support.

"Oh, wow, all right, then," Annie responded. "We know there is an awful lot more to do but your words of encouragement...well...just... thank you."

"I am also honored by your faith in what we are doing." Matty offered. "And I know we will not rest until we have a complete solution."

"That's all we ask of you," Dr. Sanders answered, nodding and smiling. "That's all we ask of you. In my humble opinion, the world has just added two more outstanding, pioneering scientists to its ranks. And, believe me, the world needs them."

"That's a second from me," Plother said, as he walked over and gave each young woman a hug.

CHAPTER TWENTY-TWO

O VER THE NEXT TWO MONTHS Annie and Matty continued working at a furious pace. Both spent enormous amounts of time and energy struggling, and succeeding, to bring their research on the pampousa leaves to a point where they could, with their professors' help, begin publishing in peer review papers their results and conclusions.

In addition, Matty completed the last of her academic requirements, while Annie actually found time, mostly in the small hours, to add more chapters to the Curie biography. Both also, with Virginia's assistance, had to write their dissertations for presentation to the Academic Board.

Annie, now acutely aware that time was of the utmost relevance with regard to completing the book, actually made great strides. She was now almost three-quarters of the way through and the latest chapters sent to Renée Coutage in Paris came back with glowing comments.

In these chapters Annie had covered Marie's stay in hospital for depression and a kidney ailment a month after receiving her second Nobel Prize. For most of 1912 she avoided public life, but after a brief visit to England with her friend and fellow physicist, Hertha Ayrton, she returned to work in her laboratory in December, a break of fourteen months.

By this time, early in 1914, Marie was appointed director of The Curie Laboratory in The Radium Institute at The University of Paris. Unfortunately, the Institute's important work was interrupted by the war, since most of the researchers were drafted into the French Army. It did not fully resume business until 1919.

Annie was most pleased with the section covering World War 1. In these pages she felt elated describing Marie's massive contribution to France's war effort. She told of Marie noticing an injured soldier's best chance of survival was to be operated on as soon as possible. She saw a desperate need for field radiological centers near the front lines to assist doctors, medics and nurses make crucial, accurate decisions regarding diagnosing the condition of limbs that could be saved rather than amputated.

To further understand the problem, Marie quickly studied radiology, anatomy and even automotive mechanics. Her ultimate aim was to develop mobile x-ray units, which she managed to do by acquiring vehicles and generators to transport the units in the field. These units quickly became known as 'petites Curies' or 'little Curies'.

Annie was delighted when Renée Coutage sent photographs of Marie during the war, which gave Annie an even better understanding of the conditions under which she carried out her important contribution.

So impressed were The Red Cross with Marie's innovations and insights that it appointed her director of its Radiology Service, which in turn enabled her to establish France's first military radiology center by late 1914.

The biography continued with Annie joyfully writing that Marie was assisted in her war effort by a military doctor *and* her own seventeen year old daughter, Irene. During the rest of the war they managed to set up to twenty mobile radiology units and over two hundred facilities in field hospitals. It was an amazing achievement, with over one million soldiers treated during the conflict. Unfortunately, as Annie sadly noted, the French Government once again failed to recognize the massive contribution she had made.

Indeed, the French National Bank even refused to accept her proposed donation of her Nobel medals to help with the war effort, but she did buy war bonds with some of her prize money.

As the chapters went on, Annie wrote of the important events that continued to shape and cement Marie's legacy in the world scientific community. In 1921 she toured the United States, giving speeches and lectures, and being warmly received at The White House by President Warren Harding, who presented her with, of all things, a gram of radium. But one accolade she refused was an offer by the French Government of a Legion of Honour award.

Finally, in 1922, her academic colleagues voted her as a fellow of the French Academy of Medicine. Annie spent a long time on this particular chapter, explaining the significance of this honor in light of Marie's previous exclusion from most French academic societies just because she was a woman.

Her fame and scientific credentials now made her world renowned. This also thrilled Annie beyond measure considering the harsh treatment she experienced early in her career from numerous governments and agencies. To this end, she traveled abroad, giving talks and lectures in such places as Belgium, Brazil, Spain and Czechoslovakia.

By mid April, Annie had completed the first fifty-five years of Marie's amazing life. She now had four months left to complete the work and submit the manuscript to her publisher. And now, there was no doubt in her mind she would be able to do just that.

The discovery of the unknown particulate in the pampousa leaf provided Annie and Matty with a moment of levity. If it was unknown, it must also be nameless. Both professors suggested they come up with a scientific appellation that suitable embodied both the substance and the discoverers. Annie and Matty kicked the idea around for several days in their off time.

"All right," Annie suggested one evening as they finished dinner, "how about KizCav?"

Matty, not usually given to hilarity, almost fell off her chair laughing.

"I am sorry, Annie, but that sounds like a tin of dog or cat food. *Give your pet KizCav and watch it grow big and strong!*"

Annie feigned terrible disappointment, frowning and wiping away a non-existent tear.

"Okay, then, your turn."

Matty thought for a moment before saying, "I think the name should include its botanical root…chlorophyll. And, since both our names end in an 'o', I think we should call it *Oo Chlorophyllia.*"

Annie grinned broadly.

"Oh, I like that. Yes, let's call it that! *Oo Chlorophyllia.* It has such a ring about it. Such mystery."

Their two professors concurred and proceeded to register the name with the appropriate scientific bodies. It was an awe inspiring moment for the young researchers…actually having a botanical strain named after them.

Annie and Matty's dissertations to the Academic Board both centered, obviously, on the work they had done trying to solve the parasitic disease in Norambuland. Annie's would concentrate on the immunity effect the newly named *Oo Chlorophyllia* had on the residents of Area 5, through the rain and river water collected from the pampousa trees.

Matty, on the other hand, at Virginia and Dr. Sanders' recommendations, zeroed in on the deleterious effect the *Oo Chlorophyllia* had on the parasites themselves and how this particulate was able to actually repel them.

Virginia, Jim Plother and Dr. Sanders all spent a great deal of time helping the two doctoral candidates with their preparations, even going as far as throwing negativity and doubt upon their plentiful evidence in an effort to simulate the kind of intense questioning and scrutiny the young women would no doubt encounter before the actual board.

But Annie and Matty handled the sessions with clear reasoning and persuasive documented analysis, as well as describing in detail their methodical, logical and scientific next steps in producing a vaccine capable of defeating the parasitic disease. All three advisors were now convinced the Academic Board would certainly approve the awarding of Doctor of Science degrees to these two outstanding candidates.

Before their appearances in front of the board members to defend their scientific positions regarding the disease, Annie and Matty received some astonishing assistance in their fight against the parasite from an unlikely source.

It was Matty who broke the news.

"Annie," she began, excitedly, "I have heard this morning from my sponsor at G.L.O.B.E., the organization that has paid for my education. One of their main financial benefactors has apparently heard about our work in Norambuland. This person, who I understand is very rich, wants to help us. My sponsor says he is willing to provide all the necessary funding for our clinical trials here at Fitzgerald."

"What!" Annie responded, hardly believing her ears. "He wants to do what?"

"To pay for our continued research into solving this disease. And that is not all. He also is prepared to pay for the cost of the vaccines to be given to everyone. Oh, I cannot think that this is real but my sponsor says it is."

"Is he some kind of billionaire or something?" Annie asked, raising her eyebrows.

"I do not know but I think all of our benefactors like to remain anonymous."

Annie, speechless for a few seconds, finally said, "Matty, this is *huge*! I mean, instead of going to outside sources and facilities, we'll be able to complete the work right here, at Fitzgerald."

"Yes, I understand that, which is what makes this so wonderful. My sponsor also told me this person would like to establish the facility in my country, now managed by Joyce, as one of the best in all of Africa. This is truly like a gift from the gods."

"We have to let Virginia know right away," Annie insisted, still amazed by the news. "Will there be something official coming to confirm this?"

"Yes, the university will hear directly from G.L.O.B.E."

Two days later, a confirmation letter from the organization did indeed arrive detailing the precise, generous nature of the gift from the anonymous donor. The Board of Governors, in fact, the whole university, was stunned by the gesture. Going forward, it meant Fitzgerald would no longer have to rely on outside entities to complete the important research it had begun on any number of areas now and in the future. Specifically, for the ongoing hope of developing a vaccine to combat the parasitic disease, it meant all the clinical trials could now be conducted at the university rather than being outsourced to another facility.

Virginia was ecstatic when hearing the news and immediately suggested an attractive opportunity for Annie and Matty.

"I would like to recommend to the director of our scientific lab that both of you play intrinsic roles in this next crucial step. Hopefully, you will have your doctorates in a few weeks, so I see no reason why you shouldn't continue what you started. No one knows this disease or the work you've done on the pampousa leaf better than you. It doesn't make sense to have someone else try and navigate the road you've already taken." With a huge smile, she said, "I hope you'll agree because I can't begin to tell you how proud I am of you for what you've accomplished in a relatively short space of time."

Momentarily shocked by Virginia's kind words, the two young women looked at each other and nodded enthusiastically.

"Just try and stop us!" Annie blurted out, grinning and high-fiving Matty. "Just try and stop us!"

Their appearances before the Academic Board to consider their doctoral applications came at the end of April. The night before, they ate dinner together and talked about how far they'd come and their hopes for the future.

"Without meeting you, Annie, I do know I would not be where I am now," Matty began genuinely, her eyes never leaving Annie's for a second. "You took me under your wing without even thinking about it. You put your faith in me when you could have turned the other way like some other people would have done. You are a true friend and I will never forget what you have done for me. It has been, and is, an honor to work with you. Thank you. Thank you, so much."

Annie, truly humbled by Matty's heartfelt words, responded with some of her own.

"When I went to Harvard for that conference I could not have known I would be privileged to meet someone like you, a person full of grace, humility, strength and a caring, thoughtful heart. But that's what I found in you, Matty. I know we've traveled on this journey together but if it wasn't for you being at that conference none of it would ever have happened. I owe you so much. You have literally changed my life...for the better, I might add. And I now know this is only the start of our time together. You and me...well...I think the sky's the limit."

The warm hug they shared seemingly lasted forever as the tears of joy reminded them that what they had was special beyond words.

The two sessions before the Academic Board each lasted a full four hours. The board members acted as Devil's Advocates, challenging, dissenting and casting doubt upon Annie and Matty's well documented evidentiary assertions. After being suitably schooled by Virginia, Plother and Dr. Sanders on exactly what to expect from the Academic Board, the two young candidates defended their positions with sound reasoning, calm logic, pure science and, in the end, irrefutable analysis of their conclusive findings. Indeed, most of the board members congratulated them at the end of their particular session on their impressive presentations.

The next two weeks went agonizingly slowly for Annie and Matty as they waited for the board's decision on whether to award them Doctor of Science status. Virginia told them not to worry but the two young women refused to count their chickens.

In the meantime, they continued their hard work on the parasitic disease, finally clearing all the hurdles necessary to push the process through to the clinical trial stages. It was a momentous moment and one which now cemented their belief that this dreadful disease could really be defeated.

The gathering, on a bright, early May morning in Virginia's office, brought together Jim Plother, Dr. Sanders, Virginia and two nervous young women eager to finally learn the Academic Board's decision.

"First," Virginia began, quite seriously, "the board did recognize the valuable work you both have accomplished on the parasitic disease."

To Annie, this introduction did not sound promising. She frowned as she listened to Virginia, now fearing the worst.

"Second, the board wishes you to know how impressed they were with your dissertations."

Now Annie felt the wind had shifted somewhat in their direction. She braved a smile.

"And third," Virginia continued, teasingly hesitating for what seemed like an age, "they have conferred upon both of you a Doctor of Science degree! Congratulations!"

For a brief second the news did not sink in. But then Annie and Matty were smothered in warm hugs and embraces from their mentors, as well as being referred to as 'doctor' for the first time. It was a moment that mattered for both of them.

CHAPTER TWENTY-THREE

—————※ ※—————

"D'YOU THINK THEY'D COME?" ANNIE asks, hopefully. It was a delicate question because she suspects Matty's parents may not have the resources to fund such a trip. They had been discussing their graduation ceremony and, naturally, Annie wondered whether Mr. and Mrs. Kizembouko would be willing and able to attend such a momentous occasion for their daughter.

"I have been in contact with them," Matty answers, in a measured tone. "They have told me they will do their best but it may not be possible."

"Matty," Annie responds emphatically, "you are about to become a doctor! *A doctor!* They *have* to come. They just *have* to!"

Diffidently, Matty says, "My parents are not rich. I fear such a journey would be too much for them to bear. I cannot ask them to sacrifice too much for me especially since they also have my siblings to care about."

Annie leaves it at that for now but decides she will talk to her parents to see if they can help in some way.

"What is this?" Matty asks, two days later, as Annie smiles and hands her an envelope.

"Open it."

Carefully, Matty tears the red paper and pulls out a graduation card. She reads the printed congratulatory words on the front before opening the card. Inside she finds another, smaller envelope and some heartfelt words written by Blythe and Clive, Annie's parents.

Dearest Matty,

Congratulations, Doctor, *on your wonderful achievement. We know how hard you have worked and the sacrifices you have made to make your dream come true. We are so very proud of you. We hope the enclosed gift will enable you to fulfill some more of your dreams.*

With much love,
Blythe and Clive

"Oh, your parents are very wonderful people saying such grand things about me. I am sure I am not that worthy."

"Yes, yes you are," Annie tells her, before saying, "Well, aren't you going to open the envelope?"

Again, Matty carefully opens it and removes a check. For the longest time she just stares at the piece of paper.

Finally, she exclaims, "No, no, this cannot be! It is too much money for your parents to give me."

The check is for five thousand dollars.

Annie beams, hugs Matty and says, "They wanted you to know how special you are and what you have achieved in such a short space of time is really amazing. Now, maybe, your parents will be able to make the trip."

"Oh, I still cannot believe what I am seeing," Matty answers, tearfully. "I am truly blessed. And, yes, I will call my parents immediately and tell them the good news."

Graduation day is set for the second Saturday in May. Two days before the event Mr. and Mrs. Kizembouko arrive from Africa and are met at the airport by Matty and Annie. It's a joyous reunion for the Kizemboukos, who remain a close-knit family despite Mrs. Kizembouko's difference of opinion about Matty's education and future direction.

"We'll drop you at the hotel," Annie tells them, "to let you get settled in and then tonight my parents would like to take you to dinner. They are also staying at the same hotel."

Mrs. Kizembouko reacts a little surprised.

"That is very kind of them but we do not wish to be an imposition. They are very busy people, I'm sure. We should look after ourselves."

"Maman," Matty intercedes, "Annie's parents are also here for our graduation and they would like to meet and get to know you. Annie has told them how kind you were to her when we were home in October and they would like to offer their kindness in return."

"Then we accept, of course," Matty's father speaks up ahead of his wife. "We, also, are so looking forward to meeting your parents, Annie. Tell your parents 'thank you'. We would be honored to eat with them."

"Well, not only them," Annie says, jokingly. "We'll be there, too."

"So much the better," Mr. Kizembouko responds, smiling. "It will be like a party."

The evening's dinner at the hotel actually goes off without incident. Clive and Blythe break the ice by giving their guests warm hugs, which temporarily surprises Mrs. Kizembouko. But, she responds with a wide smile and a gentle bow before offering her hand.

The conversation is light and centers on the upcoming graduation.

Blythe looks directly at Mrs. Kizembouko and says, "This is such a great moment for our girls. Doctors," she says, shaking her head, "who could ever have known?"

"It is true," Mrs. Kizembouko answers. "We are very blessed."

"And the work these two young ladies are doing," Blythe continues, "...just amazing."

"Oh, yes, that is for sure," Matty's father agrees, beaming at Matty. "We are so very proud of Mathilde as you both must be of your daughter."

Clive frowns, glances at Annie, before he adds, while laughing, "Even though she's a pain sometimes."

Annie swats her father's arm and the whole table breaks out in smiles.

"We'd be happy if you came with us to the ceremony," Blythe offers. "And afterwards...a small celebration lunch?"

"That would be perfect," Mrs. Kizembouko concurs.

"I was also thinking," Blythe wonders, "if you would allow us to take you to see some of the sights in New York City tomorrow. That is, if you're not too tired."

Mr. Kizembouko claps his hands, "Oh, my word, Mrs. Cavallaro, my prayers have been answered. I was hoping we might be able to see some wonderful sights. Yes, yes and yes again!"

Mrs. Kizembouko turns towards her husband and with raised

eyebrows says, "Do not forget we need to spend time with our daughter, Papa. That is very important, too."

Sensing a dispute brewing, Blythe tries to calm the waters.

"It would just be in the morning...the sightseeing, I mean. Then you'd have the rest of the day with Matty."

"The actual Statue of Liberty!" Matty's father exclaims, as though the other conversation hadn't taken place. "Oh, it would be a dream."

"That's settled, then," Clive jumps in, also hoping to smooth some feathers. "Why don't we meet for breakfast and then go from there?"

The Kizemboukos graciously accept the kind sightseeing offer and the rest of the dinner is spent talking with the daughters about the current state of the fight against the parasitic disease.

"I think they really enjoyed it," Blythe tells Annie the next evening. "Even Matty's mom seemed impressed and...should I say...thrilled to see all the sights. Pictures galore, of course, so a lot of new memories made."

"Mom, Dad, thanks so much for doing that. I know Matty appreciated it, too. Wonder how she's getting on now?"

In their hotel room, Mr. and Mrs. Kizembouko are discussing with Matty her future after graduation the next day.

"You have told us nothing of your plans, Mathilde, once your schooling is over. We think it is important for you to come home and share what you have learned in your own country."

"Maman," Matty begins cautiously, "I still have my duties here at Fitzgerald to attend to. Annie and I are very much involved with the clinical trials and all that comes after them. There is a lot of work still to do with the disease. And, one of the benefactors from G.L.O.B.E. is providing the funding for our school to continue the research here until a cure is found. My professor has invited Annie and myself to be a big part of that. I would like to honor them for giving me such a wonderful opportunity."

"So, what I am hearing from you," Mrs. Kizembouko says, "is that you are not coming home. I must say that is a very big disappointment to us. You are needed in Norambuland to deal with all sorts of problems our people have. Your duty, my daughter, is to your own country first. Yes, I am very disappointed in your decision."

"But Maman I *am* working to help our people. Finding a cure for this parasitic disease is what will help stop our people from dying. We are now coming into the summer months and it will begin to kill our people again. It is very important that I stay here." Matty surprises her mother by her determined look and her determined argument.

"Very well, but I would like you to tell us that when you have found this cure you will return home. Will you promise me that?"

Mr. Kizembouko listens to this back and forth with rising dismay. He understands what his wife is trying to say but he also feels that Mathilde, at her age and with her now advanced degree, should decide her future for herself.

"Mother," he begins, gently nodding, "how old is our dear daughter?"

"She is twenty-six, of course," replies Mrs. Kizembouko curtly, who assumes by his question that he is going to defend Matty's position.

"And is being twenty-six in your eyes an 'adult'?"

"She is an adult, yes," agrees his wife.

"And as such is she permitted to make certain decisions about her future life?"

"She is, but..."

"No, dear Mother, there are no buts. I ask you to cast your mind back to when you were Mathilde's age. Were you not a fierce defender of your personal liberties? Did you not also believe in deciding your future life for yourself despite the fact that your own mother thought she knew best for you?"

Mrs. Kizembouko's face is now set in stone, her lips pursed, her frown dark and heavy. She well knows what her husband has said is true.

"I want her to be of value to her own people. That is all."

"But, dear Mother, again...this is not your choice. It is Mathilde's, just as you made your own choices despite your own mother's disapproval. All I am going to say is...have faith in your daughter to do what is best for her and her country. After being a dutiful daughter for so many years and working so hard to obtain such a distinguished education, you should only be of support to her now."

Matty listens to her father's words and is filled with gratitude and appreciation for his understanding. She hopes what he has said will make a difference to her mother's attitude towards her. She bows her head in anticipation of her mother's response.

"Yes," she hears her mother say, "you are correct, Papa. I am ashamed of my behavior. It is time for me to allow Mathilde her own life. I know she will always do what is best for herself and her country. Mathilde," she continues, as she holds out her hand to her daughter, "please come."

Matty lifts her head and quickly walks into her mother's arms. She immediately feels a new sense of closeness with her mother.

Mrs. Kizembouko eventually holds her at arm's length and says with genuine warmth and love, "Go forth, my beloved child and do for the world what you can. That is all I ask of you."

Matty can only smile as she listens to her mother's words before tears of sheer joy fill her eyes.

It is a glorious Saturday, May, morning as Annie and Matty prepare for their graduation into the doctoral ranks. A family breakfast concludes with Mr. Kizembouko thanking the Cavallaros, and especially Annie, for all the help and support they have shown to his daughter.

"Miss Annie," he begins, holding out his hand towards her, "you have always behaved like a true friend to Mathilde. You had your own studies to take care of and yet you took our daughter under your wing and steered her on the path to a rich and rewarding education. And you have also been her partner in the desperate fight to find a solution to our country's dire sickness problem. It would have been so easy for you to turn your back and to concentrate your considerable skills on other matters that better concerned you. But you chose to help our people, indeed all the people of Africa, in their hour of need. You are truly a saint. We," he says, nodding in his wife's direction, "shall never forget what you have done for Mathilde and for us. Thank you."

Annie, by this time, is red in the face and feels humbled and not a little embarrassed by Mr. Kizembouko's kind and flattering words. But the table waits for her to respond.

"You're very kind, Mr. Kizembouko, but I'm not sure I deserve all the wonderful things you said about me. I will say this...meeting Matty, getting to know her, seeing how dedicated she is to improving the world in some way, working with her almost day and night for the past year...well, it's me who should be grateful here...to her. She has made me look at things in a totally different way...for the better, I might add...as well as showing me what kindness and service to others really means. I know you are so very proud of her and so am I. She's nothing but the best."

Annie goes over to Matty's place and the two young women embrace for the longest time. The parents actually applaud and not a few tears are shed. It is definitely a moment that matters to all concerned.

The keynote speaker at the graduation ceremony is Dr. Gail Stephens, who lectured at Harvard when Annie and Matty first met at a conference they both attended. Her presence at their graduation is an added bonus for them.

Dr. Stephens' address to the graduating class is funny, purposeful and contains a plea to those graduating in the science spectrum. *"So please, please do what you can to use the knowledge you have acquired at Fitzgerald to make a difference, to be of value and to try and further the benefits of science for the good of all mankind."*

She finishes her speech with a surprise reference to Annie and Matty, saying, *"Sometime ago I was fortunate to meet two extraordinary young scientists who, today, are receiving their doctorates. Annie Cavallaro and Mathilde Kizembouko certainly embody all the traits I have referenced with regard to using a scientific education to benefit others. Indeed, I am sure there are few people here at Fitzgerald who have not heard about their astonishing research into the deadly parasitic disease now devastating Norambuland, in Africa, which, incidentally, happens to be Mathilde's home country.*

"Their hard work and long, grueling hours have finally paid off. Clinical trials for a vaccine are now about to begin. But none of this would have been possible without a tremendous amount of detailed investigatory work, including a month-long trip to the infected area. This is precisely what I mean when I beg you all to use your education for the benefit of others, no matter where in the world that need arises.

"So, special congratulations to Annie and Mathilde, and may your careers in research be long and productive. The world thanks you."

At this point, as Dr. Stephens sits down, the audience breaks out into loud applause and whoops of triumphant yells. Annie and Matty smile and diffidently bow their heads.

After the Bachelor and Master Degrees are handed out, the twenty-five doctoral recipients are called to the stage, one by one. When Annie and Matty take their turn, they are congratulated first by Jim Plother and Dr. Michelle Sanders, next by Dr. Gail Stephens and finally by

Professor Virginia West, who has the honor of presenting them with their diplomas. Both sets of parents are on their feet, clapping and hugging each other for all they are worth. This is a moment none of them will ever forget.

CHAPTER TWENTY-FOUR

O VER THE NEXT TWO MONTHS work on the clinical trials proceeded at a fast, but measured, pace. Annie and Matty became integral members of the team, learning a lot as well as adding their unique knowledge to the process.

The weather in Norambuland had turned from the rainy winter season into fully fledged summer, meaning the climate was primed to support a new wave of the parasitic disease. But the Health Ministry, with its newly acquired knowledge and understanding of the problem facing the population, now instituted measures to hopefully mitigate somewhat the ravages of the disease. People who worked outside or spent any time at all in the open air were now instructed to wear government issued goggles to protect their eyes. So far, this mandate had not been widely accepted and the number of cases and the number of deaths remained high.

The workload, while still heavy and demanding, did allow Annie and Matty some down time to pursue their other duties and interests. Matty spent a lot of that time on a new initiative which Jim Plother had suggested. It involved using her now vast biotech knowledge to study ways in which she might help the farmers in her country better utilize the resources at their disposal. Matty embraced the idea wholeheartedly since it was another concrete way in which she could assist her people. It also would please her mother who felt this was exactly the way her daughter should use her education.

The other interest Matty pursued came as quite a shock one day to

Annie who noticed Matty with a pad in front of her and what looked like lines of poetry.

"Are you writing poems?" she enquired, surprised.

"Well, I am trying, but the words are failing to flow right now."

"Oh, wow, Matty, you are a mystery woman," she said, with a giggle. "Poetry, eh? I'm impressed."

"It has been something I have done since I was a little girl. But I fear I am not so good, but it is very enjoyable for me."

Hesitantly, Annie asked, "Care to share? I'd love to see."

"Oh, it is just scribble right now, a poem for my mother and father, but yes, if you would like."

Annie took the pad, grabbed a seat and began reading. Her eyes widened and a pleasant smile crossed her face.

"Oh. Matty, this is *so* good. Do you have more?"

"Probably a whole drawer full," she answered, laughing. "They would take you years to read."

Annie reread the words to herself...

> *We must point ourselves towards the sky*
> *and hope.*
> *We must point ourselves towards the stars*
> *and dream.*
> *For only in this way will we reach our true desires.*
> *For only in this way will we understand exactly who we are.*

"This is for your mother and father?" Annie asked.

"It is, yes. I was trying to find a way to explain my reasons for pursuing the path I have chosen. I thought perhaps this would tell them how I feel."

"Well, I think it's beautiful and I'm sure they will, too. Oh, Matty, you are one talented lady."

"I am sure I am not that but I am hopeful this poem will help my mother overcome her objections."

"Oh, it will, Matty. I'm convinced it will."

Annie's spare time was now exclusively taken up with trying to finish the Curie biography. She only had two months left in which to turn in the manuscript to her publisher. She again reviewed her last few chapters which had taken her to 1922, when Marie was now almost fifty-five years old. Despite her long, illustrious career and despite the first signs that something may be wrong with her health, Marie continued to do important scientific work as well as maintain a rigorous personal schedule.

Annie, by this time, knew Marie's life as well as she knew her own. She understood these last few chapters would be difficult to write since they dealt with the final eleven years and Marie's eventual death. But on the bright side, Annie looked forward to chronicling those years, which were filled with more triumphs and personal achievements.

The next chapter Annie began by writing...

After her European travels in early 1922, Marie was honored to be asked to become a member of The League of Nations newly created International Committee on Intellectual Cooperation. This was a prestigious position and one which she embraced with dedication, seriousness and a real sense of purpose. In fact, her valued contribution was constantly acknowledged by the other prominent researchers and scientists on the Committee like Albert Einstein. So respected was she that she maintained her seat on the Committee until her death in 1934.

Reading those words filled Annie with a real sense of pride. Finally, here was proof that Marie was regarded by her peers as one of them. How she wished she could tell Marie how she felt.

One of Marie's proudest achievements came in 1923 with the publication of her biography of her husband, Pierre. This was her chance to describe not only their working life together but also their personal commitment to each other. The book covered his early life as a boy educated by his father and who showed, early on, a strong aptitude for mathematics and geometry. By the age of sixteen he received his Bachelor of Science degree. At eighteen, he earned his Master's Degree from the Sorbonne – a remarkable achievement – and in 1895 a Doctorate from the University of Paris with a thesis on magnetism.

> 'How little did I know when our friend, Josef Wierusz-
> Kowalski, introduced us that it would lead to some of the
> happiest moments of my life', Marie wrote. Indeed, Pierre
> took her into his laboratory as his student and soon became
> to regard her as his muse.
>
> Pierre's initial proposal of marriage was refused by
> Marie. But undaunted by this setback he proposed again
> telling her…
>
> 'It would be a beautiful thing, a thing I dare not hope
> if we could spend our life near each other, hypnotized by our
> dreams: your patriotic dream, our humanitarian dream, and
> our scientific dream.'

For someone like Annie, who had yet to experience that kind of closeness with another human being, this declaration by Pierre touched her heart with such admiration for him at not being afraid to essentially bare his soul. Marie's biography of her husband was well received, both in and out of the scientific community, for describing a life of discovery, service and, of course, love.

In the next chapters Annie concentrated on Marie's continuous research into the benefits and expansion of radiography, as well as conducting important studies into the treatment of neoplasms, or the abnormal growth of cancerous tissue, by the use of radioactive isotopes.

The final chapters of the biography covered the rest of Marie's important milestones, including…

> In 1925, one significant event occurred. Marie returned to her
> home country of Poland to begin the formation of Warsaw's
> Radium Institute. For Marie, this moment brought her great
> joy, not only for the scientific benefits the institute would
> confer, but also for honoring one of Pierre's maxims when he
> proposed to her…'our humanitarian dream'. To be back in her
> native country, and to bring with her all the knowledge and
> experience she had garnered down the years, overwhelmed
> this now nearly fifty-eight year woman to the point of tears.
> She had kept the faith with her parents; she had fulfilled their
> every wish for her; she had honored them with her service to
> mankind. The Institute would finally open in 1932.

In 1929, Marie toured the United States for the second time. By now the very mention of her name in America was greeted with awe and reverence for her many outstanding accomplishments, including two Nobel Prizes, her monumental discoveries and a host of prestigious international awards. She lectured at many of the respected universities and gave in depth scientific talks to institutions and medical academies. Her stature as one of the century's great minds was now firmly established for all time.

By August, Annie finally completed the Curie biography, sending the last three chapters to Renée Coutage in Paris for her comments. These chapters included Marie's election in 1930 to the International Atomic Weights Committee, on which she served until her death; the award of the Cameron Prize for Therapeutics from the University of Edinburgh and, of course, Marie's eventual death on July 4th, 1934.

This last chapter proved the most difficult to write for two reasons; it necessarily had to record Marie's sad passing, and it signaled Annie's completion of a piece of work that had affected her in so many different ways. So, while she felt elated to have managed to successfully chronicle an amazing life, she also experienced enormous sadness that the project had come to an end and she had to say a final goodbye to an old friend. Nevertheless, she accomplished the task with focus and objectivity.

Annie started the chapter with…

For the last time, in early 1934, Marie visited Poland to mainly recall and remember where her life had begun. The visit was joyous and fulfilling, meeting old friends, touring The Radium Institute and giving a few scientific talks. The journey was hard for Marie whose health now affected her abilities.

And she ended the chapter with…

The damaging effects from ionizing radiation were completely unknown as she conducted her research projects. Not only did Marie not use any safety measures, but she often carried about her person test tubes containing radioactive isotopes.

She would store them away in her desk drawer, even noticing the faint light the substances emitted in the dark.

To further jeopardize and compromise her health, Marie, during the massive assistance she gave to the soldiers during World War 1, was exposed to X-rays while working at the field hospitals and with the mobile units.

When her health markedly deteriorated, Marie entered the Sancellemoz sanatorium in Passy, Haute-Savoie where, on July 4th, 1934, she died from aplastic anemia, believed to have been caused from her long-term exposure to radium, and which caused massive damage to her bone marrow.

Marie Curie, researcher, scientist, discoverer, two-time Nobel Prize winner, daughter, sister, wife and mother was interred at the cemetery in Sceaux, alongside her husband, Pierre.

In 1995, in honor of their scientific achievements, the remains of both were transferred to the Panthéon in Paris. Their remains were sealed in lead because of the risk of radioactivity. Marie Curie was the second woman interred at the Panthéon but the first to be enshrined on her own merits. All of her papers, even her cookbooks, are kept in lead lined boxes because they are still so radioactive.

As the last word hit the page Annie sat back in amazement that she had actually managed to finish a book. *A book, for goodness sake. I've written a book!* Although a lot of work still remained to be done on it, and she was sure her publisher would critically edit it before a final printing was approved, Annie thought her achievement impressive and worthwhile. She hoped the book would be widely read and hopefully inspire budding scientists to pursue their dreams.

Closing her laptop, she reached for her phone and called her parents. Her mother's face soon appeared before her, smiling and happy to hear, as always, from her precious daughter.

"Hi, Doctor," Blythe teased, "what's up?"

"It's done, Mom. I've finished the book!"

"Oh, Honey, that's just great. What happens now?"

"I'll send it to my agent and he'll pass it onto the publisher. God, Mom, I can't believe it's finally done."

"Are you happy with it?" Blythe asked, seriously.

"You know, I am. I really am. I don't think I could have done much better."

"Then I couldn't be more pleased. I know how hard you've worked on it despite all your other commitments. Good job, Baby. Give yourself a huge pat on the back. Your dad and I can't wait to read it."

"I keep thinking back to second grade when Mrs. Wilmott assigned us a writing project. She asked us to imagine ourselves in twenty years and what we'd be doing. Even then, Mom, I remember having very specific dreams and hopes, among them were being a scientist and writing a book."

"Oh, yes," agreed Blythe, "I, too, recall that assignment. In fact, I still have it."

"No way! Really, Mom?"

"Yes, I'll send it to you. You'll be amazed at how accurate you were even then."

"I guess sometimes things can turn out for the best..."

"If you work hard enough," Blythe interrupted. "And you have, Sweetie. You certainly have."

"Thanks, Mom. You and Dad have always supported me, always made me believe I could do anything. When I think of poor Marie and what she sometimes went through in her career...well...it just shows what determination and perseverance can do. She was so brave, so dedicated to science and helping people. I reread what I've written sometimes and I'm still in awe of her."

"Talking of determination, how's the vaccine coming along?"

"Clinical trials have started. If all goes well in the next few months we should get government and WHO approval."

"Oh, Honey, that's wonderful. You and Matty must be so excited by what you've achieved."

"If it all works," Annie replied, with a chuckle. "Anyway, I just wanted you and Dad to know about the book. Is he okay?"

"Sure. Still at work right now but I'll tell him your good news when he gets in."

"All right, Mom. You two take care. Speak soon. Bye."

"Bye, Doctor," she teased again. "Bye."

CHAPTER TWENTY-FIVE

I N THE EIGHT MONTHS SINCE Annie completed the Curie biography
so much had happened. Now April of the following year, the summer
was once again beginning its sweep across Norambuland. But this year
was different from last because of the major advances achieved with the
parasitic vaccine.

The clinical trials had gone surprisingly smoothly and in November
both Annie and Matty travelled back to her home country to begin the
vast vaccination program. Joyce Obuna, who now ran the Norambuland
facility, along with considerable assistance from her staff and the Health
Ministry, capably set up an impressive program designed to give eventual
protection to the country's nearly six million residents.

Unfortunately, the previous summer saw an enormous number
of new cases, resulting in thousands of deaths. Also, depressingly,
the disease had now spread to other parts of West Africa, making
containment harder than ever.

Annie and Matty spent almost a month in Norambuland supervising
and administering the vaccine to all areas, including Area 5 which,
although seemingly immune from the disease, nevertheless needed the
protection just in case.

Generally speaking, the residents greeted the shots with enthusiasm,
with over ninety-six per cent of the people taking the inoculation. Those
who did not were strongly advised to take other precautions to prevent
infection.

Now, with the summer in almost full swing, the researchers, doctors and, in particular, Annie and Matty, waited anxiously to see if the vaccine stood up to the promised results.

In late April, Joyce Obuna face-timed with both young women, announcing some extremely good and promising news.

"In all areas of the country I am very pleased to report to you, Annie and Matty, that there have only been twenty-five new cases. Our doctors in the hospitals have formulated new treatments to lessen the progress of the disease. Some are working and some, unfortunately, are not. We have seven deaths, with the other eighteen patients doing as well as can be expected. It seems the vaccine is working as it should, although other parts of West Africa, as you know, are not so fortunate."

Big smiles spread across Annie and Matty's faces as Joyce's information sunk in.

"Oh, Joyce, that is such good news to hear," Matty commented joyfully. "Thank you for updating us. And yes, we understand about some other parts of West Africa and you can be assured we are rushing supplies of the vaccine to them as soon as possible. Our benefactor from G.L.O.B.E. has promised every financial assistance to you until everyone who wants the vaccine can have it."

"That person is a gift to us all," Joyce offered. "Without their participation we would still be in the dark ages."

"We would also be nowhere, Joyce," Annie jumped in, "without all the dedicated hard work you and your team have done over these past long months. I can think of no one better to run this program."

Joyce bowed her head and thanked Annie and Matty for their kind words before adding, "But none of this would have been possible without all you have done. You two young ladies have literally saved this country from disaster and certain ruin. Honestly, my dear friends and colleagues, we owe you more than we can ever repay."

After the call ended Matty was justifiably upset that the disease had now spread to other parts of West Africa.

"I am worried that the supply of pampousa leaves will suddenly be affected by a fire or bad storm destroying the trees. Part of my new research is centered upon genetically modifying other trees more abundant all over Africa so that we may transfer, in some way, *Oo Chlorophyllia* to them and therefore make it never run out."

"Matty, from what you and the team have told me, you are well on your way to solving that problem," Annie reassured her. "In fact, your latest test results indicate you may soon be ready to transfer some of the new modified saplings over to West Africa."

"Yes, that is true. Professor Plother has been very helpful and thinks we can start shipping them out in the next two weeks."

"And, I understand they have been altered to be fully mature in two years after planting. Until then," Annie continued, lightly, "we have enough, I think, to satisfy our needs. Please, don't worry."

"You always have a way of making me feel better," Matty confided. "Yes, we have made great strides, so I will be confident that all will be well."

It was an early April call out of the blue which stunned Annie into thinking it must be some practical joke. Her agent was on the line and he gave her some staggering news.

"Are you sitting down," he asked, "because, Annie Cavallaro, this is going to blow your mind?"

Annie was actually still in her lab working diligently alongside three co-researchers on tweaking even further the new version of the vaccine.

"Oh, all right," she answered, surprised by Peter Corbett's call. "Hang on a sec, let me take this outside."

On her way out Annie feared the worst, thinking for some inane reason her publisher had decided to pull the biography despite the fact they had already sent her several early hardback editions back in February. And then, in March, they launched a full-scale release of the book, which had received rave reviews from most of the prominent literary magazine, newspaper and on-line critics.

Apart from her parents, whose opinions she valued above all others, she heard directly from Renée Coutage, Curator of The Curie Museum in Paris, who had been so instrumental in helping Annie with specific details for the book. Her parents loved it and were actually in awe that their daughter had produced such an impressive piece of work.

Renée, also, heaped massive praise upon Annie's endeavor, telling her how accurate, compelling and heartfelt the narrative was in all its forms. She invited her to visit her in Paris as soon as possible, reminding her that she had something special of Marie's to show her. Such high praise from an esteemed scholar thrilled Annie almost beyond words.

But now Peter Corbett was on the line with some obviously important, if not depressing, news.

"Okay, Peter, yes, go ahead. Sorry about that."

"You, young lady, *Doctor* Cavallaro, have been nominated for a Pulitzer Prize!"

"What? What did you say? No, that's not possible," Annie declared, insistently.

"Well, yes it is. I have the official list of nominations in front of me and you're on it. Congratulations!"

The moment took a while to sink in but after it had Annie asked a few questions.

"How did I even get there? Who put my name forward, Peter? And what happens now?"

"Your publisher on my recommendation submitted your entry, which isn't that big of a deal since almost anyone can send in a name with the required fee. So, everyone at that stage is just an entrant. Then, a jury sifts through the works and narrows the list down to three names. Those people now become the final nominees. Once that happens, their work is duly considered by the Pulitzer Prize Board which eventually selects the winner. That'll be announced towards the end of the month."

"Honestly, I'm lost for words, Peter. The project was basically my way of honoring and shedding some light on a remarkable woman scientist, who most of the world probably doesn't even know or realize what amazing discoveries she made in her lifetime. I really wrote it for me, Peter. She's been like a guide since I began my career."

"Well, whatever the reason, you've produced a stunning biography, so take the accolades."

As Annie's day wound down after hearing Matty's upbeat report on the progress of the modified pampousa saplings, her phone buzzed into life. Peter Corbett's face appeared on her screen.

"Peter, hi. What's up?"

They hadn't spoken since his call in early April telling her about her Pulitzer nomination, which she had largely put to one side.

"Hope you're sitting down again, Annie, because I'm about to blow your mind again!" Before Annie could respond, Peter shouted out, "You won! The Pulitzer for best biography...you won the damn thing! You!"

His words were clear but Annie's mind didn't quite grasp the moment.

Frowning and shaking her head, she answered, "My Curie bio won? What? Really?"

"Yes, really. I'm sending you over a copy of the official certification. You, young lady, are now a Pulitzer Prize winner. How about that!"

After several more seconds of disbelief, her face broke into a broad smile.

"I guess all those late nights and early mornings were worth it after all," she joked. "But I'm humbled, truly. She's the one who should be honored. All I did was to write about her life."

"Yes, but in such an amazing way. Don't forget that."

"So, what happens now?"

"There'll be a ceremony at Columbia University soon. They're the ones who administer the whole Pulitzer thing. You'll be honored, given a certificate and a check for fifteen thousand dollars."

"Wait. What? Fifteen thousand dollars?"

"That's correct. You'll be hearing from them officially with all the details, but in the meantime, congratulations, Annie, this is a huge deal. And," he added, joyfully, "it'll do wonders for the book sales."

"Honestly, Peter, I'm literally speechless."

"I understand. It must be overwhelming. Not many authors receive this honor and, I must add, extremely rare for a first-time writer to get one. On the other hand, Annie, you wrote an amazing biography…really."

"I'm going to need a little time to process this, Peter. I hope you'll be at the ceremony with me to calm me down and hold my hand."

"Of course, wouldn't miss it for the world. Now, why don't you call your parents and friends and tell them the news? They shouldn't hear this from anyone but you."

"Oh, you're right. Thanks, and thanks, Peter, for all you've done for me. I know it wouldn't have happened without your guidance and expertise."

"You're welcome, Annie. I'll be in touch. Bye."

"Dad, hi!" Annie almost screamed down the phone, as her face appeared before her father.

Immediately he imagined the worst, that some major disaster had befallen his daughter.

Frowning back at her, he answered, "Annie, what's up? Are you all right?"

"Yes! Is Mom there, too?"

"I'll go get her, hang on."

"Hi, Sweetie, what's the matter? Your dad said you sounded frantic."

"I've won a Pulitzer," she yelled again, "for the Curie bio! Peter Corbett, my agent, just called to tell me."

Both parents shouted out their congratulations.

"Oh, Honey," Clive offered, "that is just so marvelous. I never expected this."

"Me, neither," Annie agreed. "I mean, I thought it was good but not *that* good."

"Well, we've both read it and I've got to say we thought it was just wonderful. But a Pulitzer," Blythe said, surprised, "didn't even cross my mind. Who put you up for it?"

"Apparently, my publisher, on Peter's recommendation. There's a ceremony at Columbia University and I want you guys to be there."

"Try keeping us away," Clive jumped in. "Wouldn't miss it for the world."

"And, I'm also getting a check for fifteen thousand dollars! Can you believe it?"

"Then dinner will be on you," Blythe joked. "Oh, Honey, we are so very proud of you. I know keeping up the writing on this was difficult given your other commitments, but you did it!"

"Talking of other commitments, Joyce Obuna called a couple of days ago from the facility in Norambuland with some very good news. Although it's still early in the summer she told us that the number of new cases and deaths are down significantly. Apparently, the vaccine is working like a charm and the people are very enthusiastic to get it. On the down side, though, it seems the disease has spread somewhat to other parts of West Africa, so that's quite disturbing. But G.L.O.B.E. has assured us they will support our efforts there, so that's good news, too. And Matty has been working hard on modifying other trees to eventually produce *Oo Chlorophyllia*, because she fears, quite rightly, that the natural supply of pampousa leaves will not be enough. She's about ready to start shipping some of those saplings to West Africa so they can begin planting. So, you see, things are generally moving in the right direction."

"Oh, Baby, that is such good news," Clive responded, cheerfully. "Maybe, finally, you can kiss this disease goodbye?"

"Let's hope so, Dad. It's been a long, difficult fight but now there's definitely light at the end of the tunnel."

After a few more 'catching-up' moments everyone said their goodbyes, with Clive and Blythe promising to attend the Pulitzer Prize ceremony at Columbia.

CHAPTER TWENTY-SIX

$\longrightarrow$ ❋ ❋ $\longleftarrow$

The Pulitzer Prize ceremony, including a modest reception and luncheon, was held at Columbia University in the middle of May. A little over three hundred people attended the event for the presentation of the awards in twenty-seven categories. Most were for excellence in journalism, but several were for drama, music, fiction, biography, auto-biography and a few Special Citations and Awards in the arts.

Annie was accompanied by her agent, Peter Corbett, her friend, mentor and colleague, Professor Virginia West, her mother and father, Blythe and Clive Cavallaro, and her close friend and fellow vaccine discoverer, Matty Kizembouko. She was grateful to them all for supporting her at such a nerve-racking occasion.

After lunch, the Pulitzer Prize Administrator made a few welcoming remarks before introducing the chairman of the Pulitzer Prize Board. After his welcome and general congratulations to all the nominees and winners, the awards were handed out.

Despite the long list of awardees, the afternoon flew by and soon the prize for outstanding biography was presented. To Annie's surprise, the Administrator called upon Virginia West to make the presentation to Annie.

Virginia made a gracious, warm and moving speech to the audience which, in part, detailed Annie's achievements in both her professional and private life. Annie felt humbled hearing Virginia's words, but also proud of her accomplishments. It was a moment she would cherish for the rest of her life.

The final award of the afternoon was in the Special Citations category, this time honoring someone from the arts.

"The Pulitzer Prize Board does not usually give out an award for documentary film making," the Administrator began. "But this year their attention was especially drawn to *'The Passage of Time'*, a documentary made by Ingrid Strauss and Zack Jeffreys.

"For those of you who are not familiar with the documentary, and, I have to say, you must have been living under a rock not to have seen this masterpiece on Public Television, it tells wonderful stories of some residents living in a nursing home, whose lives may have been forgotten. That was the first half; the second half concentrated solely on the amazing life story of ninety-one year old, Josephine Benson, who, among other things, was nominated for an Academy Award at the tender age of twenty and, then some seventy years later, she actually won an Oscar for Best Supporting Actress for the movie *'The Good Woman of Harlem'.*"

After a few more remarks, Ingrid and Zack took the stage and accepted this rare Pulitzer Prize for documentary film making.

As the post-reception wound down, Peter Corbett sought out Annie to introduce her to his friend and fellow agent, Glen Griffith. He, in turn, had two people in tow, who he introduced to Annie and who she recognized as the recipients of the prize for documentary film making.

"I'd like you to meet Ingrid Strauss and Zach Jeffreys, Annie, who would like to talk to you about your Curie biography." Turning to Ingrid, he said, "She's all yours."

Ingrid and Zach put out their hands which Annie tentatively shook, still confused about why two film makers would want to speak with her, particularly about her book.

"Hi, Annie, it's a real pleasure to meet you," Ingrid began, pleasantly. "This is Zach Jeffreys, Director of Photography on all my projects and all around good guy."

"Yeah, sometimes," he joked. "But, absolutely," agreed Zach, still clinging to her hand, "it's an honor. Oh, sorry, better let you have your hand back," he joked again, as everyone laughed. The moment magically broke the ice.

"I saw your wonderful documentary," Annie said, nodding. "Watched it with my parents. We were blown away by the stories you told and especially Josephine Benson's. She was such an inspiration."

"Indeed," agreed Ingrid. "Everything you saw about her life was true."

"Congratulations on your Pulitzer, as well. You certainly deserved it."

"You, too," Zach responded, "which is why we'd like to talk to you about your magnificent biography."

"Oh, okay," Annie replied, somewhat bemused.

"Yes," Ingrid added, "I would very much like to buy the rights to it."

"What? You want to buy the rights to my book? May I ask why?"

"We both feel it would make a great full length feature film."

"You mean, like a movie?"

"Yes, a movie. I've just finished directing my first film and I'm looking for my next project. Also, we're very interested in possibly making a documentary about the work you've done on the African parasite disease. My agent, Glen, has been speaking with your agent who told him about your journey...well, Dr. Kizembouko's journey, too," she added, looking at Matty, "from first finding out about the devastation until now when you've secured a vaccine. And in between, we understand both of you obtained your doctorates. It's an amazing story and needs to be told."

Annie and Matty were dumbstruck by Ingrid's words.

"But we are only doing the work we are trained to do," Matty offered. "We do not think we are anything special."

Annie nodded in agreement, before saying, "Matty's correct. Our efforts were just a natural progression of our education, but if you think..."

"Oh, we do," Ingrid interrupted. "As I said, it's a story that needs to be told. And talking of stories that need to be told, can we get back to your Curie biography for a moment? What a life she led; what hardships; the misogyny and unfairness she suffered; her *two* Nobel prizes; the amazing discoveries and her World War 1 service to France...I mean a scriptwriter couldn't come close to making this up."

"It's true," Annie conceded, "she had an amazing life..."

"Which needs to be told in a major movie," Zach broke in. "And we'd love to be the ones to make it."

Annie just shook her head before Peter and Glen added their two cents' worth.

"As your agents, we'll broker a deal that suits all of you," Glen proposed.

"Which will be generous to all parties," Peter added, with a smile.

"And we'd like you, Annie, to be a consultant on the movie, since you obviously know more about Marie's life than any of us. If you'd be prepared to work with our scriptwriter, then we'd be thrilled," Ingrid proposed.

"Oh, okay, but all of this is a bit overwhelming right now. Can you give me some time to think things over?"

Ingrid smiled and nodded knowingly.

"Yeah, I know how you feel. When I was offered the chance to become an assistant director for Marvin McCullen, I thought it was a joke. Then, when it wasn't, I kinda turned to jelly for a while. But he and his staff were more than kind and supportive of me and now here I am directing movies for a living. We'll take good care of you. You have my word on that."

"Yeah," agreed, Zach, with a mile-wide grin, "and I'm a real good holder of hands."

Everyone laughed before Annie asked, "How long will you need me for? I have a trip to France lined up to be shown around the Curie Museum in Paris and, of course, Matty and I are still involved big time in tweaking the vaccine."

"There's a Curie Museum?" Ingrid asked, surprised.

"Yes and the curator has become a good friend of mine. In fact, she helped so much with the book."

"Any chance I could tag along?" Ingrid wanted to know. "I'm sure there's so much I could learn for the movie. When are you planning on going?"

"Actually, in about two weeks and, yes, that would be great to have you come."

"And since you're an advisor for the film, I'll cover all the costs of the trip. How does that sound?"

"Sounds wonderful," agreed Annie, surprised. "It'll be for about five days and I've also been asked to give a couple of talks at the Université Paris Cité and the Sorbonne."

"No way!" exclaimed Ingrid. "The Sorbonne...amazing."

"Yes," Annie replied, raising her eyebrows, "not sure I'm up for that yet, but Marie received her doctorate from the university and was the first woman professor there, too. And her husband, Pierre, got his master's degree from the Sorbonne and he also received his doctorate from the university. So, in some ways, it'll be like walking in their shoes for me. I'm terrified but also excited."

"And again, I know exactly how you feel," Ingrid confessed. "First day on set of the first movie I directed...totally scared out of my mind. It was only laid back, ultra mellow Zach here," she said, turning towards her friend, "who convinced me I could do it. *'Just dive right in, Ing,'* you said, right? *'You can do this.'* So I did and, although I hate to admit it, he was right...yet again," she groaned, rolling her eyes in mock disapproval.

Everyone laughed and Annie immediately felt very comfortable with Ingrid and Zach.

Peter Corbett suggested the whole group, including Blythe and Clive, go out for a celebratory dinner, to which everyone agreed, and where these nascent friendships could be solidified and expanded upon.

The two weeks until Annie was due to fly to France with Ingrid passed by in a whirl of activity. She was correct when she said she still had massive commitments to tweaking the vaccine with Matty and the other researchers at Fitzgerald. Virginia kept her foot down firmly on the pedal, which reminded Annie not to be swayed by outside influences no matter how seductive and glamorous they might seem.

But Annie was nothing if not dedicated. She regularly kept in touch with Joyce Obuna in Norambuland, who told her the vaccine program was still in full swing and being almost fully accepted by the citizens. She did, however, sound a note of alarm with regard to the spread of the disease to other parts of West Africa.

"My field officers are extremely worried, Annie, by the rise in cases outside of my country. The deaths are also rising quite rapidly, so there is cause for considerable concern. We need to speed up the arrival of the vaccine shipments, but I know that the production is already straining."

"It is, but we are all working around the clock to make sure you have what you need. We have actually opened another facility here at Fitzgerald and their first shipment is due to be sent out tomorrow."

"Good. That is very good," Joyce agreed. "Thank you. We are also worried about the supply of pampousa leaves. We have harvested so many some of our trees are beginning to look quite bare."

"Matty actually brought that to our attention and she has been working hard to genetically modify other species so that they can produce *Oo Chlorophyllia*. That experiment has gone better than we expected and she's sending out her first shipment of saplings in the next day or two. Of course, they will take two years to mature but we have enough supplies to last us until then."

"Oh, that is very good news to hear. To realize we shall never run out of the leaves is more than wonderful."

After some more upbeat reporting by Joyce the two young women said their goodbyes in the knowledge that the arc of the parasitic disease was now rapidly descending.

Ingrid was not kidding when she told Annie the studio would cover all the costs associated with their trip to Paris. When they met at the airport Ingrid warmly greeted Annie before steering her to the first class lounge.

"We're flying first class?" Annie asked, surprised.

"Indeed," Ingrid responded, with a wide grin. "There's really no other way."

Sitting comfortably in plush chairs, they were served lights refreshments by an attentive attendant.

"This is more than I expected," Annie offered, as she sampled one of the delicious pastries set before her. "But I'm not going to complain."

"Good, because you deserve it, not only for the wonderful Curie bio, but also for the…the…I don't really know the right word here…the awesome work you've done on that horrible disease. So enjoy it, Annie; you've earned it."

"Well, I'm not sure about that," Annie answered, a little skeptically. "Renée Coutage, the Curie Museum curator gave me a lot of help with the book and, of course, Matty and the whole parasitic disease team, both here and in Africa, have worked diligently to solve the problem. I was just another cog in the wheel. Really, Ingrid, you should know it was and always has been a team effort."

"With you at the helm," Ingrid responded. "Anyway, I want this trip to be fun for you, despite the dreaded talks you're giving," she continued, with a laugh. "It'll hopefully give you a chance to relax for a while."

During the long plane ride the two accomplished young women shared almost non-stop conversations about themselves and their lives, making each feel more and more comfortable with the other.

At one point Annie asked Ingrid, "So, are you and Zach a couple?"

Ingrid burst out laughing before saying, "More like brother and sister actually. Oh, don't get me wrong, Zach's a great guy and I certainly couldn't have made either the documentary or the movie without his cinematic brilliance, but no, we're not a couple. He has his private life and me mine. Why d'you ask?"

"He just seemed like a really nice guy and kinda cute, too," Annie answered, now wishing she hadn't mentioned him at all.

"Yes, he is but our relationship is purely professional." With a sly smile Ingrid added, "Why, you interested?"

Annie shrugged before saying, "Well, I'm not looking but you never know."

"Then let me tell you that he's one hell of a man. Really. He reminds me so much of Josephine Benson's fiancé, Milton Sewell, in the documentary. He was a gentleman to his core, never, ever tried to take advantage of Josephine in any way, shape or form. Such a tragedy for both of them when he was killed in the Korean War." Ingrid shook her head as if hearing Josephine's description of that awful time in her life when she was told the news about Milton's death.

"Zach is the same," she continued. "He has never made a pass at me or said anything remotely inappropriate and we've spent a lot of time together, including many late, late nights. Honestly, Annie, he'd be a great catch."

Diffidently, Annie glanced away. Secretly, in the back of her mind, the thought surfaced that perhaps she'd contact Zach when she returned to the States. That thought made her smile in surprise at what she was feeling. She quickly changed the subject and the two talked for a while about Ingrid's documentary.

"You know, she left her Oscar to me," Ingrid revealed.

"What? Josephine gave you her Oscar?"

"She did. Left it to me in her will."

"Oh, wow, that must have been a moment for you."

"It was. It's something I'll treasure always."

"Well, of course. Where do you keep it?"

"Since I'm on the move a lot, it's in my bank box. But every now and then I'll go in just to see and touch it. The moment is always magical but also sad at the same time."

"I can imagine. She was…what…ninety something when she won it?"

"Ninety-two. Just amazing."

"As was your documentary, Ingrid. So talented pulling all that history together. And I loved all the other stories. You surprised me so much with what some of the residents revealed. Who could have known?"

"I know. I used to pinch myself sometimes when I was listening to what they were telling me."

"Do you still keep in touch?"

"Whenever I'm back that way I always pop in. Trouble is, the numbers keep dwindling, unfortunately. But I think those that are still around really appreciate being remembered."

The journey slipped by relatively quickly and, after some welcome shut-eye, the two extraordinary young women finally found themselves at Orly Airport at nine the following morning. Ingrid had arranged for a car to meet them, which soon whisked them away to their hotel.

CHAPTER TWENTY-SEVEN

—❋ ❋—

ANNIE AND INGRID'S TRIP TO Paris was a whirlwind affair beginning on the afternoon of their arrival with an amazing meeting with two of Marie's grandchildren, Hélène and Pierre, both now in their nineties but still continuing their passion for all things scientific.

Renée Coutage, who met Annie and Ingrid for lunch, told them of the arranged meeting after welcoming the pair with excitement bordering on frenzy.

"I am so happy to finally see you in person," Renée began, hugging and kissing each of them on the cheek. "Annie, you now are an old friend to me and, Ingrid, it is such a pleasure to meet such a famous film director. Annie told me about your important documentary and your new film, both of which I have seen and admired. Thank you for coming all this way and for possibly making a movie of Marie's life."

Ingrid smiled, surprised to hear Renée's kind words, which she felt were no where near the actual truth.

Before she could protest and set the record straight about her nascent film career, Annie cheerfully responded to Renée's warm words of welcome.

"I know, Renée!" she gasped, equally thrilled to actually be meeting the person who helped her so much with the book. "This is a dream. Thank you for inviting us over."

"And I second that," Ingrid jumped in, "and thank *you* for saying those nice things about me which I'm not sure I deserve, especially the part about being a *famous* film director. Don't really think so, yet," she added, as they all laughed.

"Well, let's just say you are on your way to becoming a legend and leave it at that, shall we?" Renée countered, as Ingrid bowed theatrically. "Now, I thought we could spend the day tomorrow going through the museum. There is much to see; much I want to show you. The tour, hopefully, will give you, Ingrid, a real sense of who Marie truly was. There is so much information available to help you plan your movie. But that is tomorrow. For the rest of this afternoon we will be going to a private house where her grandchildren are waiting to meet you."

The nonagenarians, nuclear physicist Hélène Langevin-Joliot and her biologist brother, Pierre Joliot-Curie, warmly welcomed Annie and Ingrid into their home. For Annie, in particular, coming face-to-face with relatives of Marie Curie bordered upon the surreal.

Pierre, being only two years of age when his grandmother died, unfortunately had no discernable memories of her, but Hélène, who would have been seven, remembered her quite vividly.

"Always busy. Always anxious to research new things and always pushing me to learn, learn, learn," she confided, with a smile. "She was not given to frivolity and could be very stern with those who were, but with us she was always warm and grandmotherly."

Annie asked some polite questions regarding Marie's stature as a world-renowned scientist and Nobel Prize winner.

"How did she manage being famous?"

Hélène waved her hand in the air before saying, "She would have none of that, I can tell you. For her, it was only important that her work spoke for itself. Anything else was just wasteful nonsense."

Ingrid was more interested in Marie's final months, weeks and days.

"Did you ever realize how sick your grandmother was? I know you were only seven but how did she handle her illness around both of you?"

Hélène thought for a moment as if trying to look back through the years of her memory to relive those days.

Finally, she answered softly, "She was always very brave and, of course, being so young, we were naturally shielded from a lot of her distress. But I did notice how tired she used to get, which was strange because she usually had so much energy. She reduced her work load, I remember, because she began spending more time with the family.

"Towards the end, before she went away into the sanatorium, she was always so tired, always just wanting to lie down and sleep. Honestly,

I think she knew she was dying and being the practical, no-nonsense person she was, she accepted that as a purely logical scientific fact, similar to the ones she had pursued most of her life. I think she was at peace. That's what I think; she was at peace."

Before they left, Annie, Ingrid and Renée were served coffee and delicious French pastries. For Annie, the moment all the while still seemed unbelievable, that here she was in the same room as people who actually knew, played with, laughed with and talked to Marie Curie. Her link to Marie was almost complete.

Later, Renée agreed with Annie's thoughts, telling her, "I know how you feel. When I first met them after I'd become Curator at the museum, it was as if I was staring right into Marie's eyes. They come often now but the feeling is always the same…incredible joy and wonderment."

The next morning, after a breakfast of coffee and flaky croissants at their hotel, Annie and Ingrid made their way the few blocks to The Curie Museum, which Renée had closed to the public for the duration of their visit.

In the cab on their way over Ingrid expressed how grateful she was to Annie for letting her come on the trip.

"This has been a real eye-opener for me, Annie. As much as I loved your biography, just talking to Renée and Marie's grandchildren has brought her life into a new dimension for me. I've been thinking a lot about the actress I need to portray her. The one quality that is essential is the ability to make Marie both studious and human at the same time."

Annie nodded before saying, "Indeed. You always have to remember her scientific struggles as well as her private setbacks and tragedies. Do you have anyone in mind?"

"Yes, Faye Salatini. She was one of the other four actresses nominated for Best Supporting Actress when Josephine Benson won her Oscar. Her performance in *Flowers and Wine* was outstanding and she's gone on to star in several other big box office hits."

"Oh, I loved *Flowers and Wine*. And, yes, that actress was *so* good. That movie was hard to watch sometimes…harrowing and tragic…but she was very believable and you really felt sorry for her in the end."

"Well, that's who I'd like to play Marie. She has a great range. If we can persuade her, I'd like the two of you to get together so she can get a real feel for Marie's overall character. After writing that bio I'm guessing you now 'know' her better than almost anyone."

"Okay, Ingrid, this is getting weirder by the minute. First you want to buy the rights to the book, then you want me as an advisor on the film and now you want me to sit down and coach an Oscar nominated actress. Really? I'm a research scientist not a film producer," Annie conceded, with a laugh.

Ingrid laughed, too, before saying, "Listen, one thing I've learned in this business is to always try and know and understand a character inside and out. From reading your book and coming here with you to the museum, I can maybe acquire a reasonable idea of who she was. But you, you've studied the woman for years, so I can think of no one better to guide us through this project. Your knowledge and insight will be invaluable, believe me."

"Just as long as you don't want me to *appear* in the movie," Annie replied, shaking her head.

"Oh, how about a small cameo," suggested Ingrid, facetiously. "Wouldn't that be fun?"

"No, no it wouldn't, so don't even go there!" countered Annie.

"All right, no cameo, but please help me out as much as you can."

Smiling, Annie agreed, which settled the matter once and for all.

Renée Coutage met Annie and Ingrid at a side door to the museum, located in the former premises of The Radium Institute's Curie Pavilion, on the rue Pierre et Marie Curie.

"Welcome, welcome," she enthused. "We have the whole place to ourselves, so I want you to take your time and see everything. It's not a huge museum but, oh my, it contains some wonderful exhibits. C'mon."

For the next three or four hours Renée led them on a journey that traced Marie's life from birth to death. For both Annie and Ingrid, just being able to see such history thrilled them almost beyond words. Ingrid gleaned so much new information about her life; information that would prove invaluable to the making of the movie.

"This is Marie's small office as it was," Renée informed them, as the women studied the furniture, souvenirs of her trips, some of her scientific text books, pictures, of which there were several of Pierre, an old black telephone, dark, wooden bookcases and other fascinating objects. For Annie, knowing Marie had lived, worked and breathed in this space filled her with so much emotion. In fact, she half expected Marie to suddenly appear from the next room.

"And this adjoining room was her small, personal laboratory," Renée continued explaining, "which as you can see, contains various sorts of apparatus which was used by both Marie and her daughter, Irene."

"Irene also won the Nobel Prize," Annie informed Ingrid. "Unfortunately, it was in 1935, the year after her mother's death."

They next visited a chemical lab complete with flasks, test tubes and other equipment used at the time. Again, Annie marveled at seeing the actual materials Marie used to carry out her research.

Ingrid was also fascinated by the numerous framed posters, newspaper cuttings and photographs, some taken a hundred years ago showing Marie at her desk or at work in her lab. One poster even advertised various beauty products containing radium, the risks of which were not known at the time. Another glass frame contained notes that showed the Curies' calculations of the atomic mass of radium. The case was lead lined because of the possibility it might still be radioactive, explained Renée.

"Yes, I wanted to ask about that," Annie said, remembering how dangerous the Curies' research was. "I know they were around radium and radioactive matter all the time, handling it and using it in experiments. In fact," she added, turning to Ingrid, "her aplastic anemia was caused as a direct result of her exposure to radium."

Ingrid shook her head before replying, "That's just a tragedy, working with chemicals and elements that you have no idea how dangerous they are."

"Just to reassure you," Renée jumped in, "her laboratory was decontaminated in 1981, so we are quite safe, but some of her other things like her cookbooks, notes and research books are still considered radioactive. They are kept in a safe, secure area, which is where we are headed now."

Renée saw Ingrid's look of apprehension at the prospect.

"Oh, you do not have to worry," she responded, with a sly smile, "everything is behind lead-lined, brick and glass walls. And, Annie, this is where the surprise I promised you is kept. C'mon."

After punching in her entry code, Renée escorted them into the secure room, which was light, airy and full of exhibits both professional and personal of the Curies. Marie's cookbooks, research notes, glass vials, and a host of other objects, including some personal letters written by the two scientists to each other, were studied intently by Annie and Ingrid. Finally, Renée led them to a separate lead and glass case.

"I remember you telling me, Annie, when you and Matty were first trying to figure out why a particular area in her country seemed to be immune from the disease, about your theory of the pampousa leaves absorbing rain water."

"Yes," agreed Annie, "I do recall telling you that. And the theory turned out to be correct. After a while the leaves would discharge the water, which now contained a substance only found in the pampousa tree, into the river, which in turn would be used by the nearby residents."

"And you also told me," Renée continued, "you collected the rain water as it dripped from the leaves into sterile bottles, and that is how you eventually found your solution to the disease...in a bottle of rain."

"That's right, I did."

"And that's when I mentioned I would have a surprise to show you when you visited here."

"You did, and I'm so intrigue because you said there was an amazing coincidence with Marie."

"Well," Renée offered, pulling aside a curtain she had made especially for the occasion, "here it is."

Annie and Ingrid found themselves looking at an old fashioned glass specimen bottle inside which was a small piece of dark material in a clear liquid. The moment seemed anticlimactic until Renée explained.

"When Marie and Pierre eventually discovered the element radium, she wanted a protective way of preserving what little they had. She thought, mistakenly, that rain water was the purest of all water and, so, took to sealing up the radium in bottles of rain. When you related to me how you collected your samples I smiled because I knew that was exactly what Marie had done all those years ago. Amazing, non?"

"Oh my god!" Annie exclaimed. "That is *so* cool."

"Like completing the circle," Ingrid offered. "I love it."

"Here," Renée said, handing Annie an envelope, "I took a picture of it for you to keep as a reminder that sometimes science moves in mysterious ways."

"It's almost as if Marie was guiding your thoughts and your hands," Ingrid added. "You're right, Annie, this is *so* cool."

As the tour ended, both young women thanked Renée profusely for showing them around.

"I cannot tell you how much this will help with the movie, Renée," Ingrid assured her. "And once it's finished I hope you'll be my guest at the premiere?"

"Oh, ma chère, I would love to be there. Thank you."

"Then consider it a date."

Annie hugged her friend for the longest time, finally telling her, "I can never repay you for all the assistance you gave me for the book, Renée. It's reassuring to know, with your help, I didn't get too many things wrong!"

They all laughed before Renée finally said, "No, thank you, Annie, for shining a fresh bright light on one of the most remarkable women in scientific history. All I ask of you is to try and be the same."

The next two days for Annie and Ingrid were taken up with Annie's talks at the Sorbonne and the Université Paris Cité. The previous evening over dinner, Annie expressed her trepidation at the prospect of speaking in front of such distinguished people. But Ingrid reassured her, relating her own utter nervousness when called upon to speak, first before the nursing home audience at the premiere of her documentary, and then on the promotional tour for her debut full-length feature film.

"As hard as it may seem, it is definitely something you get used to. The key, I found, is knowing your subject matter. I would suggest you make some notes and have them with you. Stick to what you know. You are so smart, Annie, so just be yourself, don't try and be too cutesy, and you'll be fine. There may also be questions asked and, again, stick to the facts, give the answer then move onto the next one. I'll be in the front row, so if you need a friendly face…there I'll be."

After listening to Ingrid's advice Annie felt better and more confident. In fact, her talks went far smoother than she could have imagined. At the Sorbonne, the audience members were attentive, receptive and very engaged with her descriptions of the journey she and Matty took to solve the parasitic disease problem. Her time flew by and before she knew it the whole thing was over. Ingrid warmly congratulated her on a job well done.

The talk at the Université Paris Cité was quite another event altogether. This audience consisted of faculty, scholars and academics, as well as research staff and post-doctoral students from the Curie Institute, one of the leading medical, biological and biophysical research centers in the world. There were also doctors from the hospital associated with the Institute, specializing in the treatment of cancer. However, Annie, after her successful talk the day before at the Sorbonne, actually looked forward to the moment.

In the speech, she raised her game, detailing precisely and minutely the intricacies and specifics involved in her and Matty's ultimate resolution of the disease.

She finished by stating, "Ultimately, our success was due to all the scientists who have gone before us. And as I stand here, in the hallowed halls of the Curie Institute, one person in particular is close to my heart and always will be. So, in closing, I would like to say 'Thank you, Marie, for making it all possible. Thank you'." The applause lasted a full three minutes, which embarrassed Annie beyond measure.

As she was being congratulated by a number of people, including Ingrid, a small, bespectacled man approached her, introducing himself as Dr. Michel Dansante, one of the directors at the Institute.

"Docteur," he began, courteously, "please forgive my intrusion but I wanted to compliment you on such a fine speech. Dr. Michel Dansante," he continued, holding out his hand, which Annie tentatively shook, "and I am a director of the Institute."

"I'm very please to meet you, sir," Annie replied, respectfully.

"I have been speaking with some of my fellow directors and we are more than impressed with you and Docteur Kizembouko's remarkable discovery of a vaccine for the parasitic disease. So much so that we are prepared to offer both of you one year Fellowships at the Institute, where we sincerely hope you will be able to pass on your knowledge to some of our research students. The Fellowships come with a generous stipend and, of course, we would cover all of your housing and other needs."

Annie looked at this man as though suddenly he had sprouted another head.

Taking a while to answer, she finally said, "Are you serious, Dr. Dansante; a Fellowship here at the Curie Institute?"

"Why, yes indeed. Your credentials are impeccable and for one year you and Docteur Kizembouko would be able to impart your critical and considerable knowledge to some of our post doctoral students. Your contribution would be invaluable. But, please, take your time in deciding. Tell your colleague of the offer and let me know when you can."

He left Annie with all the necessary details before making his exit. Immediately, she sought out Ingrid to relate the news.

"Oh, well, really Annie, it's a no-brainer. A Fellowship *here* would be gold for you and Matty. Think of all the good you can do inspiring others. Plus, this is a first-class research facility so you'll be able to also work on some of your own projects. So I say…take it!"

That night, Annie slept not a wink. All she thought about was the fantastic offer and what it might mean for her future in the scientific world. Her only worry was persuading Matty to come along for the ride. She was aware her friend had plans to return home to Norambuland, but she hoped that could be delayed for a year. She wasn't optimistic but all she could do was ask.

The next morning, before they were due to leave Paris for home, Annie and Ingrid made a quick visit to the Panthéon, in the Latin Quarter, where Marie and Pierre's remains had been transferred in 1995 to honor their scientific achievements.

The mausoleum, which is dedicated to the most distinguished French people, stands atop the church of Montagne Sainte-Genevieve in the center of the Place du Panthéon, and was constructed between 1758 and 1790.

As she stood in the rotunda Annie regarded this shrine as the last, tangible link to her heroine. To realize Marie was somewhere close to her at that moment filled her with joy almost beyond belief. A huge smile crossed her face as she nodded to herself and burst out laughing.

"What? What is it?" Ingrid asked, puzzled at Annie's reaction.

"I've found her at last. I've really found her."

CHAPTER TWENTY-EIGHT

AFTER THE PARIS TRIP THERE was so much for Annie to discuss with so many people. Her first priority was to seek out Virginia West, essentially her overall boss at Fitzgerald, to relate the offer of a Fellowship to her and Matty. In Annie's eyes, Virginia had always supported her right through to becoming a doctor, as well as now making her an integral part of the university's research team. She regarded Virginia not only as a mentor but a close friend. Virginia had also been instrumental in securing Matty's transfer and ultimate progression to her doctorate. Quite simply, Annie owed Virginia a lot.

"So, sit yourself down and tell me all about Paris," Virginia said, as a nervous Annie came into her office.

"It was *so* amazing, Virginia," Annie began, positively. "Really, it exceeded my wildest dreams." She went on to describe the meeting with Marie's grandchildren as well as the tour of The Curie Museum. "I think Ingrid gathered so much knowledge and information for her film."

"I'm glad it was a success," Virginia offered, before adding, with a sly smile, "and the talks you gave at the Sorbonne and the university were just great. Good job, because I know how traumatizing they can be sometimes."

"Yes, they went better than I expected, but how do you know how I did?"

"Oh, I have my ways," Virginia replied, with a laugh. "A colleague of mine lives there. He recorded them and sent them over. Really, you gave wonderful presentations."

"So, I didn't make quite the fool of myself as I thought?" Annie answered, surprised by Virginia's revelation.

"On the contrary...very professional...very doctoral. I'm so proud of you."

"Thanks, Virginia, that means so much coming from you. Which brings me to a delicate situation I'd like to discuss."

"Oh, sounds intriguing. I'm all ears."

"After my speech at the Université Paris Cité, a director of the Curie Institute sought me out. He was very complimentary and told me he and his other directors wanted to offer Matty and me one-year Fellowships at the Institute. They thought our experience and knowledge solving the parasitic disease would be extremely beneficial to their post-doctoral students. He also offered a generous stipend and would cover housing and other expenses." Annie was out of breath after her non-stop description, which she wanted to get out in one, unbroken passage. She waited, heart-in-mouth, for Virginia's reaction. It didn't take long in coming.

"Oh, Annie, that is so fantastic!" she gushed. "I'm fully aware of the Curie Institute and the amazing work they do. I believe there's a hospital attached that treats all forms of cancer, so I'm sure they'd welcome your help there, too."

"So, you're not upset?"

"Upset? No, why?"

"Because it would seem like we'd be abandoning Fitzgerald after all you've done for us."

Virginia laughed before saying, "Listen, this is an opportunity not to be missed. Working in that kind of environment, passing on your knowledge and gaining invaluable experience is what scientific research is all about. And it doesn't mean you two are done with Fitzgerald for ever. They'll always be a place for you here, you know that. But this is a great chance for you to broaden your horizons, which is so important in our kind of work. So, no, I'm not upset, I'm thrilled. Take the offer... that's an order," she proclaimed, smiling.

Annie felt immediate relief. Ever since Dr. Dansante offered her the Fellowship she dreaded having to tell Virginia. But now...well...now everything was okay. She could breathe again.

That evening, Annie sought out Matty and invited her to have dinner. She could hardly contain her excitement at the prospect of informing her friend about the Fellowship offer.

Need to tell u all about trip, she texted. *Can u come over for dinner tonite?*

Matty replied immediately. *Yes, want to hear all. B there at 8.*

Over spaghetti and salad Annie related most of the highlights of the Paris visit. Matty, thrilled for her friend that she'd had such a successful and rewarding time, was given no inkling of Ingrid's definitive decision to make a film of the couple's vaccine journey, nor of the offer of a Fellowship. Annie, almost bubbling over, finally broached the subjects.

"Gathering information and background for her movie wasn't the only reason Ingrid came along," she continued, cautiously. "She told me she's fully committed to putting together a documentary about us."

"Us?" Matty queried. She faintly recalled Ingrid mentioning this before.

"Exciting, eh?"

Matty frowned before saying, "I am still not sure we deserve a documentary. We only followed what we were trained to do."

"Matty, you're always downplaying yourself. What you *did* was help solve a devastating disease. My feeling is a documentary would not just tell the story but be a sort of teaching tool to other researchers to show what is possible."

Matty thought over Annie's words.

"Yes, you are correct again. I just hope I will not be required to be in the documentary too much. I would not want to spoil it!"

Annie playfully slapped Matty's arm.

"So, is it all right if I let Ingrid know we are comfortable with her proposal?"

Matty nodded and smiled.

"Yes. If it inspires other researchers, then I am happy."

With that hurdle navigated, Annie decided to see if she could go two for two.

"When I was in Paris, after I'd finished my talk at the university, one of the directors from the Curie Institute approached me," Annie began, slowly. "He said some nice things about my speech and how he and his whole facility had been following the progression of our research into the parasitic disease. That in itself amazed me knowing other esteemed researchers had been watching our every step."

"That is a very big compliment," Matty agreed, nodding her head and smiling.

"But then," Annie continued, "Dr. Dansante, from the institute, made us a startling offer."

Matty cocked her head, not quite yet understanding what Annie was saying.

"Made us an *offer*?" she queried.

"That's right," Annie beamed. "They want to give each of us a Fellowship for a year with all expenses paid!"

Still Matty did not fully comprehend the implication of the word 'offer'.

"But what does that mean? I do not understand."

"It means, they want us to go and work at the institute for a year to essentially pass on our knowledge of solving the parasitic disease to their post-doctoral students. *And*, there's a hospital attached to the institute that specializes in treating all forms of cancer. We're also invited to study there and be a part of their groundbreaking research into new curative therapies."

Annie waited a few anxious seconds for Matty's response. She feared the worst but hoped for the best.

Finally, Matty answered, "My mother will be disappointed but, yes, this is an opportunity not to be missed. To study at such a fine institute is a dream. We are very lucky."

"So, I can tell Dr. Dansante we'll accept?"

This time, Matty beamed before saying, "Of course, and please let him know how grateful I am for his kindness."

"I will, but Matty he's making this offer because of what *we* have to give. *He* should be grateful to us," she joked. "Are you one hundred per cent sure?"

"I am. Oh, Paris for one year…yes, it is a dream."

By July, Annie and Matty's duties at Fitzgerald wound down enough for Virginia to grant them the whole month of August off before they set out for Paris in September. The three of them went out for a farewell dinner, which Virginia described as a temporary parting.

"You're only on leave for a year," she stated, wagging her finger and laughing. "You're duty bound to bring back all you've learned to Fitzgerald so we can continue to use you like our research rats.

"But, seriously, this is a wonderful opportunity for you both. The Curie Institute is world-renowned, cutting edge technology and first class personnel. I know you will fit right in."

In some ways it was a sad moment for Annie and Matty. They had spent most of their higher level education at Fitzgerald and leaving now seemed like abandoning an old friend. Annie spoke for them both.

"Not seeing you nearly every day, Virginia, will be so hard to take," she began, almost mournfully. "What we've learned from you both professionally and personally…well…I can't begin to tell you."

"Yes," agreed Matty, "without you inviting me to Fitzgerald and streamlining my doctorate pathway, I do not know where I would be at this moment. And you have treated me like a member of your family, which I will never forget."

Virginia, eyes wide open at the praise, wagged her finger again.

"Listen you two, this is beginning to sound like some sort of obituary!" she smirked. "It's always been a two-way street; you have taught me so much, too. So, you have my complete blessing. Take in as much as you can and impart everything you've learned to those who will now look up to you. You are now the teachers not the students. And, oh my god, Paris for a year, I'm jealous already!" she concluded, with a fake sneer.

August now became a busy month for the two new doctors. Matty decided to visit her parents to tell them in person about her Fellowship in Paris. She no longer feared her mother's reaction, since confidence in her ability to forge her own future path now overruled any objections her mother might make. Fitzgerald, Annie, Virginia and the successful research into the parasitic disease had turned a once tentative young student into a self-assured, proud and balanced individual. Matty, for the first time in her life, felt totally in charge of herself.

For a few days at the beginning of August, Annie also took a trip home to see Blythe and Clive. There was much to tell; much to catch up on.

"The trip to the Curie Museum and finally meeting Renée," she began, shaking her head, "just amazing." She went on to describe the exhibits as well as being introduced to Marie's grandchildren. "Brilliant people, who certainly followed in her footsteps. Both in their nineties now but still active and involved."

"And you said when we spoke that your talks at the Sorbonne and the university went well despite being nervous…and who wouldn't be?" Blythe offered, holding out her hands. "Annie, we still can't believe you did that. I mean…the *Sorbonne*."

"I know. Have to pinch myself sometimes," she replied, before bringing up the offer from Dr. Dansante. "I didn't mention this before because I wanted to tell you in person, but something else mind-blowing happened at the end of my talk at the university."

Clive and Blythe looked at each other completely bemused by their daughter's admission.

"Okay, are you going to tell us or do we have to play twenty questions?" Clive asked, with a smile.

Annie playfully batted her dad's arm before saying, "Well, there were a lot of important people from the Curie Institute at the talk, and one of them, a Dr. Dansante, who is a director there, offered Matty and me…wait for it…a one-year Fellowship each!"

"What," screamed Blythe, throwing her arms around Annie's neck, "are you kidding?"

Annie went on to tell her parents about the institute's first-class research facilities as well as the role of the attached hospital. She also told them what Dr. Dansante had offered in terms of their teaching his post-doctoral students, as well as allowing them to participate in the hospital's various cancer programs and research. For Clive and Blythe the information seemed overwhelming.

"When do you leave?" her mother finally asked, knowing full well Annie had already decided to take the offer.

"Next month, mid September."

For the next few minutes her parents praised their daughter upside down and inside out for accomplishing everything she had in her relatively short life.

"So proud, we are," Clive gushed, taking Annie into his arms. "So very proud."

"Will you come over and visit at Christmas?" Annie almost pleaded. "I can't go a whole year without seeing you guys."

"Oh, you bet," her mother confirmed. "I have a long break from school, so we're already packing," she added, with a laugh.

The rest of her time at home was spent in closeness, sometimes doing mundane mother/daughter, father/daughter things.

"Can't you stay another few days?" pleaded Blythe, the evening before she was due to leave.

Annie shook her head. "Wish I could but the rest of the month is going to be taken up with Ingrid's '*Marie*' movie. She wants me to sit down with the actress playing her, as well as the scriptwriter. It's all a bit of a rush because Ingrid wants to start shooting in Paris in November or December. I tell you, there's just no rest for us major movie producers," she said, wide-eyed and giggling.

CHAPTER TWENTY-NINE

⟶⟶✳ ✳⟵⟵

"**A**NNIE, IT'S MY PLEASURE TO introduce Faye Salatini," Ingrid began, as she ushered Annie into a small conference room in the New York hotel she was calling home for the next two weeks. Ingrid and Faye had flown in the previous day from Los Angeles, together with Jason Houghton, the scriptwriter on the *'Marie'* movie. Annie had driven from home that morning and would spend the best part of the next two weeks sharing her knowledge with Faye and Jason. Ingrid's Director of Photography, Zach Jeffreys, was currently in Paris scouting out possible location sites with her producer on the film, Sonia Myers.

Annie, very nervous on two fronts – meeting a famous actress in person and being involved in a totally foreign environment – smiled warmly as Faye got up and shook her hand.

"So pleased I am to finally meet you," Faye offered. "What a wonderful biography. I can hardly wait to get started."

As she spoke, Annie quickly studied this fresh-faced, dark haired young woman, immediately thinking Ingrid had chosen wisely in selecting her to play Marie. She was by no means a stunning beauty and yet her sharp features certainly mirrored Marie's usually stern, expressive face. Annie could see Faye easily taking Marie from young woman to her eventual death and all the stages in between. At once, she relaxed somewhat, already feeling comfortable in Faye's presence.

"Oh, thank you," Annie replied, as Ingrid guided them to a couch. "I saw you in *Flowers and Wine*," she confessed, handing back a compliment. "I loved your performance. Some of those scenes were difficult to watch but you were so believable."

"And that's why she gets paid the big bucks," Ingrid interjected, as they all laughed. "By the way, Jason Houghton, our scriptwriter, wants to meet with you next week, so right now it'll just be us three girls."

Over the next two hours Ingrid outlined her vision for the movie as Faye and Annie listened intently. The film, Ingrid said, would largely follow Annie's biography but, of course, would contain fictional dialogue and family scenes to give Marie's life personal and intimate content.

"My ultimate aim is to present her as the complete person she was," Ingrid explained. "She achieved such greatness with her intellect and scientific discoveries but she also suffered from a lack of respect particularly from her male peers. I want to show how she overcame the bias and misogyny prevailing at the time. It's no wonder she suffered depression at various points in her life." After asking and receiving Annie's positive take on her proposal, she then left them to talk while she sought out Jason to see how he was progressing with the script.

"Oh, wow, this is going to be more complicated than I thought," Faye said, frowning earnestly. "So many sides to her character. I hope I can pull it off."

"Yes," agreed Annie, not quite sure how to respond to a famous actress admitting doubt on her abilities, "but you must have so much experience playing different people."

"But they're fictional characters," Faye answered, shaking her head. "Marie is a different proposition altogether." Looking directly at Annie, she continued, "I think it would help me and the movie if I picked your brains."

"Oh, okay," Annie agreed again, before saying, "but I'm not sure how that will help."

"Annie, you probably look at me and think because I'm famous I have this innate understanding of everything under the sun," she offered, laughing. "But to be honest I really know shit. I've been acting since I was a kid so all I've ever known is what I've managed to acquire through roles and scripts. I mean, I had so many different tutors growing that it all became just a blur...learning stuff, I mean.

"But you, you're a *doctor* for heaven's sake, at what...twenty something! So, yes, you telling me how you did it will help me so much playing Marie. If you don't mind – and whatever you tell me will of course stay between us – I want to hear basically your life story. I mean, you pretty much stamped out a deadly disease singly-handedly for a start! So, c'mon, yes, I can learn so much from you," Faye stated insistently.

"Well, not quite single-handedly," Annie corrected, with a laugh. "Matty Kizembouko deserves half the credit, too"

"See, that's what I'm talking about…your collaboration with Matty, just like Marie and Pierre. You've been there, in that situation. Trust me, it will help a lot."

Annie still found it hard to rationalize that this famous actress wanted to hear all about her life. But she did realize that in some way her short life in research did somewhat mirror Marie's. She could see Faye's point and, if it helped make the movie more realistic and relevant, she could hardly say no.

The two women from different backgrounds, professions and experiences spent the next four days in close contact, discussing both Marie and Annie's life in minute detail. This closeness resulted in the pair becoming fast friends and comfortable with each other in ways that surprised them both.

Towards the end of their time together, Faye particularly wanted to discuss the harsh, bias treatment Marie suffered over a number of years in France and from the scientific world as a whole. There were exceptions but they were few and far between.

"Annie," she said softly, almost afraid to broach the subject, "in light of Marie's scientific ill treatment mostly because she was, first, a woman and second, a foreigner, can you at all relate to those situations?"

Annie cocked her head, thinking hard about something she'd never really thought about.

Finally, she responded, "Because I'm Asian American and obviously look different?"

Faye nodded and shrugged before saying, "Yeah, sorry to ask but I just wondered."

"Well, I've never thought of myself as being different. As I told you, I was adopted as a baby so this is the only country I've ever really known. My parents, I guess, have always protected me from the 'meanies' and, as far as I can remember, I've never been personally attacked because of the way I look except…except…," Annie paused and became suddenly quiet. She glanced away from Faye as if seeing in her mind's eye a moment she'd all but blotted out.

"Sweetie, oh, I'm so sorry," Faye exclaimed, seeing the pain in Annie eyes. "Just forget I asked, really, it's none of my business."

But Annie turned back and shrugged, saying, "It was a long time ago now, but there was an incident in high school that certainly hurt at the time. I was fifteen, it was the end of ninth grade and they were handing out academic prizes. I excelled at math, was in an advanced placement program and loved everything about the subject. My GPA was close to ninety-nine, ahead of the next person by almost three points.

"The math award was named after the French mathematician and philosopher, René Descartes, and lo and behold my name was called. My math teacher, I remember, made a lovely speech…a little over the top for poor, shy me at the time…and I walked away with a gold trophy and a certificate.

"School wasn't over for two more days and when I returned the next morning a few kids…not my friends, by the way…actually made some sly, hurtful comments, some behind my back and a few to my face, basically saying I was the teacher's pet and I only won because of the way I looked. Some of it was racial and it actually made me cry.

"But my friends supported me one hundred per cent, as did my teachers and, of course, my parents. They all told me I'd won the prize fair and square, that the way to deal with those mean guys and girls was to ignore them, always hold my head up high and be proud of my accomplishments. And that's what I did. I even took the trophy out every now and then," she continued, laughing, "just to look at it and remind myself that I'd worked really hard and earned it.

"So, imagine my surprise all these years later, when I was researching Marie's life, to find out that's exactly how she responded to her harsh treatment. She knew her worth and wasn't about to let anyone deny her rightful place among them."

Faye actually left her seat and gave Annie a huge hug.

"You're a much better person than me," she offered. "I would've just told them to eff off," she said, sneering and giggling as if they were in the room. "But, yes, your story is going to be a great help when I come to shoot those scenes. I now know exactly how to play them. Thanks so much for sharing, Annie. I can only imagine how difficult that moment must've been for you."

As their time together drew to a close, both realized how much the other would bring to Ingrid's movie.

"Being with you these past few days," Annie started, nodding her head in appreciation, "just tells me you are so right for the part. Your Marie will be outstanding in every way. Ingrid is so lucky to have you."

Faye actually felt herself tearing up at Annie's kind words. She well knew that without her new friend's knowledge and meaningful input she would have only done a mediocre job at best.

"No, Annie, you're the one who deserves the praise here. And you can rest assured that all the while I'm making this film, your voice and guidance will be with me the whole time, seeing me through, scene after scene. I couldn't have done this without you, Sweetie. I just couldn't."

They spent their last evening together with Ingrid, bringing her up to speed with the incredible progress they'd made. After listening to their upbeat, positive comments, Ingrid knew she had a *tour de force* on her hands if she didn't mess it up.

Most of the following week for Annie was spent with Ingrid and scriptwriter Jason Houghton. He already had a first draft outline but was unsure which important events in Marie's life he should cover since there were so many.

"From reading your book, Annie," he began, slightly frowning, "it's clear we have to pare down her life to the key moments. I think this outline does that but I need you and Ingrid to review what I've written with sharp, critical eyes."

That evening, Ingrid and Annie went over Jason's first effort scene by scene and line by line. Generally speaking, Annie felt he had certainly covered most of the aspects of Marie's amazing life, but thought he hadn't done enough to convey the hardships and mistreatments she'd suffered by both her peers and the French government. She also felt he had glossed over her major contribution to France during World War 1.

Ingrid immediately agreed, saying, "Her whole life was basically a fight one way or another. I think he definitely needs to tighten up that aspect and make it a general and continuing theme throughout the movie."

They went late into the night making copious notes in the script's margins, but when they finally wrapped up at four in the morning the result of their marathon effort pleased them almost beyond words.'

"See, this is why I insisted you be an advisor on the film," Ingrid offered, warmly. "I wouldn't have thought of half of this and, consequently, the movie would have suffered accordingly. Annie, thank you, not only have you written a fantastic book but your critical eye here will hopefully make a good movie great."

Annie, taken aback by the compliment, replied wide-eyed, "So glad to help, Ingrid. Have to admit when you first asked me I wasn't too sure. Hollywood and all that seemed way out of my league. But I'm actually enjoying the experience. I only hope Jason won't take offence at our comments," she laughed.

"Oh, don't you worry about him. He's very professional. He usually takes feedback in stride and knows it'll make the final shooting script that much better. Now, it's late, so let's get some sleep and go see the man in the morning."

Jason did indeed welcome their input, telling them their comments now gave him a better understanding of Ingrid's ultimate vision for the film. In the next few weeks he would submit no less than seven rewritten scripts, each one of which was carefully scrutinized by Annie and Ingrid. The eighth became the winner and Ingrid scheduled shooting to begin in Paris in late November.

Towards the end of August, Matty returned from visiting her family in Norambuland, as well as spending a few days at the research facility catching up with Joyce Obuna and the rest of the staff.

"And how was your mother?" Annie asked, curious to hear, because she knew Matty would have had a difficult conversation about her Fellowship in Paris.

Matty grinned and nodded mischievously, before saying, "I am going to Paris. That is all I will say." She then added, "I have her blessing and she told me it was a very good thing that I studied French in school for five years."

"So, no guilt trip?" Annie asked.

"I am now a Doctor of Science," she answered, throwing out her chest, a huge smile creasing her face, "and completely my own person. That is all I will say."

They both laughed before Annie gave her friend a heartfelt hug.

"Good, Matty, I'm so pleased for you. And tell me about your visit to see Joyce and the crew."

"It was mostly positive news. The cases in my country have fallen very sharply. Most people have been vaccinated and the hospitals are almost back to normal. However, the neighboring countries are still experiencing difficulties, but with the vaccine becoming more widely available, thanks to our dear benefactor, they are confident next summer will be greatly improved.

"Joyce and her staff have done very fine work. The planting program for the saplings we sent over has been embraced fully. There are now rows and rows thriving in all parts of the country. Our schoolchildren are the ones who have been doing the planting, which has taught them so many lessons. They have been told the story of your 'bottle of rain' and now in each classroom one bottle has pride of place," she added, with a big smile. "And," she continued, "The Health Ministry has officially renamed the research facility as 'The Dr. Annie Cavallaro and Dr. Mathilde Kizembouko Research Centre. It is a great honor. When you can make a visit in the future, they have promised to give us a big celebration and an official unveiling."

Annie just shook her head at this news that they would have the facility named after them.

"Honestly, Matty, I wonder sometimes if I'm dreaming all of this. Now a research center named for us? Unbelievable!"

But Matty tried to explain what she and Annie now meant to her country.

"No, Annie, it is only a small token of their appreciation for solving the parasitic disease. We are now held in very high esteem as pioneering scientists. I am grateful for their recognition because it means others will want to follow in our footsteps."

Annie nodded as she began to understand Matty's sensible rationale.

"You're right, of course. It's just that I've never thought of myself in that way."

This time it was Matty's turn to give the self-deprecating lesson.

"You have reminded me…several times, I have to say," she offered, with a huge smile, "to be proud of my achievements. Now I am telling you to do the same. You have studied hard to become a doctor. You have come to my country's rescue in its hour of need. You have written an amazing biography of Marie Curie, which has earned you a Pulitzer Prize, and you are now advising Ingrid and Faye as they make their film.

"Miss Annie," she continued, giggling, "I tell you, you are one truly awesome woman, who I am proud to call my friend."

After listening to such heartfelt praise, Annie took the accolade with grateful thanks, hugging her colleague like the sister she now regarded her to be.

CHAPTER THIRTY

THEY ARRIVED IN PARIS IN mid-September and within a few days had settled into a comfortable, two bedroom apartment on the rue de la Seine, a couple of blocks from the Curie Institute.

Friendly staff, along with director, Dr. Dansante, welcomed them warmly with an evening of meet and greet, which immediately made Annie and Matty feel part of this great institution. The next day was a day of orientation, touring the whole facility as well as making a quick visit to the hospital next door.

Dr. Dansante outlined the broad wishes of his board for their Fellowships, which for the most part consisted of teaching and mentoring post-doctoral students, lecturing and minutely detailing their journey and subsequent resolution of the parasitic disease, and also spending time at the hospital to learn and advise about the new approaches and therapies concerning all forms of cancer. In essence, they were now considered adjunct professors at the Institute.

Matty was especially pleased to see students from so many different countries and backgrounds being brought together in one common cause; to make the world a better place. The two young women soon gained the confidence and respect of the students, who were engaged, absorbed and always inquisitive. The first week was exhausting but so rewarding; different but exhilarating.

As September gave way to October, Annie caught up again with Ingrid, Faye, Zach and the rest of the film crew at the weekend. Ingrid, confidently excited with her project, gave Annie a complete rundown on where things stood.

"Script all done. No major changes from the last one I sent you. Locations secured, including fantastic help from Renée at the museum, who is allowing us to shoot a lot of the indoor scenes there. Costumes are period pieces but our wardrobe department has all that sealed up. We're currently in rehearsals and tomorrow, if you're free, I'd like you to come down and see things for yourself. Critical eye and all that," she offered, smiling. "And bring Matty. I haven't seen her for ages."

"At the museum, right?"

"Yes, we start early, around eight."

Sunday morning found Annie and Matty inside the Curie Museum watching Ingrid tightly control rehearsals. Faye, miraculously transformed into Marie, ran through scene after scene almost effortlessly, but with all the characteristics, determination and aura of the real Marie. It was an impressive performance which had Annie just shaking her head with admiration.

"This next scene," she heard Ingrid say, "is when Marie returns to her lab after her husband, Pierre, has been killed in an accident. Annie," she said, turning towards her friend, "I would love your feedback on this."

"Oh, okay," Annie replied, a little startled that she was being asked to comment. "I'm all ears and eyes."

As the scene progressed with Faye playing Marie with a sadness bordering on a tearful breakdown, Annie frowned and gently shook her head. As the scene wound down, Ingrid looked at her with open hands.

"What d'you think?"

"As devastated as she was by her husband's death," Annie answered, trying hard not to sound too critical, "she returned to work determined as ever to continue her research with the same mental toughness she always showed. So, in my humble view, depicting her as near to tears and finding it almost impossible to carry on...well, I don't feel that would be an accurate portrayal of her at that time."

Ingrid and Faye listened intently, finally nodding in agreement.

"So, you're saying," Faye offered, "play her more sternly, more preoccupied with the work and much less emotional?"

Annie nodded, hoping she hadn't been too critical, particularly of Faye's performance, which, as usual, was forceful and believable.

"Yes, I just know she would have gotten up in the morning convinced that Pierre would have wanted her to carry on with their work as soon as possible."

"You're right, Annie, I should have pulled back on this," Ingrid agreed. "From what I've read, seen and all that you've told me, that's exactly what she would have done. Good catch. Thank you."

The rest of the session went by without major criticism from Annie. In fact, from what she'd seen in these rehearsals, she realized Ingrid and Faye had Marie's persona just about spot on. That in itself was a relief, since she wanted the movie to be a true reflection of her biography.

Annie and Matty conducted their lectures, experiments and lessons mostly in tandem, with each assignment being carefully planned so as to move the whole learning process continually forward and at a reasonable pace. The work, by its very nature, was demanding, challenging and unfamiliar in ways the students had not experienced before.

Matty suggested it might be a good idea for each of them to hold a two-day symposium once a month, dedicated to a particular biotech medical subject that was close to their heart.

"Oh, I love that!" Annie concurred. She remembered the Harvard conference they attended, when out of the blue the keynote speaker, Dr. Gail Stephens, began talking about a deadly disease in Norambuland. That was the first she'd heard of it but it subsequently led to them seeking a cure. "And that way we'll be able to cover some lesser known but equally important areas of research. Good idea, Matty."

Since their days were full, demanding and at times tiring, they did their best in their off hours to explore the city and have a little fun. On one such excursion Ingrid, Faye and Zach joined them for a day of casual, carefree comradery.

They took a boat ride on an iconic Bateau Mouche on the Seine; went as far up the Eiffel Tower as possible to experience the stunning views of Paris; took in the fabulous art at the Louvre Museum; went to the top of the Arc de Triomphe, and finally ended up at the Palace of Versailles. In between, they ate lunch at a chic café on the Left Bank.

Matty, especially, found it difficult to express her amazement at seeing all the sights she'd only read or been told about.

"This really is a dream come true," she gushed, shaking her head. "I cannot believe I am really here seeing all these wonderful places."

It was a moment that stopped the others in their tracks, as they realized how lucky they were having opportunities they took for granted all their lives, while Matty had never experienced the same possibilities growing up in Africa.

Zach, smiling, put his arm on her shoulder, before saying, "Well, believe it, Matty, because you're really here and you've earned it."

Dinner was back at the Eiffel Tower restaurant, a laid-back affair which finished off a perfect day perfectly.

The following Monday saw Annie and Matty attend the hospital next door for the first time. Dr. Dansante, an attending physician at the facility, briefly showed them around before handing them off to Dr. Suzanne Pangloss, the chief researcher at the cancer hospital.

Suzanne had been anxious to meet the pair after learning about, and keenly following, their parasitic disease solution.

Graciously, she said, "This is an honor for me…for all of us here…to have you willing to participate in our studies and therapies. While we have made great strides in the fight against most forms of cancer, there are some that still elude our fingers and brains. And while we mostly concentrate on cancer, we also have smaller research teams studying ways to combat Parkinson's and Multiple Sclerosis. It is a very exciting place to be."

Annie nodded enthusiastically before saying, "We are really here to learn although our research also centered on tissue, cell and blood analysis. So, yes, I'm sure there are areas that overlap and we'd be happy to share what we have with you."

"Also," Matty added, "we are very interested in exploring the more extreme forms of diseases because we feel if they can be lessened to some extent then it might be possible to apply those discoveries down through the system to attack the less severe forms. And so your work with Parkinson's and MS is of great importance to us and we wish to learn as much we can while we are here."

"Good," Suzanne agreed, "then that is the way for us to proceed. Now, let me take you into our main laboratory so you can meet some of our senior researchers. You will, of course, have full access to all of our equipment as well as being provided with anything else you need."

The lab tour and introductions to their new fellow researchers only added to their confidence and excitement that the next year spent at the Curie Institute and neighboring hospital would create a fantastic, innovative atmosphere for all concerned.

"It's what we've talked about, Matty," Annie remarked, later that evening over dinner. "A chance to possibly make some real breakthrough discoveries that will benefit a wide range of people."

Matty smiled broadly as she shook her head, saying, "To think how far we have come in so short a time is very hard to believe. But I think we are only at the beginning of our long, difficult journey. I am reminded of something you told me your Marie once said. I remember you quoted her as saying, '*I was taught that the way of progress was neither swift nor easy.*' That is exactly how I feel. We still have much work to do."

In an elegant oak paneled room in Stockholm, Sweden, an eclectic group of scientists and academics gathered to make a decision that would alter forever the trajectory of the lives of complete strangers. It was mid-October and the members of this dedicated committee had been sifting through recommendations, discussing, sometimes heatedly, the pros and cons, the for and against, the worthy and extraordinary, while trying hard to put their own personal feelings to one side and just judge the matters before them in rational but definitive ways, so as to leave no doubt that their ultimate decision was the correct one.

It was a process of elimination, of weighing the considerable evidence in each case against the other, of choosing the highest value and the greatest impact to the world at that given time. The decision, obviously, was almost impossible given the diversity of contributions, but at the end of their deliberations the members' vote was unanimous.

Soon after, the statement announcing the result was prepared and agreed upon, and the next day, at the Karolinska Institute, it would be read to the world by the committee chairman.

CHAPTER THIRTY-ONE

—※ ※—

T HE MOMENTOUS AND INFLUENTIAL STATEMENT was made at precisely eleven o'clock Swedish time, from the Karolinska Institute by the smiling chairman of the Assembly, who announced…

Four hours to the south, at three o'clock in the afternoon in Norambuland, Mrs. Kizembouko had just returned home to her bungalow in Brannisville after visiting the local market for groceries for her family's dinner. Barely in her house more than a few minutes, she suddenly heard a loud commotion outside and eventual banging on her door. The noise didn't seem threatening, just joyful and uplifting. People were singing, clapping and chanting her daughter's name.

"Whatever is the matter with all of you!" she exclaimed, as she carefully opened the door, frowning and not amused.

"Come! Come!" people cried out, as they rushed forward and gently led her to where the mayor of Brannisville stood, holding a piece of paper in his hand.

"Mrs. Kizembouko," he began, a wide grin creasing his happy face, "this is indeed a great and wonderful day!"

Mrs. Kizembouko stared at the mayor with a look of thunder that said, *What on earth is going on here?*

"Oh, yes, indeed," the mayor continued, before realizing Mrs. Kizembouko had no idea why he and all her fellow villagers had come to her house. "You do not know?' he asked. "You have not heard the great news?"

"News, what news?" she answered, bemused and still unsmiling. "I have heard nothing."

It was then that he told her and it was then that she nearly fainted.

Blythe and Clive Cavallaro slept soundly at five o'clock in the morning in New York. As the sun began rising and peeking through their bedroom curtains an hour later, the couple stirred, said *good morning* to each other with a kiss, arose and started preparing for the doings of their day.

It was a normal workday for them both; Blythe teaching her third grade class and Clive dealing with a difficult defense in a drunk-driving case. The day promised nothing out of the ordinary, except that it was life, their life and, as such, things sometimes happen that nobody can foresee.

After a leisurely breakfast, some small-talk and easy banter, Clive went to the den to finalize a brief he'd been working on the night before and, which, he was due to present in court later that morning. He settled into his comfy chair, took out the relevant papers, found his pen and began scanning and altering the important documents.

In another part of the house, Blythe also prepared for the day. Although her daily schedule was almost routine…check homework, math, music, recess etc…she had some last minute lesson plans she needed to go over before leaving for the short drive to school. After that task was accomplished, she clicked on her phone to quickly scan the main news stories of the day. It was at that moment she let out a scream so loud Clive came running from the other room. He found her, shaking and holding the phone out in front of her for him to see.

"Read this! Read this! Read this!" she continued screaming, as she pushed the phone almost into his face.

It was a little after three o'clock in the afternoon at the research facility in Norambuland. Joyce Obuna, Kip and Philippe sauntered out of the conference room having solved a couple of problems with the vaccine distribution Joyce had been concerned about. As they rounded the corner to enter the lab another member of staff almost bumped into them.

"Oh, thank goodness I have found you!" she began, breathlessly. "You all have to come with me right now. It is very important." She hurried off to the break room with the others following at a trot.

Inside the break room, the young woman turned on the huge

television, saying, "You have to watch this," as she pressed the play button on the remote.

For a few seconds, all Joyce, Kip and Philippe saw was a well-dressed man in front of a microphone, addressing a small crowd in some sort of ornate hall. After some preamble the man reached the main point of his speech.

It was then that Joyce, Kip and Philippe just stared at the screen before turning towards each other, their faces on fire with wide smiles, and voices so loud their yells and screams drowned out the television man's last remarks. They hugged and danced like crazy people, shaking their heads and hardly believing what they had just heard.

At Fitzgerald University, Dr. Virginia West, awake and ready at five in the morning, kept an eagle eye on all the news feeds as she waited impatiently for the announcement. She hoped beyond hope that it would be what she wanted to hear.

Five months ago she, the Board of Governors and the whole faculty submitted their proposal to the powers that be in Sweden, in a nomination that stretched to fifteen pages. It was an impressive document, supported by other academics from around the world. All they could do was offer up the two worthy nominees and leave it to a committee to decide the outcome.

Now, at a little after five, the breaking news flashed onto the screen. She punched the air, reached for her phone and hit the number.

At a little after eleven in the morning at the Curie Institute, Annie and Matty were oblivious to the uproar happening in other parts of the world. They had just finished instructing a group of pre and post doctoral students on the intricacies of intra cellular analysis pertaining to cross matching and elimination, when Suzanne Pangloss burst into the room.

"Whatever you're doing, stop right now!" Suzanne ordered, her fingers pointing at the two young doctors.

Instantly freezing, they frowned at Suzanne, wondering what on earth was happening. She stepped close, hugging them both tightly.

"Mon Dieu, it's just been announced!" she exclaimed, smiling broadly, her hands out in front. "Congratulations, mes amies!"

Still bewildered, Annie responded, "For what, Suzanne? What are you congratulating us for?"

It was then Suzanne told them the stunning news.

They sat, calmly now, holding hands, shaking their heads, still hardly believing what they now knew.

Finally, Blythe said, "The *Nobel Prize*? Clive, this is not real, surely?"

"Honey, it is," he insisted. "We've checked all the reliable sources and that's what they're all saying. Our baby has won the Nobel Prize for medicine."

"We have to call! We have to call right now! Give me the phone."

As soon as Suzanne broke the news, Matty put in an urgent call to her parents in Norambuland, where Mrs. Kizembouko had finally recovered from her bout of near hysterics.

"Maman!" Matty shouted down the phone, "I have some very exciting news to share with you and Papa."

"We have heard! We have heard!" Mrs. Kizembouko replied. "Is it true? Is it really, really true?"

"It is, Maman, it is. Annie and I have won the Nobel Prize for medicine."

"The mayor and all the townspeople came to our house this morning to tell us. It was a joyful occasion, but we did not want to believe them until we had heard it from you," her mother explained. "Now I can breathe again and tell you how proud we are of you and Miss Annie. It is truly a momentous day for all of us and our beloved country."

Mr. Kizembouko then took over the phone, telling Matty how overjoyed he was.

"You, dear, sweet child, are truly worthy of this great award. What you have done in your life, how hard you have attended to your studies and all the sacrifices you have made for our country tells me these honorable people in Sweden have made the correct choice." It was then he became so emotional he had to hand the phone back to his wife.

Matty told her mother she had to go since so many people were wanting to speak with her and Annie, but that she would call again soon.

"Sweetness, you are a blessing," her mother said softly. "Never forget you are a true blessing."

Annie answered her mother's call right away, desperately anxious to share this moment with the two people who meant most to her in the world. Ever since Suzanne informed her and Matty about the prize, Annie had been inundated with well wishes, congratulations and calls and texts from a dozen different people.

One of those calls, from Virginia, came in immediately after the official announcement.

"Virginia! Virginia!" she yelled, as Virginia beamed on the other end of the line. "Have you heard?" she asked, before catching herself. "Well, of course you have, otherwise you wouldn't be calling."

Calmly, Virginia answered, "Nobel Laureate, now, my, my," as she giggled down the phone.

"You did this, didn't you?" Annie pushed, excitedly. "No one else could've known all the details."

"Might have had a little something to do with it, yes," Virginia replied, still smiling.

"Oh, Virginia, I don't know what to say. It's all so overwhelming."

"I understand. I do. But you and Matty have earned this. Never, ever forget that, okay?"

The warm conversation eventually ended with Annie receiving a firm commitment from Virginia to attend the official ceremony in Sweden in December.

"I promise I'll come," Virginia confirmed. "In fact, try keeping me away!"

Now, at last, she was able to talk with her parents, see their faces and let them see her reactions in real time.

"Oh, Sweetheart," Blythe almost shouted at the screen, "Oh, Sweetheart. This is *so* amazing, *so* unbelievable!"

"I know, Mom, I know. I'm still trying to get my head around it. I mean, the *Nobel Prize*?"

"We're going to have to make an appointment to talk to you in future," Clive joked, trying to bring some levity to the moment. "It's just wonderful, Honey, and well deserved, I might add."

"Thanks, Dad, but I don't know about that."

"These folk don't make mistakes," Clive answered, firmly. "They would've looked at things from every possible angle before deciding. So, yes, very well deserved."

"How's Matty handling this sudden fame?" Blythe considerately asked.

"About the same as me...stunned and disbelieving. But she's spoken to her folks and they were so happy for her and her country."

"They'd better be," Clive joked again. "This is an awesome moment for her, too."

"They want us to each give a lecture sometime before the actual ceremony, which is in December. I guess it's one of the requirements along with the prize. Matty thinks we should do them a couple of days before the presentation so our folks can be there, too."

"Oh, that would be wonderful," Blythe offered. "We want to see the whole shindig from start to finish."

Annie went quiet for a few seconds before saying, "I'm going to be really nervous, you know, at the ceremony."

"Only natural," Clive said, nodding. "This is a big deal."

"I mean, about meeting the King."

"Who?" Blythe asked. "What king?"

"Only the King of Sweden. Apparently, he makes the actual presentation to us."

"Oh, wow, even better," Clive exclaimed. "That's a moment none of us will ever forget."

"Dad, thanks," Annie frowned jokingly at the screen, "I just told you I'm going to be nervous and you pile more you know what on me!"

They all laughed before Blythe said, "Sweetheart, we will be right there with you the whole time. You will be fine. Promise."

After another brief pause, Annie almost whispered, "I just want you to know that I owe everything to you. I wouldn't be where I am now without you always supporting me and loving me as much as you do. I know it's not much but I just wanted you to know that."

Everyone became teary-eyed at Annie's heartfelt remarks. It was a moment that mattered for all of them.

The last people to congratulate Annie and Matty were the most raucous. Renée, Ingrid, Faye, Zach and Sonia arrived at their apartment armed with bottles of champagne, noise-makers and their own yelling, screaming voices.

There were hugs, kisses, high-fives and plenty of easy banter and jokes galore. The noisy celebration lasted two hours before Ingrid reminded her crew they had an extremely early start the next morning. Before leaving, she drew Annie and Matty aside.

"What a finish this will make to the documentary I'm planning for you two. I mean, Nobel Prize winners…it couldn't get any better than that!"

In the quiet of the rest of evening, when the hubbub finally stopped for a while, Annie and Matty spent a peaceful few hours just talking.

"I still can't really believe it," Annie mused. "Just saying *the Nobel Prize* kinda freaks me out. I mean…*the Nobel Prize!*"

"Yes," Matty agreed, shaking her head, "I keep wondering if they announced the wrong names."

"My dad said they don't get these things wrong, and Virginia nominated us because she said we deserved it. But still…"

"I think we need to let the idea slowly sink into our heads and into our hearts," Matty contended. "Perhaps when we are actually in Sweden for the ceremony it will suddenly become real."

'When I first heard, I immediately thought of Marie and how she must have felt. And then I thought in no way can I compare with her. She has always been the real deal to me."

"And yet, here we are," Matty conceded, "Nobel winners in our own right."

"What d'you think will happen to us now?" Annie asked. "I mean, the prize also comes with like a million dollars."

"I would very much still like to work with you," Matty offered. "There is so much to be done in the world."

"Me, too. I couldn't imagine not having you as a partner. I already have some ideas but let's leave them for another day."

And they did. They toasted themselves with coffee, hugged and later tried to deal with their restless sleep.

CHAPTER THIRTY-TWO

I T IS A COLD DECEMBER day in Stockholm, with the temperature hovering just above freezing, as Annie and Matty anxiously await the arrival of their parents' planes at the Arlanda airport. Clive and Blythe are due to land first, with the Kizemboukos arriving an hour later.

Since the announcement of the Nobel Prize the young doctors' lives have mostly been like hurricanes caught in the middle of typhoons. As well as trying to keep up with their regular duties at the Curie Institute and the hospital, they constantly dealt with interviews, dinner invitations, and numerous job offers from all over the world. In addition, Annie still spent time assisting and advising Ingrid, when she could, with the *Marie* movie, which had begun filming in November. All in all, their lives were now chaotic but strangely exhilarating.

Their parents were the last to arrive in Sweden for the lectures and ceremony. Virginia flew in a few days before to help with their speeches, while Renée, Ingrid, Zach, Faye and Sonia came the day after, since Ingrid needed to secure permission to film the Prize ceremony for her eventual documentary of Annie and Matty's incredible journey to the Nobel.

But now, the two most important people in Annie's life come hurrying down the concourse, as she and Matty run to meet them. The moment is all hugs and kisses; smiles and a few tears.

"Sweetheart, sweetheart, sweetheart!" Blythe continues yelling, as she engulfs Annie in her arms.

Matty is swallowed up by Clive before the roles are reversed. Bags are collected from baggage claim before the daughters briefly leave to meet and greet Matty's parents. They arrive on time and another emotional, heartwarming moment plays out.

The Cavallaros welcome the Kizemboukos like old friends and the whole group takes a shuttle to their hotel. At dinner, a lively, warm atmosphere eventually enables them all to relax, to catch up with each others' lives and bestow more praise on their daughters. Later, each family spends some quality time alone.

"You are indeed a blessing," Mrs. Kizembouko lovingly tells Matty, as they sit close and she holds her hand. "To think we are the parents of a Nobel Prize winner. My, oh my, yes, what a blessing."

"But you are *my* blessings, Maman and Papa," Matty responds, rubbing both their hands. "Without you always there to guide me I know none of what I have achieved in my life would have been possible."

"We have surely helped along the way, child, but you have been the one to study hard and work hard all your life. Maman is correct when she says you are a blessing."

"And we know this is only the beginning of a glorious career for you. Tell me," Mrs. Kizembouko asks, "what are your plans when the Fellowship at the institute is over?"

Matty dreads these types of questions because she clearly remembers the difficult moments they have caused between her and her mother. She decides this time is not appropriate to divulge what she and Annie have been discussing.

"I do not yet have a plan, Maman. So much has happened in the past few months I sometimes do not get much time to think about that."

"Yes, I understand," Mrs. Kizembouko says, nodding and frowning, "but you are now regarded as a distinguished person in our country and, as such, you will be expected to serve and contribute to its wellbeing. Mathilde, there will be many opportunities for you to work elsewhere but you must always be thinking of how best you can be of value to your own country."

"I do understand my responsibilities, Maman, and I will make sure my future research benefits our country as well as the whole world."

It is a non-committal statement which Matty hopes will satisfy her mother's insistence she return to Norambuland. Matty knows that will probably not happen but at this moment she doesn't want to engage her mother in a dissonant discussion. Fortunately, her father steps into the fray.

"Maman, it is time to leave the girl alone," he advises, firmly. "Talk about what she will do and when she will do it can wait for another time. This is only a moment for celebrating. We are here with our daughter for a very short time to give praise for her magnificent achievement. So let us do exactly that and leave all other talk for another day."

Matty is relieved to hear her father's kind, wise words. She quickly glances at her mother who, surprisingly, is nodding in agreement.

"You are correct, Papa," Mrs. Kizembouko tells her husband. "I just wanted our child to know where her responsibilities lie. That is all."

Secretly winking at his daughter, Mr. Kizembouko answers, "She well knows that, Maman. Oh, yes, she knows that very well indeed."

There is no such tension with the Cavallaros. In fact, the talk is all about Annie and Matty's ambitious plans after the Fellowship is over.

"We've been tossing a lot of ideas around," she begins, positively, "but what we've both decided we'd like to do is run our own research laboratory. Right now we're dependent on other facilities, but with the prize money, the cash from the film rights I sold to Ingrid for the book and my royalties, we think we'll have more than enough to get going. Plus, Virginia has already assured us Fitzgerald will willingly be a partner, supplying us with whatever we don't have.

"Also, we'd be adjunct professors at the school, which means we'd have a steady stream of super qualified students to teach and mentor, which will be so important with the in-depth research we want to start doing on some of the less well known diseases."

Blythe and Clive are listening intently as Annie's mouth and brain move along at a mile a minute. Both are overly impressed with the vision and scope of their daughter and Matty's agenda for their futures.

"Would you need a building for the new lab?" Clive asks.

"Oh, yes, we'd want something that was completely ours and something we could expand."

"I can always help with the legal side of that," he confirms, an offer which is music to Annie's ears.

"Oh, thanks, Dad, that'll be great."

"And," Blythe jumps in, "if you need, you know, any extra financial help to get going, we'd be glad to chip in… a little," she offers, with a sly grin.

"Oh Mom, thanks, too, but we're going to try and manage things on our own. Of course," she continues, laughing, "should we get stuck then..."

"How d'you think Matty's folks will take to her doing this and not going back home?"

"Guess we'll find out soon," Annie answers, with a shrug. "Over the past few months she's really started sticking up for herself. She's like a totally different person in that respect, so I don't imagine she'll suddenly cave...at least...she better not!"

"You've been a really good friend to her, Sweetheart," Blythe offers, nodding. "You set a great example by how you conduct yourself, being your own person and knowing what's right for you. She's learned a lot from you, I'd say."

Annie agrees but adds, "And she's taught me a great deal, too, about being grateful for what you have, the opportunities that come your way, humility and always treating people with kindness and understanding."

"Then it's been a two-way street," Clive acknowledges, "and the world has gained two wonderful, talented human beings."

"We're going sightseeing tomorrow with her folks," Blythe says, "while you're with Virginia buttoning down your lectures. I'll gently try and find out how the land lies with regard to your plans. But I promise not to interfere," she continues, smiling broadly.

"That would be good, Mom...the not interfering part, I mean."

They all laugh at Annie's pointed comment before hugs and kisses finish off the evening.

The next day Virginia advises Annie and Matty that the Nobel Committee has agreed they can combine their lectures into one. It will cover the whole parasitic disease from start to finish, with each of them alternating over the prescribed two hours. This is work they obviously know from every angle, but Virginia's job is to help them shape a compelling, complete but concise narrative. The process turns out to be harder than they imagined, but by the end of an exhausting all-day session, their lecture is ready for presentation.

While their daughters are occupied with the serious side of the ceremony, the Cavallaros and the Kizemboukos set out for a day touring the principal sights of Stockholm. The weather is cold but sunny as they board the tour bus.

"The buildings are so colorful and the architecture is like something out of a fairytale book," Mrs. Kizembouko comments, as they drive around the city center. "I had no idea Sweden was like this."

"And very clean, too," adds Blythe. "This is something I shall talk to my class about when we begin studying Europe next month."

During the morning the tour covers the ABBA museum, Skansen, which is a miniature exhibition of the history of Sweden, consisting of over one hundred fifty buildings brought from all over the country, including churches, schools, shops, a zoo and workshops full of craftspeople demonstrating glassblowing and pottery.

For lunch, the tour stops at Gamla Stan, which is the Old Town of Stockholm, complete with cafes, shops and cobblestone streets.

Over delicious, hearty soup and crusty bread, Blythe gingerly asks the Kizemboukos how they are feeling about Matty's great success.

"We are very proud, of course," Mr. Kizembouko answers. "To think our blessed child has won such a prestigious award is more than we could ever have hoped for."

"I know," Blythe agrees. "They have come so far. It is amazing, really."

"And they have far to go still," Mrs. Kizembouko adds. "I feel their journey is just beginning. Tell me, do you know your daughter's plans when the Fellowship has finished?"

Blythe swallows hard and takes a few seconds to think over her answer. She decides to be definitive, to let Mrs. Kizembouko know Annie has marked out her path and by implication it will no doubt include Matty.

Brightly, she begins, "You are right, Mrs. Kizembouko, this *is* just the beginning for both our daughters. It was so fortunate they met when they did otherwise none of what they've achieved together would have happened. Annie so values your daughter's brilliant mind and the way her intellect has looked at some of the problems they've faced with a new perspective."

Although every word Blythe utters is true, she is tending to lay the compliments on a tad too thickly.

Even so, she continues, "I just want you to know how much Annie appreciates and loves working with your daughter. As for Annie's plans after the Fellowship has finished, well, all I know is she is determined to continue her research career in her own laboratory, if possible. And I feel sure Matty would be welcome to join her."

Mrs. Kizembouko listens carefully. She is certainly no fool and realizes Blythe's daughter has probably told her parents a great deal more than what Blythe has indicated. She also understands the tight bond now established between the two young doctors and, for all intents and purposes, they both would like it to continue.

"My daughter, too, continually expresses her admiration for Miss Annie. She feels she would not have progressed to where she is today without your daughter's constant help and guidance. It seems they were destined to work together. The only hope I have is that at some time in the future Mathilde will return to our country and serve it as the honorable citizen she is."

"Perhaps at some point they both will do that," Clive offers. "They are still so young and the world, so to speak, is at their fingertips."

Mr. Kizembouko, who has also been listening intently to the conversation, joins in to support Clive's remarks.

"That is so very true, Mr. Cavallaro. For us, all we really would like for our daughter's future is that she is happy and productive. It seems you wish your daughter the same."

Mr. Kizembouko's words effectively put an end to any further comments from his wife. The matter was settled…Matty would be free to make her own choices.

The rest of the tour around the sights of Stockholm continues to amaze them all. After lunch, the bus takes them to The Royal Palace, the official residence of King Gustaf of Sweden, where they are lucky to catch the changing of the guard. Mrs. Kizembouko stares in wonder at the huge rectangular, brick building and shakes her head in disbelief at the staggering number of windows.

Close by, they all admire the imposing architecture of Storkyrkan. The medieval Stockholm Cathedral, built in 1279, hosts all the royal weddings and funerals. Again, their jaws drop at the magnificence of such an impressive religious shrine.

By now, their sightseeing is almost over except for a ride called Skyview.

"Are you afraid of heights," Blythe asks Mr. and Mrs. Kizembouko, "because this ride will take us about three or four hundred feet into the air?"

They are all looking at the Avicii Arena, the world's largest spherical building, also called the Globe.

"Not at all," Mr. Kizembouko answers, as he nods enthusiastically at his wife.

"That is very easy for you to say," Mrs. Kizembouko replies, doubtfully, "since you are always scaling the high peaks at home, but I am willing to go with you."

Everyone smiles as they climb aboard a glass gondola, which will take them on a thirty minute ride on the outside of the Arena. The ride is smooth but Blythe tentatively takes hold of Mrs. Kizembouko's hand to reassure her.

At the top, the three hundred sixty degree view of Stockholm is spectacular. They leave their seats and gather at the windows of the gondola, oohing and aahing like small, excited children. It is a moment none of them will soon forget.

Back at their hotel, over tea and Swedish scones, they are chattering about the tour when Mrs. Kizembouko says something that catches Blythe and Clive by surprise.

"We have had such a very wonderful time today with you and I feel we are now very good friends. It would please us if we could be less formal with each other. My name is Nandi and this," she says, turning to her husband, "is Mosi."

"Oh, yes, we would love that, too," Blythe offers, warmly. "Clive," she states, as she looks at her husband, "and I'm Blythe."

It is a touching moment that ends a memorable day for all of them

While their parents are enjoying the sights of Stockholm, Annie, Matty and Virginia are polishing and fine-tuning the joint lecture they are to give tomorrow.

"I think it would be a good idea to start at the beginning of the parasitic disease," Virginia advises, "and then take it in turns to explain in detail the steps you took which finally led to a solution. Remember, you only have two hours so precise and clear is the order of the day.

"A lot of this stuff you presented for your doctorate dissertations so, obviously, it is familiar ground for you but not for a lot of those gathered to hear you speak."

Five hours of review and strict editing goes by quickly. It is agreed Matty will lead off the lecture by holding up a bottle of water and saying the words *A bottle of rain. This is what ultimately solved the devastating parasitic disease.*

Finally, they are all in agreement and pleased with the content and concept for the lecture.

"Good," Virginia advises. "Let's leave it at that and good luck tomorrow. I know you'll both do a great job."

CHAPTER THIRTY-THREE

TWO DAYS BEFORE THE DECEMBER 10th Nobel Prize Ceremony, Annie and Matty delivered their joint lecture to an esteemed audience of Nobel committee members, representatives from the Swedish Medical Academy, academics from around the world, a host of invited guests and, of course, the families and friends of the recipients.

After formally being introduced by their colleague and member of the International Scientific Committee, Dr. Virginia West, Matty took to the podium to begin the lecture. Her demeanor exuded calm and confidence as she looked out over a sea of distinguished guests staring back at her. She turned towards Annie sitting nearby and smiled knowingly.

"Good evening, most honorable guests," she began, her voice strong but controlled, "my name is Dr. Mathilde Kizembouko. Along with my friend, colleague and fellow researcher, Dr. Annie Cavallaro, we are this year's joint winners of the Nobel Prize in Physiology or Medicine."

Immediately she was interrupted, as the audience burst into a round of applause. After nodding and gracefully bowing, she picked up a laboratory bottle full of water.

"This," she emphasized firmly, "is where it all started, with a simple bottle of rain." After a pause, she corrected herself and smiled. "Well, perhaps not just a simple bottle of rain." She glanced quickly at Annie who nodded back with a justifiable grin.

For the next fifteen minutes Matty shared with the rapt audience the genesis of the parasitic disease as it started to devastate Norambuland.

At the point where she first met Annie, she stopped and handed the microphone over to her friend.

In the audience, a proud Mr. and Mrs. Kizembouko squeezed hands and looked at each other with wide smiles and whispered praise.

Annie now stood before the gathering, poised and ready to continue the story.

"We met at a summer conference at Harvard and that chance encounter changed not only our lives but the lives of millions of Mathilde's people. That moment and this bottle of rain, as well as the keen observation of Mathilde and our other local researchers in West Africa, are the reasons the parasitic disease is well under control in all areas of Africa."

She spent the next twenty or so minutes explaining the importance of Area 5 in Norambuland and the subsequent discovery of the beneficial effects of the pampousa leaf.

The lecture continued with Matty and Annie alternating accounts, until Matty finished their talk at the point when the vaccine was approved and widely distributed. In turn, they both thanked the audience for allowing them to discuss in detail this remarkable achievement. As they sat down, virtually every person in the auditorium stood and applauded the speech. The two young doctors turned and smiled smiles which said *I think we did okay.*

Virginia was the first to congratulate them, followed by their parents and friends. At least twenty members of the audience patiently lined up to offer their comments, compliments and gushing approval. To say the moment was overwhelming would have been a huge understatement and, the scary part was, it wasn't even the actual Nobel Prize ceremony. That would occur two days later, on December 10th, the traditional day to hand out the awards.

"A *dress* code?" Annie asked Virginia, as she frowned and looked at Matty. "What sort of dress code?"

"Tuxes or suits for the men; dresses or gowns for us."

"And you're telling us this *now!*" she continued, with a friendly sneer. "I was going to wear pants and a tee shirt."

"We'll go shopping this afternoon," Virginia offered. "Lots of great places around here."

The dress expedition lasted three hours, but at the end both Matty and Annie found perfect solutions. Matty's was full length, cream colored with a high, respectful bodice. Annie chose a simple, black dress, knee length and slightly off the shoulder.

"You both look so stunning," Virginia exclaimed as they exited the dressing room, "I'm going to have to up my game. Now all we need are the shoes. C'mon."

That part of the process turned out to be a lot easier and by six that evening Annie and Matty put on a fashion show for their parents. Needless to say, the Cavallaros and the Kizemboukos could hardly believe their eyes at the sight of the two beautiful young women standing before them. Again, it was a moment that mattered.

The Nobel Prize Award ceremony took place on the afternoon of December 10th. Family members, guests and other dignitaries gathered in the magnificent Stockholm Concert Hall at least an hour before the ceremony was to begin. The Swedish Royal Philharmonic Orchestra, situated on one side of the huge stage, entertained the growing audience with an eclectic selection of tunes past and present.

The Hall was richly decorated with an abundance of colorful floral displays, while the blue carpeted stage set depicted Swedish architecture of white arches, balconies and ornate balustrades. Murals of past Swedish life and modern paintings completed the impressive, formal spectacle. A large bust of Alfred Nobel dominated the side of the stage where the Nobel Laureates would be seated, while a dark wooden podium took center stage for the official speeches.

Annie and Matty waited in an ante room, along with the other Laureates in physics, chemistry, literature and economics. The awardees congratulated each other and generally made small talk until an usher escorted them to their seats on one side of the stage.

Surprisingly, both young women showed few signs of nerves. As they waited for the event to get underway, they took time to look at their grand surroundings and marvel at the imposing Hall and its eloquent scenery.

"Can you believe this is really happening?" Annie whispered. "I mean, look at this place."

Matty nodded and smiled before saying, "It is very beautiful and I feel we are so lucky to be here."

Almost before the words left her mouth, six red-uniformed trumpeters stood on one of the balconies and heralded the arrival of the King and Queen of Sweden. Everyone stood as the royal couple was escorted to their place of honor and the orchestra played the Swedish National Anthem. At its conclusion, King Gustaf bowed before he and the queen took their seats.

The mistress of ceremonies for the event, Astrid Eriksson, the executive director of the Nobel Foundation, walked to the center of the stage and began her warm welcome.

"Your majesties, Nobel Laureates, families, friends and distinguished guests, it is my honor to greet you all on this most auspicious occasion – the awarding of this year's Nobel Prizes.

"Alfred Nobel hoped his legacy would always benefit humankind. These recipients," she continued, turning to face the awardees, "as all the previous winners have, certainly fulfill Nobel's vision; a vision that encompasses the human mind and spirit to work and strive for a better world.

"It is now my pleasure to introduce the chairman of the Nobel Foundation, Karl Heinz Larsson."

The chairman spoke eloquently for ten minutes about the importance of these awards and how this year's honorees have honored Nobel's quest for always expanding the boundaries of science, literature and economics.

After the chairman, Astrid introduced one of Sweden's premier opera singers, Kristina Andersson, who performed an aria from *Die Fledermaus*.

Once her thunderous applause died down, Astrid returned and welcomed to the podium the director of the Royal Swedish Academy of Sciences, who lauded the winner of the Prize for physics. At the conclusion of his speech, the recipient stepped forward and received his medal and diploma from King Gustaf. Obligatory pictures were taken of the smiling pair before the ceremony moved on.

Next, Niklas Bergman, a Swedish classical guitarist, seated near the orchestra, played a haunting rendition of *Autumn Leaves*, which left the audience spellbound and certainly captured the essence of the occasion.

After the chemistry Prize was awarded, it was time for Annie and Matty's big moment. Astrid introduced a member of the Nobel Assembly at the Karolinska Institute to briefly describe their achievement.

As the representative walked to the podium to address the audience,

Annie quietly reached out and held Matty's hand. Each of their beaming smiles let the other know how proud they were of their monumental work, and how proud they were of each other. It was difficult to know whether either heard all the accolades strewn upon them at this moment, since overwhelming emotion threatened to engulf them both.

"…and their progression towards an eventual vaccine for the parasitic disease," the speaker continued, "in truth, was a modern day miracle. Their massive contribution to the compendium of knowledge of new, tropical diseases is one that cannot be measured." After another five minutes of similar praise, the speaker ended with the words, "This year's recipients of the Nobel Prize in physiology or medicine are not only worthy, but now rightfully take their place alongside those pioneers who have gone before as true equals."

As the speaker stepped aside, King Gustaf mounted the stage as Astrid called upon Matty.

"This year's joint Nobel Prize in physiology or medicine goes to Dr. Mathilde Kizembouko of Norambuland."

Matty, elegant and calm, stepped forward, bowed and shook the king's hand, before taking the 18ct. gold medal and the heavily ornate diploma from him. She proudly held the medal up for the world to see. Astrid then motioned her to one side as she announced Annie's name.

"This year's joint Nobel Prize in physiology or medicine goes to Dr. Annie Cavallaro of the United States of America."

A beaming Annie walked purposefully towards the king, bowed and shook his hand before receiving her medal and diploma. The two new Laureates stood on either side of him as the official photograph was taken. They then returned to their seats to watch the presentations for literature and economics.

Once the ceremony finished and the king and queen departed, family and friends gathered around to offer their congratulations.

"My blessed daughter!" Mrs. Kizembouko exclaimed, as she hugged Matty. "You are an inspiration to us all." She turned to Annie, embraced her tightly and said, "Miss Annie, what a gift you are. You and Mathilde will always be remembered."

Blythe and Clive did much the same, as did Renée, Ingrid and the rest of the group. More official photographs were taken, while everyone pulled out their devices for selfies. For Annie and Matty, the moment seemed surreal and mostly a blur.

The Nobel festivities continued in the evening with a glittering banquet held in the Blue Hall of the Stockholm City Hall. The King and Queen of Sweden attended, along with other members of the royal family and a mere thirteen hundred or so invited guests

It was an elegant affair, complete with a touching speech by the king, as well as stunning, delicious, but unusual dishes, superbly prepared by the chefs to honor each of the home countries of the laureates.

Sitting together, the Cavallaros and the Kizemboukos marveled at the Swedish display of lavish hospitality bestowed upon the award winners, their families and guests.

"It is indeed an honor to be a part of such a wonderful occasion," Mrs. Kizembouko remarked, as she squeezed Blythe's hand. "It is almost like a fairytale."

Blythe nodded. "I know exactly what you mean, Nandi." Then, touching her heart, she continued, "So hard to put into words. You are right when you said we are all blessed."

The celebratory dinner finally wound down around eleven o'clock. Each of the families had early travel plans the next day; Clive and Blythe back to the States; the Kizemboukos home to Norambuland and Annie, Matty, Renée, Ingrid and her group all back to Paris. Their final goodbyes took until midnight, as laughter, tears, hugs and heartfelt sentiments filled the lobby of the hotel with sincere, raw but rich emotions.

As she lay in bed, not thinking, just reliving the day over in her mind, Annie still found it hard to believe she was now a Nobel Laureate. When she was writing the biography of Marie Curie, the part of her story that most amazed her was the fact that Marie won *two* Nobel Prizes. At the time, that feat seemed almost incomprehensible and out of reach. She certainly never, ever contemplated the idea that one day she, too, would be awarded such a prestigious honor. But here she was, at age twenty-eight, a recipient.

Annie wondered how Marie felt and if she also had thoughts of worthiness and doubt; value and humility? Indeed, she decided, she would have, and then she would have immediately dismissed them to continue and concentrate on the next problem up ahead. That is what Marie actually did and that is what Annie decided she would do, too. With a now settled mind, she drifted off into a well-earned, exhausted sleep.

CHAPTER THIRTY-FOUR

———❧ ❧———

I N THE WEEKS AND MONTHS after Annie and Matty became Nobel
Laureates, The Curie Institute's directors spent a considerable amount
of time trying to woo them into making their Fellowships permanent.
The offers were generous, both in terms of the scope of the teaching
opportunities and in the remuneration. They were even offered seats on
the board of directors.

But despite the attractiveness of the overtures, Annie and Matty
had already decided that starting their own laboratory, in conjunction
with Fitzgerald, was the path they wanted to pursue.

To further cement their ambitious plans, the philanthropist who
had supported Matty in her efforts to become a doctor, and who also
bankrolled the development and distribution of the parasitic vaccine,
heard of their plans and offered liberal financial help in setting up and
running the lab. It was help they could not refuse.

By the middle of May it became time to say their farewells to the
Curie. They were feted with an elaborate dinner and made roaming
ambassadors for the Institute. A bronze plaque was even unveiled
in the main laboratory honoring their Nobel Prizes, as well as the
contributions they had made during their tenure. It was placed next to
the one dedicated to Marie, which almost emotionally overwhelmed
Annie for knowing she was now forever linked to her heroine.

Ingrid's movie of Marie Curie's life, based on Annie's biography,
finally wrapped up shooting in April. All through the process, Ingrid

relied heavily on Annie's knowledge, intuition and reliable input, especially in those scenes that depicted Marie's struggles against prejudice for merely being a woman and a foreigner.

"We're ready to begin the editing part now," Ingrid informed Annie, "which is tiresome but necessary to make a good film even better. That'll begin back in LA in a couple of weeks. But right now, I'd like to show you some of the rushes if you have time and give me your feedback on how we've done so far."

"Love to," Annie replied, "if you think it'll help."

"Oh, no question. Can you manage an hour or two tomorrow evening?"

"Sure. Seven okay?"

"Absolutely. I'll ask Zach to drop by and pick you up. See you then."

The next evening lasted not two hours but close to four. Once she started looking at the rough shoot, Annie became totally immersed in the process and the movie. In fact, her analytical mind offered several suggestions to improve or tighten a few scenes which Ingrid considered and embraced.

"Looks like I've got to be looking over *my* shoulder now," she joked, "or you'll be taking over the director's role from me!"

At the end of the evening Annie could not believe the amazing job Ingrid, Faye, Jason, Zach and the rest of cast and crew had done with her book. The film grabbed her immediately with its true-to-life portrayal of Marie, her struggles, triumphs, as well as her losses and immense courage.

"Ingrid, oh my," she gushed, "this is just so…so…beautiful. You've managed to capture her in exactly the way I think she was. And Faye… oh…oh…what a fantastic performance. I really thought I was watching Marie in all her elements. Really, you've blown me away."

"From you, that means everything," Ingrid replied, giving Annie a huge hug. "Once the final cut is made, probably by late June, I'll fly up too see you with a copy. We'll have a private screening just for you."

"Really, you'd do that for me?"

"As I said before, no movie without you. I'll bring Faye and Zach with me and we'll make it a party. How's that sound?"

"Perfect. Just perfect. Oh, Ingrid, I can't wait to see it."

By the time Annie and Matty returned to Fitzgerald it had been almost six months since they'd seen Virginia at the Nobel ceremony in Sweden. There was much catching up to do and so much to discuss regarding the opening of their own laboratory. Although still adjunct professors at the university, technically they were no longer under Virginia's auspices. But, since she had offered help and an almost joint partnership with the school, they both felt involving Virginia as much as possible would be the right and respectful thing to do.

For her part, Virginia had already secured a prime location near the university, and since Annie's father had offered his legal expertise, she started him on the complex road of acquisition, permits and all the rest.

While all these arrangements took place, Matty flew back home to Norambuland for a brief visit with her family. She intended to tell her folks about her and Annie's plans to run their own lab and, for once, experienced none of the old feelings of nervousness or apprehension. In fact, since winning the Nobel Prize, she now knew her mother would no longer try to dictate her future.

The reunion was a joyous, emotional occasion, with the whole seven days full of closeness, honesty and appreciation. Nandi Kizembouko even asked her daughter about her future plans in a way that suggested she already understood Matty would not be returning home any time soon.

"Precious, you must tell us," she began one evening, as they enjoyed the beauty of their garden, "what you and Miss Annie are intending to do now. Is it still the laboratory idea that Mrs. Cavallaro hinted at to me when we were in Sweden?"

Beaming, Matty quickly and firmly answered, "Yes, Maman, it is. We are very excited at the prospect." She went on to describe the details and the hopes she and Annie had for working diligently on tropical diseases, as well as looking for solutions to some of the more traditional, yet persistent, ones.

"I know you wished me to return here," Matty conceded, "but the work we will be doing will benefit all parts of the world. We are very excited at what possibilities may lie ahead."

Nodding, her mother offered her own seal of approval.

"Mathilde, blessed child, whatever you do and wherever you go, we want you to know you always have our support and love. You are now a very wise woman and, as such, are in charge of your own destiny."

Her mother's words seemed like pearls and diamonds to Matty's ears. She had waited a long time to hear them but at that moment the past did not matter in the least. A long-standing hole in her heart had been filled by one of the two people she most loved in this world.

As soon as she returned from Norambuland, Matty joined her friend and colleague on a visit to Annie's parents. They arrived on Memorial Day weekend, a three-day affair which gave Blythe and Clive a lot of free time to reconnect, listen and generally appreciate the rapid, ever-changing lives of these two, now famous, Nobel Prize winners. It was also the opportunity Blythe had been hoping for to execute a surprise she'd been planning for some time. But that would come later. Right now, what mattered to the family most were closeness, fun and relaxation.

"We were thinking about a gentle hike in the state park after breakfast," Blythe offered. "And then lunch at Willow's on Garner's Lake. Would you guys be up for that?"

"Yes, that'd be great, Mom. Matty?"

Matty nodded enthusiastically, before saying, "Walking in the woods has always been one of my favorite things to do. It would be a lovely experience, thank you."

"And then tonight," Clive jumped in, "we thought we'd take in the concert at the bandstand in town. There's a group of local singers and performers putting on a show. Nothing too grand, Matty, but always a good time."

"My mom and dad usually embarrass me, Matty," Annie joked, "by joining and singing at the tops of their voices, but...other than that... it's a lot of fun."

The day unfolded gently with a refreshing walk in the woods. During the hike Blythe intentionally fell in step with Matty, while Annie and her father marched on at a faster rate.

"How was your visit home?" Blythe asked, nonchalantly, hoping Matty wouldn't think she was intruding.

"It went very well, thank you. I am pleased to say my maman has finally accepted the fact that I am a woman in my own right." She smiled broadly at Blythe after surprising herself with her candid comment.

"Oh, Matty, that is wonderful. You know, sometimes it is difficult for us parents to realize our child has finally reached adulthood. I know I held onto Annie for a long time before I could let go completely. I'm sure your mother always had your best interests at heart. For some of us it takes a little longer. Oh, I am so pleased things have finally worked out for the best. It is one less thing you have to worry about."

"Annie has been such a good guide and example for me," Matty replied. "You and your husband are to be congratulated for raising her in the correct manner. I have learned a lot from her."

Blythe stopped and embraced Matty for the longest time.

"I want you to know, now and for always, what *you* have brought into her world and ours. You are, and always will be, a part of our family."

For the rest of the hike they held hands, each silently basking in the glow of respect and closeness. Lunch, later, was full of talk, laughter and fun, while the concert at the bandstand had them all singing along with the rest of the rowdy crowd. Matty had not experienced many moments like these in her life, and she suddenly felt freer, more alive and blissfully happy.

The three day holiday weekend ended on Monday with the local Memorial Day parade. The event was a first for Matty and one she enjoyed since it reminded her of the colorful, noisy, musical celebrations she participated in whilst growing up in Norambuland. It brought a pang to her heart and a lump to her throat as she watched scores of marching children, dressed in their softball, Little League, Girl Scout or Boy Scout uniforms, having the time of their lives. She suddenly remembered times gone by when she was one of those kids in a country far away. Perhaps, she thought, we are not so different after all.

After dinner, Blythe had a surprise for her two girls, which she had been bursting to tell them ever since they arrived.

"Tomorrow," she began, "is back to school day for me...and for you, too."

Annie frowned, not understanding the inference.

"For us? What d'you mean, Mom?"

With a fake sneer, Blythe answered, "I'd like you both to come in with me if you're not too busy with your new found fame."

Annie swatted her on the arm while Matty wasn't too sure if she was serious or not.

"What, to hang out in your class like last time?"

Blythe nodded. "That and a couple of other things you can help me with."

"Mom," Annie questioned, "what have you got up your sleeve?"

"Nothing. Absolutely nothing, I just thought it would be a fun day for you before you head back."

Annie glanced at Matty, who shrugged her shoulders and nodded.

"We had a very fine time in your class last time, so I would very much like to come with you."

"Good, that's settled then," Blythe confirmed. "Be ready to go at eight."

Blythe's third grade class, sitting on the carpet in front of the smart board, was introduced to Annie and Matty as, "My daughter, Miss Annie and her very good friend, Miss Matty. They will be spending the day with us and assisting with anything you need extra help with. But first, I'd like them to tell you a little bit about themselves. Miss Annie, why don't you go ahead?"

With a big smile, Annie stepped up and glanced at all the eager, bright faces staring back at her.

"Well, hi everyone, this is so exciting for me. Are you all enjoying third grade?" Hands and voices were raised confirming the fact that they were. "When I was in second grade, about twenty years ago," Annie continued, "my teacher gave us an assignment. She asked us to write about where we thought we'd be in twenty years and what we thought we might be doing.

"I loved that assignment and to this day I can remember exactly what I wrote about. Even in second grade I knew I wanted to be a scientist. I thought discovering stuff would be really, really cool. And my dream never changed all through middle school and high school. And guess what? That's right...I became a scientist. Now, I have to tell you, it wasn't easy becoming a scientist, or in my case – a biotech medical research scientist. It took a lot of hard work, going to more great schools and doing...are you ready for it?...lots and lots of homework. Yes, I know," she continued, as she was greeted with groans and moans, "but you know what? It was all worth it in the end. Now I am a scientist, and a doctor, with a pretty exciting life."

She stopped talking as Blythe moved to the front of the class and introduced Matty to the children.

"This, girls and boys, is Miss Mathilde Kizembouko, actually Dr. Mathilde Kizembouko, and she's going to tell you a little bit about herself, too. Miss Matty..."

A confident Matty stepped in front of the class, smiling and waving. She decided to sit down, cross-legged, to be on the kiddos' level. Blythe thought that gesture extremely touching, warm and inclusive. She made a mental note to do the same sometimes when she read to the class.

"You may wonder where I am from," Matty began, calmly. "I was born in a West African country called Norambuland. How many of you know where Africa is on a map?"

Several hands shot up and Blythe invited one of the students, Natalie, to go to the map on the smart board and point to Africa.

"Yes!" Matty exclaimed. "That is correct. A very good job, Natalie." She then asked Blythe to indicate where exactly Norambuland was in Africa. "It is certainly a long way from here," she nodded, smiling.

For the next ten minutes Matty enthralled the kids with the story of her journey from Africa to the United States.

"So, you see, anything is possible in your life if you are willing to attend to your studies and work hard. Are you all going to continue to do that for me?"

Every hand shot up and Matty beamed like a child herself.

"Now, girls and boys," Blythe announced, "I have a surprise for you. Who can tell me what we spent a lot of time discussing and studying in social studies last week?" Five or six hands were raised and Blythe chose Hunter to answer.

Hunter, who spoke very deliberately, replied, "Well. Mrs. Cavallaro, I think you are referring to the Nobel Prizes."

"Yes, that's correct, Hunter. Very good. And what did we say about them?"

"You told us that a Nobel Prize is a very important award and not many people win them each year."

"Correct again, Hunter. Can anyone else tell me why Nobel Prizes are given to people? I mean, it is because they're famous or good baseball players or perhaps movie stars?"

En masse, the class broke out with shouts of 'No! No!'

"What then?" Blythe asked, as Annie and Matty looked on with huge grins. "Yes Chloe?"

"I think I remember you told us they are given to people who discover or invent stuff to make people get better quickly."

"Yes, Chloe, that's exactly right. Some of them are. So, are we all agreed that winning a Nobel Prize is a pretty big deal?"

Again, the whole class yelled out 'Yes! Yes!' this time.

"Well, the big surprise I have for you is…is…Miss Annie and Miss Matty over there, *won* the Nobel Prize in medicine last December! How about that?"

A stunned silence reigned in the classroom as Blythe's magical words sunk into the children's minds. But the moment didn't last long. Yells rang out and soon the two Laureates were engulfed by nineteen excited kiddos. In years to come, these students would always recall the time they were in the presence of two Nobel Prize winners.

After lunch in the faculty room, where Blythe's fellow teachers gathered around in awe of the celebrities in their midst, she announced to Annie and Matty that they were now going to make the short trip to the high school.

"The high school?" Annie questioned, with a frown. "What are you up to now, Mom?"

Blythe laughed as she ushered them out the door. At the high school, from where Annie had graduated ten years before, the atmosphere was eerily quiet as they entered. As her mother led them through the lobby and down the long hall, Annie remembered a walk she'd done so many times. The paint was fresh, the posters and signs now totally different, but the classrooms, library and science labs seemed just as she left them the last time she walked out. Even the smell of the place was the same.

Eventually, they turned into the gymnasium which, upon their appearance through the double doors, burst into a cacophony of applause, yells and hoots from the massive audience. The raucous reception temporarily stunned both young women, who were then led to seats on the small stage.

"Mom, what have you done? What is this?" Annie asked, as she and Matty glanced at the sea of young, smiling faces.

Blythe ignored her daughter as the superintendent of the school district rose to speak.

Putting up his hand to quell the on-going cheers and whoops, he said, "Thank you, thank you. That welcome is indeed appropriate to greet our two very special guests today, Dr. Annie Cavallaro and her esteemed colleague, Dr. Mathilde Kizembouko.

"Annie graduated from Sunbury High ten years ago and is a proud Tiger, while Mathilde graduated from her high school in her own country of Norambuland, West Africa, nine years ago. Since then, these two extraordinary young women have pursued lives of learning, hard work and, most importantly for the world, careers in biotech medical research.

"They happened to meet by chance at a conference at Harvard several years ago. There they were made aware of a devastating disease running rampant throughout Mathilde's country. Almost immediately, with massive help from their school, Fitzgerald University, they set about finding a way to eradicate the disease with an appropriate vaccine.

"Fast forward two years and that is exactly what they accomplished. Now, I am pleased to say, the disease, which was also spreading to other parts of Africa, has largely been eradicated."

Annie and Matty listened to the superintendent's words with a mixture of pride and somewhat disbelief, as if he was describing the work of two complete strangers, not themselves. They quickly glanced at each other, nodded and soon put that notion to rest.

"Now," he continued, "in honor of their amazing, groundbreaking achievement, Annie and Mathilde were awarded, last December, the Nobel Prize in Medicine. You, ladies and gentlemen, are in the presence of two Nobel Laureates!"

As one, the student body stood and clapped and hooted for all it was worth.

Before he finished, the superintendent told the audience about Annie's other massive achievement.

"I must also mention that at the same time Annie Cavallaro worked diligently on the parasitic disease, she was also writing a biography of Marie Curie, herself a scientist, researcher and the winner of *two* Nobel Prizes. For this monumental work, Dr. Cavallaro was awarded the Pulitzer Prize last April, and a movie of the book, I understand, will be released later this year. So, for you budding writers out there, always remember anything is possible if you just work hard enough. Now, it is my distinct honor to introduce Dr. Annie Cavallaro and Dr. Mathilde Kizembouko."

They arose and stepped forward to a thunderous ovation that lasted all of two minutes. They smiled generously and Annie waved at some of her old teachers gathered around the gym. Neither of them was nervous, since over the past two years they had delivered many talks and speeches, and could now handle almost any situation with grace, clarity and ease.

Over the next twenty minutes, with Annie leading off, they spoke to the students about pursuing their passion, whatever that may be, as well as always remembering they were part of a larger picture in this place we call the world.

After speaking to an enthralled audience, they took questions from the students for nearly half an hour. At the finale, the principal of the high school presented them each with a citation of appreciation from the school board, as well as making Matty an honorary Tiger. Moments matter in a student's life and this one, when two Nobel Laureates stood before them, would never be forgotten.

CHAPTER THIRTY-FIVE

A S GOOD AS HER WORD, Virginia found a three-story building not a mile away from Fitzgerald, which she felt would make a perfect laboratory for Annie and Matty. After showing them around, they agreed, and Annie's father, Clive, immediately set about securing the purchase through the benefactor's foundation for one and a half million dollars. A further two million was promised by the foundation for the extensive renovations needed to turn the building into a functioning laboratory.

Over the next six months the building was steadily transformed from a shell into spacious labs, clean rooms, offices and all the necessary facilities required to run a first class operation. Fitzgerald's architects and building contractors, used to working in such an environment, soon had the whole concept transferred from the drawing board to reality. With financing being no object, every screw, nail, piece of equipment and everything else was top of the line and the very latest in technology. Even Virginia was jealous of the amazing set-up.

"I'm coming to work for you," she joked, one day in September, "if you'll have me?"

During the months before the lab was ready for occupation, Annie and Matty spent a lot of time securing the necessary federal, state and local permits for operating an independent research laboratory. This was not an easy task since stringent regulations and laws needed to be followed to the letter. Again, Clive assisted, as he helped them overcome, in some cases, areas of massive red tape.

In October, Annie received a surprise call from Ingrid, who sounded giddy and almost incomprehensible.

"Ingrid! Ingrid, calm down. I can hardly make you out."

"Sorry. Sorry," Ingrid answered, still breathless, "but I've some great news. The movie's being released next month."

This was the final theater version, not the rough cut she'd shown Annie back in July, when she, Faye and Zach had flown in from the coast. Even then, Annie thought the film of Marie's life staggeringly beautiful, touching and filled with almost every episode from the biography.

"Oh, Ingrid, that's so cool! Are you having a premiere?"

"Of course, two, in fact. One will be in New York around the middle of November. I'll let you know the exact date in a day or two. I want everyone there, if possible; you, your folks, Matty, Virginia and anyone else you'd like to invite. The other one will be the European premiere, which I'm going to hold in Paris. I'll try and persuade Renée to host it at the Curie Museum and I'd like her to bring Marie's two grandchildren. I'll get in touch with her in a few days to see if we can set something up. Will you try and attend, too?"

"Oh, sure," Annie confirmed, then after a pause, asked, "Are you happy with the end result, Ingrid?"

She almost thought she heard a sob or a catching of breath on the other end of the line.

"Annie, honestly, I couldn't be happier. Faye…well, I mean…she was phenomenal as Marie, as were all the other actors in their roles. And Zach, as usual, did the most outstanding job with the photography. Honestly, I don't think we could have done better."

"All I know is, Ingrid, you are one talented lady. Congratulations and thanks. You'll never know what this means to me."

"And I understand completely. I remember feeling exactly the same about Josephine Benson when I'd finished chronicling her life in the PBS documentary. It meant so much to me just knowing her. Oh, Annie, I'm more than thrilled for everyone that this worked out as well as I'd hoped. Now, changing the subject, how's the new lab coming along?"

"We're aiming for a February or March opening. So far, things have gone surprisingly smoothly. The contractor's done a phenomenal job with the renovations and the equipment specialist will begin installing the machines, computers and all the rest next week. I tell you, Ingrid, I still cannot believe Matty and I are doing this."

"Well, believe it, Sweetie, because it's really happening. And I know you'll be successful, but more importantly, a gift to the world of medical research."

Annie thanked her friend for her kind words before Ingrid broached another subject.

"Listen, for the next couple of months I'll be tied up doing promos for the movie. But by the start of next year I'd like to get going on the documentary about how it all began for you and Matty, the journey you've made together, the impact of your research and, of course, your Pulitzer Prize and the Nobels. And since you think you'll be ready to open the lab in February or March, it'd be great to begin there and work back. Are you and Matty still okay with this?"

Ever since Ingrid first floated the idea of making a documentary, Annie had pushed it to the back of her mind. She never quite grasped, as Ingrid did, the concept that anyone else would be remotely interested in her and Matty's story. They both did not object in principal to a film that would basically tell how they figured out their solution to the parasitic disease in an honest and straightforward way, as they knew Ingrid would. That point of view would be fine, but it was just that they felt the rest of their life stories were just not that interesting or worthy. In the nicest way possible, she told Ingrid as much.

"Okay," Ingrid answered, firmly, "just you listen to me for a moment. Number one; you and Matty have had incredible journeys. You were born in China and Matty in Africa, and here you both are now, in America, with a Nobel Prize to your names.

"Number two; when I was working on the nursing home documentary, none of the residents thought their stories interesting enough to be told. But they were wrong, as I told them at the time, especially Josephine, whose life story thrilled viewers all over the world.

"I've already told my agent, Glen Griffith, all about you two and he's started talks with PBS. He's insisting we make this documentary and won't take no for an answer. Annie, I understand how personal this will be for you and Matty, but I promise you I will treat you with the utmost respect and dignity. But, Sweetheart, this is a tale that just has to be told."

As Annie listened she realized how passionate Ingrid was about telling their stories, and she also understood that perhaps it was important for other people, particularly young girls, to know about them and be inspired to go on and do amazing things themselves.

"Ingrid, I don't want you to think I was being ungrateful, it was just that we weren't sure anybody would care. I'll talk to Matty but I'm pretty sure she'll come around, just like me."

"Fair enough," Ingrid replied, confidently, "can't ask more than that. But Annie, I'll be waiting for that call."

The premiere of the movie *Marie* was held at the New York City Music Hall on a chilly, late November evening. A sparkling affair, it had all the razzamatazz of those usually held in LA. All the stars, as well as Jason and Zach, were in attendance, along with Annie, her parents, Matty, Virginia and one late surprise guest, Renée Coutage, who had flown in specially from Paris. In pre-premiere promotions, Ingrid always gave enormous credit to Annie for producing a masterpiece of a biography. At the premiere, where she addressed the expectant audience, she echoed the same sentiment.

"We, all of us, would not be here tonight if it wasn't for my friend, Dr. Annie Cavallaro. We met, quite by chance, at last year's Pulitzer Prize ceremony, where Annie received the Pulitzer for best biography." Interrupting her, the crowd applauded with gusto that announcement.

"After reading Annie's book, I knew I just had to turn it into the film you're about to see tonight. Making this movie was a labor of love for all us as we told the...the..." here Ingrid hesitated, as she tried hard to find the right adjectives to describe Marie's life... "the amazing, stunning, tragic and heroic story of one of the most dedicated discovers the world of physics and chemistry has ever produced. The winner of *two* Nobel Prizes in different categories..." she stopped as the audience gasped at this piece of information... "I know. I know. Absolutely remarkable. She also suffered massive gender bias, misogyny and discrimination because she was a foreigner in a foreign land.

"Despite those hardships, Marie continued, year after year until her death, to work for the benefit of mankind. She was a proud mother, always encouraging her two daughters to follow in her footsteps. Indeed, her elder daughter, Irene, also was awarded a Nobel Prize in 1935, a year after her mother's passing.

"The film you are about to see was born out of love; Annie Cavallaro's love and deep respect for Marie Curie. That she is following one of her heroines is testament enough."

The audience filled the theater with loud, long applause, as Ingrid encouraged Annie to rise and take a bow. She did so reluctantly, but with a wide smile and waves to a now standing crowd.

"Making a movie is a complicated business," Ingrid continued, after Annie's accolade died down. "There are so many essential components that need to be brought together and gel as one. A great cast, an amazing scriptwriter and a wonderful, technically brilliant and hardworking crew. Fortunately, we had all three. I couldn't have asked for more from our outstanding actors, led by the Oscar nominated Faye Salatini. She *is* Marie, no question. And Alex, Chloe and Rex, my deepest thanks for such fantastic performances.

"To also make a good movie great you need a writer who understands how each character will fit into the storyline in ways that bring emotion, anger, love and all the other necessary human qualities and foibles. Jason Houghton…Oscar winner, by the way…did just that and so much more. His vision and words enabled Marie's story to be told in an honest, touching and uncompromising way. Thank you, Jason, you are simply the best. And finally, to my director of photography, Zach Jeffreys, you, too, are the best. Every frame, shot, set-up and imagery you conjured up in your mind were perfect. You will always have my deepest thanks and love."

Again, the audience enthusiastically applauded Ingrid's heartfelt remarks.

"So, now, sit back and enjoy the movie, a movie that I hope manages to encompass everything Marie stood and worked for. Thank you."

And, for the next one hundred twenty-eight minutes, they were indeed treated to a film that took their breath away for its scope, passion, spellbinding storyline and performances. At its conclusion, *Marie* received a five minute long standing ovation.

In the next two months, with the help of Ingrid and Faye's promotional appearances, *Marie* took in close to seventy-five million dollars at the box office. It was a triumph for all concerned but particularly for Annie, whose main objective in writing the biography in the first place was to bring Marie Curie's astonishing life to as wide an audience as possible.

Over dinner one evening in New York, Annie and Ingrid celebrated the film's success, which also brought positive notoriety to them both. Ingrid, it was hinted, might be nominated for an Oscar in the Best Director category, while Annie received all sorts of interesting academic offers.

"I hope you are, Ingrid. That would truly be icing on the cake. You made such a great movie."

"It would be nice, I'll give you that, but honestly, what this film has brought me is you. I just feel we're going to be best friends for the rest of our lives despite where life may take us."

Annie grinned and nodded.

"You and Matty are the sisters I never had. I can't imagine my life without both of you in it now."

"Right back at you. Now, talking about your life," Ingrid responded, with a sly grin, "the documentary? Any word from Matty, yet?"

"Oh, yes, sorry, I should've texted you. Yes, she's all for it."

"Yes! All right, we're now in January, so after I've tied some things up in LA, I'd like to begin in February. When's the lab scheduled to open?"

"Middle of March and, after that, we're going to be pretty busy for like the next fifty years."

They both laughed but there was a serious note to Annie's voice. Opening the lab was a dream come true for her and Matty, The work she envisioned them doing involved long hours, intricate, innovative research and interacting with others all over the world. But the rewards could be enormous, encompassing their progressive concepts and compassionate idealism for the ultimate benefit of humankind.

"That gives us most of February, then. Perfect. Now, Annie, one of the things I want to do is take you and Matty back to Norambuland. It's important we cover exactly where the disease hit and where you discovered the healing effects of the pampousa leaf. Are you good with that?"

"Sure, and I know Matty will be thrilled to be going home, if only for a while."

"It'll just be Zach and me going with you. D'you think Matty's parents will agree to being interviewed?"

"They're very proud of all she's accomplished, so, yes, I think they'll be okay with that."

"How about your mom and dad?"

"Ditto, so yes, but I'll talk to them."

"Good, and I'll be doing a lot of on camera interviews with you and Matty, much as I did with Josephine Benson. Are you comfortable with that?"

"If you'd've asked me two years ago I would have said no. But, honestly, we've given hundreds of them, as well as scores of speeches and talks, so, yes, I know we'll be okay with that, since this time it'll only be you asking the questions."

"Perfect. Oh, Annie, this has the makings of a wonderful documentary if I don't screw it up, as Zach always tells me," Ingrid answered, as they both laughed.

"I have no worries, Ingrid. If it's only half as good as the last one… well…it'll be amazing."

"Okay. Good. I think we'll be good to go next month."

CHAPTER THIRTY-SIX

———※ ※———

T HE JOURNEY BACK TO NORAMBULAND occurred in early February. Matty could not have been more excited to be going home to see her parents even if she wasn't too sure how they would respond to Ingrid's documentary. She thought her mother might resist Ingrid's necessary questions about her childhood and teenage years and, before Ingrid began any filming, Matty knew she would need to sit down and have a serious conversation.

Once Joyce Obuna learned of their planned trip, she immediately contacted the Health Ministry to set up the official unveiling of the newly renamed facility she now ran, as The Dr. Annie Cavallaro and Dr. Mathilde Kizembouko Research Centre. The Minister of Health himself promised to attend the ceremony and officially cut the ribbon alongside Annie and Matty. Ingrid, after hearing this news, knew she would have to include this event in her documentary, which would emphasize how esteemed these two women were now regarded in Norambuland.

It was also Ingrid's intention to trace each woman's roots basically from birth until the present time, which she knew, from discussing matters with Matty, might be a challenge given her mother's penchant for privacy. In this regard, Ingrid decided to take the bull by the horns and offer Mrs. Kizembouko a window into her concept for the film. Without telling Matty, Ingrid arranged a meeting with her mother two days after they arrived.

"Thank you so very much for seeing me at such short notice," Ingrid began, earnestly, "I'll try not to take too long."

"We will take all the time we need, child. It is an honor to meet you," Mrs. Kizembouko offered. "I have seen your other documentary and the piece on Josephine Benson was of the highest quality. Now, what is it you want to know?"

Ingrid, taken aback by Mrs. Kizembouko's plain speaking, immediately felt the ice had already been broken.

"First," she replied, smiling, "thank you for your kind words. And second, *I* am honored to be with you. Speaking with mothers of Nobel Laureates doesn't happen often," she laughed. "So thanks for sparing the time. Now, I will be very honest with you, Mrs. Kizembouko…"

"It is quite all right if you call me by my given name, Nandi. It means 'sweet' in our language, so I will try and live up to it," she said, also with a rare smile.

"Oh, all right, thank you," Ingrid answered, surprised by the candor. "Then Nandi it is. This proposed documentary is a way of telling your daughter and Annie's story of how two young, relatively inexperienced medical researchers managed to find a solution to defeat a deadly disease. The world needs to know and understand that and, also, who these people are and what extraordinary circumstances brought them together.

"So, from you and your husband I would like to ask you, on camera, about Matty's life from the moment she was born until now. I will tell her story in the most honest way I can and I would hope, if you agree to participate, you do the same. Of course, I appreciate that there may well be some details or moments you would rather not divulge and, for those, I will respect your privacy. But I am aiming to tell the whole story, blemishes, warts and all."

Nandi Kizembouko frowned and stared at Ingrid for what seemed like an age. Ingrid imagined the worst until Nandi leaned forward, smiled and put out her hand.

"I believe the words you have said. We will be happy to tell you everything we can." Grasping Ingrid's hand, she continued, "Our blessed child has done a great service to our country. Your documentary will honor her in a way she deserves."

Ingrid actually got up and hugged Nandi before saying, "Thank you. You will not be disappointed. I will not let you down."

They arranged for the formal on-camera interview to take place two days later.

Zach Jeffreys packed his film gear into the back of Kip's rugged jeep for the journey with Ingrid, Annie and Matty to the banks of the River Ballooka in Area 5 and the wondrous pampousa trees. Along the way he asked Kip to stop several times so he could take some shots of the countryside where Matty grew up. Once they reached their destination, Ingrid spent two hours directing the two young women as they examined the trees, took samples from the river and finally held up a bottle of rain, which unfortunately had arrived in earnest, soaking them all to the skin. But Ingrid could not have been happier with the outcome.

On the way back Ingrid told Matty about her conversation with her mother.

"So, you don't have to fret, Matty, your mother was most agreeable to talking to me."

"That is definitely a heavy weight removed from my mind," she replied, nodding. "Thank you for approaching her in the way you did."

"Zach and I are doing the formal interview tomorrow and if you'd like to sit in I'd have no objections."

Matty shook her head before saying, "Thank you, but I do not think that would be a good idea. My mother will be able to speak more freely if it is just her and Papa. Besides, I am sure she will tell you things about me that I cannot remember. It will be amusing and informative for me to hear those stories when I watch the documentary for the first time."

"I understand completely. My lips will be sealed," Ingrid agreed, with a laugh.

The on-cameral interview lasted all day. It was filmed at the Kizemboukos' house where they felt most comfortable. Much to Ingrid's surprise, Mrs. Kizembouko produced lots of Matty memorabilia, including a wide range of photographs, school prizes and certificates, old science projects and costumes from various native celebrations.

Ingrid was thrilled to see this treasure trove from Matty's life, which would enhance that part of the documentary beyond measure.

Both Nandi and Mosi Kizembouko chronicled their daughter's upbringing with obviously clear and rare insights, as well as touching, heartfelt anecdotes and moments from the past. At the end of the marathon session Ingrid expressed her profound gratitude.

"Nandi and Mosi, I just want you to know I've conducted many,

many interviews over the past few years but, honestly, what you have told me today, the way in which you've been brutally honest and straightforward, well…this ranks right up there with the best I've ever done. Your contribution will, I have no doubt, turn this documentary into a must-see all over the world, as well as being an incredible testament for Matty to treasure always. Thank you. Thank you. Thank you."

The joyful crowd gathered early to witness the official unveiling of The Dr. Annie Cavallaro and Dr. Mathilde Kizembouko Research Centre. Zach set up his camera at a prime location and had already captured some of the happy, noisy and colorful scenes provided by Matty's friends and family. The day was amazingly warm and even the heavy rain held off until after the ceremony was over. At a little after eleven Joyce Obuna stepped up to the microphone.

"Your Excellency," she began, addressing the Health Minister, "Annie, Matty, family and friends, we are joyfully gathered here today for the official unveiling of our newly renovated and newly named research center, The Dr. Annie Cavallaro and Dr. Mathilde Kizembouko Research Centre. No two people deserve this honor more than you for what you have contributed to our country."

Joyce gave a quick summary of their achievements before turning the stage over to the Minister.

"My friends, this is a distinct honor for me to be here with you all today for this most worthy unveiling. Miss Joyce has already told you about these two young doctors and Nobel Laureates' spectacular accomplishments and, on behalf of my government, I would like to add one more fitting description…that of saviors…saviors of our country in its most dire hour of need. I am instructed by my Prime Minister to bestow upon them our highest civilian honor, the Distinguished Service Medal. Please, ladies, step forward."

Annie and Matty were completely taken by surprise by the Minister's announcement. They rose from their seats to thunderous applause from the crowd and accepted the medals with their usual humility and grace. After they sat down, the Minister continued.

"I am also happy to inform Doctor Cavallaro that my government has made you an honorary citizen of Norambuland. Congratulations."

Annie's eyes opened wide at this news, before Matty got up and warmly and excitedly embraced her friend.

"And now," the Minister concluded, "along with Miss Annie, Miss Mathilde and Miss Joyce, we will cut the ribbon to official name this facility as The Dr. Annie Cavallaro and Dr. Mathilde Kizembouko Research Centre."

Again, loud clapping filled the morning as the four participants duly sliced through the bright, pink ribbon. It was a true moment that mattered for all concerned.

Before leaving Norambuland, Ingrid and Zach spent a day interviewing and filming Matty's close relatives, friends and teachers. These contributions helped Ingrid with Matty's back story, which would eventually provide the viewer with context and understanding of Matty's phenomenal achievements. All in all, Ingrid was thrilled with the mass of content she'd gathered on Matty's life. Now she just had to do the same for Annie.

Back in the States, while Ingrid and Zach continued working on the documentary, including interviews with Virginia, Dr. Jim Plother and Dr. Michelle Sanders, Annie and Matty received some unexpected news about the progress of their new laboratory. The completion date was set for the second week of March, which meant they had to quickly bring forward most of their plans. The first order of business had them spending a week checking and calibrating all the various machines to ensure accuracy and reliability. The work, painstaking and repetitive, filled their every waking hour but by week's end all systems seemed ready to go.

"This is just amazing," Virginia remarked, as Annie and Matty took her on a tour. "I am so jealous but so happy for you both."

"None of this would have been possible, Virginia, without your constant support, input and advice," Annie offered.

"Well, we're all in the same game here, don't forget. Fitzgerald will be relying on you to help out whenever we need it. By the way, I already have four pre-doctoral students for you. They graduate in May so that'll give them two months to get a real feel for this kind of research."

"We will look forward to receiving them, Virginia," Matty confirmed. "It will certainly take me back to my time with you and all the other professors who helped me. I only hope we will be able to provide them with the guidance you gave us."

"Are you kidding, Matty?" Virginia replied, frowning and opening her hands. "You are *Nobel Laureates*. Who better to teach them?"

Both Matty and Annie grinned at Virginia's comment, before Annie facetiously, but smilingly, answered, "We'll do our best."

Ingrid and Zach spent a week of evenings recording the formal interviews with Blythe and Clive for Annie's part of the documentary. Annie's parents, overjoyed their daughter's life was to be presented this way, were eager participants, providing Ingrid with an in-depth look into her journey from deep inside China as a baby until the present day.

"Tell me," Ingrid asked them, near the end of the interviewing process, "putting aside for the moment all of Annie's achievements, awards and various accolades, what else are you most proud of?"

Blythe looked across at her husband, before saying, "For me, it has to be the wonderful friendship she's developed with Matty. As you know, they were complete strangers when they met at that conference at Harvard, a conference, I might add, that change both their lives forever, and Annie took this seemingly lost soul under her wing. That inspired me, it really did. It wasn't only a feeling of great pride, it was also knowing this child you've raised since a baby, had become such a caring and empathetic individual who sometimes put other people above herself. For me, that was so very powerful and something I will always carry with me about Annie."

Ingrid gulped at Blythe tender words, words that she, too, shared. She then turned to Clive and waited for his contribution.

"Oh, I absolutely agree with my wife," he offered, "but my favorite memory is how well she has always treated us. As you know, we are not her birth parents, but to this day Annie has never, ever, thought of us as anything else. We are a family; she made us a family and for that I will always be grateful to her. She's just one gem of a daughter."

Again, Ingrid felt herself welling up. These testaments would bookend the documentary as no others could.

Annie and Matty's tight schedule left Ingrid with just a week to secure their sit-down interviews. She began with Annie and their conversation, light and easy, stretched over two days. Being originally from China, the earliest memories she could remember, her grade school years, her relationship with her parents, attending Fitzgerald, meeting Matty, solving the parasitic disease in Africa, winning the Pulitzer for her Curie biography and, of course being awarded the Nobel Prize, were the main topics discussed at length, truthfully and in great detail. The final question Ingrid asked was the most personal.

"And how would you rate yourself on a scale of one to ten?"

Annie frowned before grinning into the camera and saying, "Oh, thanks a lot for *that* one! I don't know, maybe an eight."

"Tell me the good and the bad of picking that number?"

Annie thought for a few seconds then answered, "I know I'm a good person but I also realize I could do better at some things."

"Like what?"

"I tend to be a perfectionist but I've learned you sometimes have to accept matters as they are and leave them at that. I don't like doing that so that's one area I need to work on. I'm also too opinionated at times. I know what I know and I feel others should act or react in the same way. That's not rational in today's world. My parents are really good at bringing me down to earth on that one," she laughed.

Ingrid smiled, too, before posing one final question.

"And now, Annie, what are your hopes for the future?"

Staring straight into Zach's camera, she replied, "The new laboratory is going to be my whole life from now on. I'm so looking forward to working with Matty and trying to help solve some of the more complex and stubborn diseases. If I can make just a slight difference to people's lives then I'll be a happy girl."

Matty's on-camera interview proceeded along the same lines as Annie's. She confirmed, with her recollections, much of what her parents had already told Ingrid. Pressed by Ingrid to reveal some of her feelings growing up in a strict home environment, Matty said she was grateful for always receiving her family's love and support. She offered no criticism as she explained to Ingrid that her youthful years contained the structure and regimen so vital and necessary for a young girl being raised in her country.

"What were some of the dreams you had as a child?"

"I do not know if I had any," she answered, smiling. "I did my best with my school work and my other time was always taken up with helping my family. We all worked either in the fields or around our home but, yes, sometimes I would dream of becoming *something*. I just did not know then what that might be."

"And how did the G.L.O.B.E. scholarship happen?"

"I think that must have been due to my teachers at my high school. One day they told me because my test marks were very good they had recommended me for university. But not the university in my country, a university in America. This I could not believe because we did not have money for such things. It was then they informed me I had qualified for assistance under this program. At that time, I hardly knew where America was and I also feared my parents would not let me go. But I was completely wrong. They said yes, that I could benefit my country by doing these studies. So, off I went.

"And after I received my degrees, I attended a conference at Harvard where, as you know, I met Annie Cavallaro."

She went on to explain the significance of that chance meeting and the subsequent journey she and Annie took together. As Ingrid wound down the interview she asked Matty the same question she had asked Annie.

"Oh, forgive me, but I do not understand what you are asking me...a scale of one to ten...what is that?"

"Okay, let me put it to you another way," Ingrid replied. "What type of person do you think you have become?"

"Oh, yes, yes, now I understand. I think I have become a good person because of all of the help I have received from so many very wonderful people. They have taught me much in my life, which I hope to share with others. Opening the new laboratory with Annie makes me very excited because we will be able to put what we have learned to very good use. It is my wish to fulfill the words of Mr. Nobel, which were inscribed on my certificate, that in some way I will, through my work, be able to benefit all mankind. That is my wish."

Ingrid wrapped up the interview with her grateful thanks to Matty for being so forthcoming and honest with her answers, which she clearly understood was not an easy proposition.

The second Monday in March found all the principals gathered at the new laboratory facility for its grand opening. Annie and Matty preferred an understated affair but Virginia would hear nothing of that. She spoke for a solid half hour extolling the virtues of her two former students, after which she insisted they, too, address the small audience. Both sets of parents were present, as well as local dignitaries and representatives from the three huge pharmaceutical companies with which the lab had already secured meaningful contracts. By early afternoon Annie, Matty, the four pre-doctoral students and the dozen or so support staff were hard at work. The dream of the two Nobel Laureates had finally come true.

In a quiet moment, the two fast friends took a few minutes by themselves to reflect on what had just happened.

"Can you believe we really did this?" Annie asked, rhetorically.

A smiling, excited and happy Matty answered her friend with her usual honesty.

"Yes," she nodded, "I can, thanks to you and everybody else who has ever helped me. Now it is our turn to repay all those kindnesses. Yes?"

"Always the wise one," Annie responded. "Always the wise one."

It took Ingrid a solid six months to complete the documentary. She and Zach took an enormous amount of time with the editing, perfecting the sequences so that the story unfolded almost like a movie. When it was finally finished she took a copy to show Annie and Matty.

"We've already sold it to PBS," she announced, proudly. "It'll be aired some time in November, but I wanted you to be the first to see it."

As they sat in one the new lab's conference rooms ready to watch, Annie asked two questions.

"Are you happy with the outcome, Ingrid?"

"Oh, for sure, I am. It's right up there with the last one, thanks to you two."

"And d'you have a title for it?"

Ingrid raised her eyebrows and smiled wickedly.

"I do. I do. It's called….. *A Bottle of Rain*."

Printed in the United States
by Baker & Taylor Publisher Services